Dedication

For many years after the expedition, my old leather-bound journal, sweat stained and tatty, lay buried in the cupboard as other exciting expeditions took pride of place. Then Ross and his girlfriend Geraldine gave us our first grandchild, Tristan Kingsley. His African name is Kalungwishi, the name of the beautiful river that flows over the Lumangwa Falls in northern Zambia. I dedicate this humble account of our family adventure to our little Kalungwishi, in the hope that soon he will adventure in his grandparents' footsteps.

Induna Ngema and Thandeka blessing Kalungwishi (aged four weeks) in the Great Hut in Shakaland.

Cape to Cairo

One family's adventures along the waterways of Africa

Kingsley Holgate

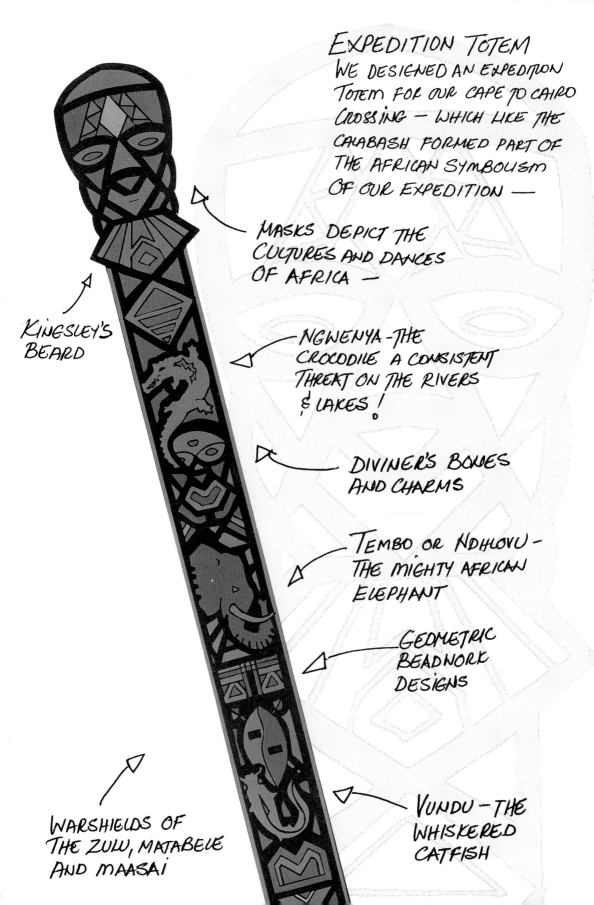

EXPEDITION TOTEM
WE DESIGNED AN EXPEDITION TOTEM FOR OUR CAPE TO CAIRO CROSSING — WHICH LIKE THE CALABASH FORMED PART OF THE AFRICAN SYMBOLISM OF OUR EXPEDITION —

MASKS DEPICT THE CULTURES AND DANCES OF AFRICA —

KINGSLEY'S BEARD

NGWENYA – THE CROCODILE A CONSISTENT THREAT ON THE RIVERS & LAKES!

DIVINER'S BONES AND CHARMS

TEMBO OR NDHLOVU – THE MIGHTY AFRICAN ELEPHANT

GEOMETRIC BEADWORK DESIGNS

WARSHIELDS OF THE ZULU, MATABELE AND MAASAI

VUNDU – THE WHISKERED CATFISH

Expedition journal

Dear Friend
Sawubona

The pages of this book are simply a copy
of the handwritten descriptions, sketches,
scribblings and ramblings in my original
leather-bound expedition journal. It was the
first one that I ever kept, and in it I attempted
to keep a humble record of our family journey
in open boats and four-wheel-drive vehicles across the
African continent. Sometimes sweat from a malaria-fevered brow
blotched the ink, and on some occasions I was simply too weary to
write, and have had to go back and fill in the gaps as best I could.

Our 1993 crossing of Africa was a turning point in our lives.
For South Africans the first wind of change was blowing
across the continent, and we were blessed to be a part of it –
a South African expedition heading across Africa armed only
with a Zulu calabash of Cape Point seawater and a scroll of
peace and goodwill.

When we departed from Cape Town, Mozambique was still
smouldering from its long and bloody civil war; the tension in the
Great Lakes was soon to explode; banditry was rife in northern
Kenya and southern Ethiopia; and the civil war raged on in
southern Sudan. Ethiopia was closed to overland travellers, and
there was virtually no overland traffic between Sudan and Egypt.
But at least there was an opening up of the African continent to
us South Africans, and so there we were, our own little diplomatic
corps, about to set out into the great unknown.

The key ingredients to our expedition recipe seemed to be blind faith, determination, humour, courage and a liberal measure of good fortune. It was an expedition that we as a family will remember forever. It opened our souls to 'Mama Afrika' and made us citizens of this great continent. Its success was the start of many other great family adventures - but for us this early expedition will always be our great 'first love'.

Please understand that I'm really just an ordinary sort of fellow, blessed with an extraordinary passion for Africa. You probably share that passion, so I guess we're kindred spirits.

Siyabonga and best wishes

Kingsley Holgate

PS The pages of this journal are best read by the light of an old paraffin lantern. Settle the legs of your favourite canvas camping chair into the Kalahari sand, smell the hardwood burning as it sparks into the starlit sky. The blackened camp kettle hisses on the coals, and you refill your old dented enamel mug with Renoster coffee laced with Captain Morgan rum. By the light of the fire you can make out the familiar shape of the Land Rover, the tent, and the old wooden camp box that Dad used. A simba roars in the distance, as you pull your chair closer to the fire and add another twisted log. Fortunately, there's a cool breeze blowing, so no mozzies tonight. I wish you safari njema as you journey with us across Africa.

How it began

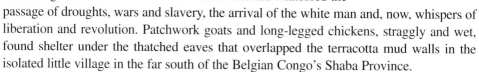

The drought had broken. The dance of the Rain Queen had opened up the African skies. Tropical rain poured down in buckets onto the roof of the unpainted corrugated-iron church set among massive hardwood trees – trees that had witnessed the passage of droughts, wars and slavery, the arrival of the white man and, now, whispers of liberation and revolution. Patchwork goats and long-legged chickens, straggly and wet, found shelter under the thatched eaves that overlapped the terracotta mud walls in the isolated little village in the far south of the Belgian Congo's Shaba Province.

I was only six years old and shared the rickety church bench with my mother Ivy May and my brothers Mervyn and Donald. I was the baby of the family, and my *velskoen*ed feet did not reach the mud floor of the church. So I was not affected by the ever-increasing flow of floodwater that ran through the building forming a large pool at the feet of my father, the Rev. Arthur Holgate. Despite the help of an interpreter who Africanized the contents of the sermon and beefed up the lyrics of the hymns, he was fighting a losing battle against the noise of the deluge on the corrugated-iron roof. It was impossible for him to keep the attention of the congregation, who were overjoyed at the coming of the first rains.

My father, a schoolmaster and lay preacher, believed that this was a good way for us to spend the school holidays. We had travelled 3,000 kilometres up from Natal in South Africa to stay with missionary friends.

On our way back through Northern and Southern Rhodesia, the rains continued and we were often forced to camp on river banks while we waited for the raging torrents to subside. Rivers that for most of the year ran dry now roared down towards Mozambique, the swirling brown waters taking dead livestock, floating pumpkins and the occasional thatched roof with them to the Indian Ocean.

My father would push long, sharpened sticks into the mud of the brown eddies on the river bank, against which he made hourly observations to see if the water level was falling. Once the family Nilometer had indicated a drop, we would all bundle into the brown 1946 Chevy. With a loud hoot of the chromium hooter-ring and the crash of the column shift, we would hit the muddy torrent armed, not only with several tons of Detroit steel, but also with a massive dose of the good Lord's providence, which my father had ensured with a lengthy prayer prior to the plunge.

I don't know when my bond with Africa first began. It might have been on those early missionary journeys through the subcontinent. Or maybe when, much to my parents' consternation, I was 'abducted' by my Zulu nanny who, after a drinking bout, decided to take me off to her Zulu home. What I do know, however, is that from an early age I became fascinated with 'things African' and, while as a young man I chose to travel the world, I could never wait to return to Africa's shores.

It was not surprising therefore that my wife Gillian and I began a successful trading business dealing in traditional African artefacts which enabled us to travel the wilds of southern Africa. However, owing to the shortsightedness of the South African government and its unacceptable apartheid policy, our world was shrinking. On my passport, how could I possibly continue to adventure? I even subscribed to an informative publication that explained how one could buy, bribe or even marry to obtain a foreign passport. But my wife, though adventurous, decided that bigamy was too high a price to pay.

Cape to Cairo - A dream is born

My fascination with Africa grew as one expedition followed another and then, on a short riverboat expedition on the Zambezi and Lake Malawi, a dream was born. What a great adventure it would be to cross the continent from Cape Town to Cairo, exploring wherever possible the waterways of Africa!

The lakes, rivers and coastline of this magnificent continent had always captivated me, and I'd read the journals of the great explorers – Livingstone, Burton, Stanley and Speke. Magical names such as the Zambezi, Shire and Okavango rivers; lakes Malawi, Rukwa, Tanganyika, Victoria, Albert, Edward and George; Lake Turkana, the world's largest desert lake; the Rift Valley lakes; Lake Tana, the source of the Blue Nile; and the mighty Nile itself. I pasted the Michelin maps of Africa together and, as north, south, east and west became a single continent, they revealed that it would be possible to cross Africa almost entirely by water, linking seas, lakes and rivers by towing boats overland between them. Fortunately, by this time South Africa was creeping along the road to democracy and we, as 'Africans', were all looking forward to a great future. Africa was opening up to South Africa after the wasted years of apartheid, and at last we were becoming part of the world at large.

For days and weeks I dreamt of nothing else. I'll always remember the day I made the final decision to go. I had slept the night in a run-down little motel in the southern Zambian town of Livingstone. Fearing that the breakfast might be worse than the beds, I popped down to the Victoria Falls for bacon and eggs at the Intercontinental Hotel, and then walked down to the falls to gaze at their splendour.

Looking across at Livingstone Island I imagined how it must have been for David Livingstone, the great missionary explorer, who had come down the river with his Makololo porters in a dugout canoe. What excitement he must have felt at first seeing this spectacle, which he named after his monarch, the queen.

As a boy I would listen to my father's stories about Dr David

9

The first European to travel from Cape Town to Cairo was not one of the great known explorers, but Ewart S. Grogan, a Cambridge undergraduate. The story goes that the father of the beautiful girl with whom young Grogan had fallen in love would not give his daughter's hand in marriage, telling Grogan: 'You're simply not man enough.' 'If I were to be the first man to complete a journey from the Cape to Cairo, would you consider me man enough?' And so Grogan took off, and in a truly amazing adventure succeeded in reaching Cairo. He married the girl and settled in Kenya. His incredible journey took place nearly a hundred years ago. His book is a great inspiration to me and will accompany us to Cairo. We take Grogan's Cape to Cairo book along with us!

Leaving the falls behind me, I continued upstream to the Old Drift where the original village of Livingstone had been situated. I sat quietly among the graves of the early pioneers, many of them victims of blackwater fever and malaria. Below, the mighty Zambezi ran swiftly, and in the distance I could see the cloud of mist that hung over *Mosi oa Tunya* – 'the smoke that thunders'. A feeling of quiet satisfaction came over me and I felt close to the spirits of the early adventurers who lay buried beside me. There and then I made the decision: we would travel across Africa from the Cape to Cairo, using inflatable boats to explore the continent's timeless waterways. To my knowledge it had never been done this way before, and I knew that it would not be easy. We would have to face banditry, as well as malaria and other diseases. The expedition would sometimes be frightening and at times I would be risking, not only my own life, but also those of my family. But the average man, I believe, lives a life of quiet desperation. Some men, as they grow older, and especially as they reach their mid- to late forties, realize the need to get out there and 'just do it'.

A small herd of giraffe passed me, walking daintily on their long legs down to the Zambezi to drink. They had not noticed me as I sat quietly in the shade of a jackal-berry tree. In the distance a lone hippo snorted indignantly while, up above, a grey loerie uttered its raucous 'go-away' cry. I felt a brief rush of adrenaline – a new adventure had begun. And so, with the spirit of the great Zambezi beside me, I drove back to Zululand via the wide-open spaces of Botswana. Ahead of me lay an adventure that would change my life.

An expedition in the making

Ross, my twenty-year-old son and one of my best friends, began doing research into boats, outboard motors, vehicles and equipment. We decided on two expedition 'rigs', each to consist of a tough four-wheel-drive vehicle suitable for carrying expedition members and kit, and strong enough to pull a semi-rigid inflatable expedition boat loaded onto an off-road trailer. All rims, wheels and tyres should be the same size and interchangeable. There should be radio communication between boats and vehicles and massive hatches for transporting fuel. Both vehicles should have powerful winches and lock-up storage spaces. We would need camping equipment, mosquito nets, expedition clothes, a fridge, maps and

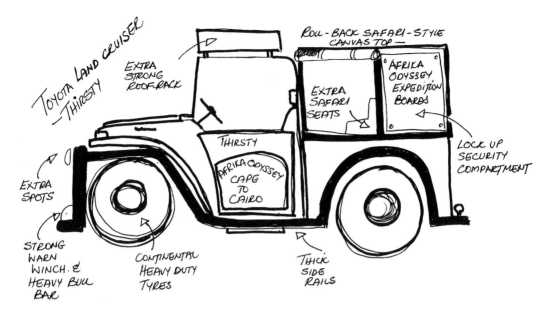

Toyota Land Cruiser – Thirsty

Extra strong roof-rack

Roll-back safari-style canvas top

Extra safari seats

Afrika Odyssey Expedition Boards

Lock up security compartment

Thirsty

Afrika Odyssey Cape to Cairo

Extra spots

Strong Warn winch & heavy bull bar

Continental heavy duty tyres

Thick side rails

reference books, food supplies, a good medical kit, fishing gear and a fistful of dollars. If you ask most expedition leaders their scariest task, they will probably tell you it's finding the sponsors and the bucks to make it happen. And so the enormous task began.

The wonderful thing about so many South Africans is that they identify with a great adventure. One of the best examples of this was Paul van der Westhuizen from Wilbur Ellis, who has spent much of his life on the Zambezi River. His blue eyes twinkled with delight as we went through the map together, looking at rivers and waterways of which he had only dreamt. This would be a world first for Wilbur Ellis's Mariner Outboards and, yes, they would gladly sponsor all the outboards and spare parts we needed, and a short Mariner Outboard engine course for Ross. The deal done, Paul shook my hand and said, 'Good luck; you're going to need a lot of it.'

Gemini manufactures strong and rugged inflatable boats that are highly suitable for expedition use. Thanks to a generous and adventurous sponsorship from Graham Symmonds and Carl de Villiers, we soon took possession of two fantastic Geminis. They had bright yellow, rigid, fibreglass monohulls, deck and transoms to which were fitted red high flotation pontoons. With their standing consoles, foot and hand straps and extra fuel hatches, these boats were to prove amazingly tough.

The small boat, a 4.7-metre Gemini Waverider with two 25-horsepower Mariners, we called *Bathtub*. She was the ideal riverboat and was constantly used to fetch and carry, to collect firewood and supplies, and for recces and fishing. She rested cozily beside her 'mothership', christened *QE2*. Six metres long with a deep V-keel and two 60-horsepower outboards, *QE2* was able to tackle high storms and massive waves, leaving little *Bathtub* to ride in her wake like a hippo calf following its mother.

Equally important were of course the vehicles. We already owned (with the bank) a hardy Land Cruiser, aptly nicknamed *Thirsty* because of her 4.2-litre petrol engine. Her days as a pick-up truck were now over, and we converted her into a canvas-topped East African safari-type vehicle with a roof-rack over the cab and a large security lock-up area behind the passenger seat at the back of the bin. Expedition boards complete

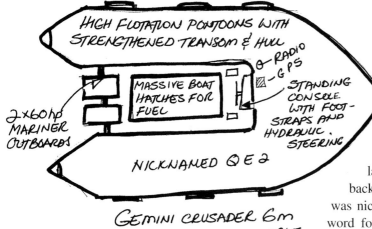

HIGH FLOTATION PONTOONS WITH
STRENGTHENED TRANSOM & HULL

O-RADIO
-GPS

MASSIVE BOAT
HATCHES FOR
FUEL

STANDING
CONSOLE
WITH FOOT-
STRAPS AND
HYDRAULIC
STEERING

2x60hp
MARINER
OUTBOARDS

NICKNAMED QE2

GEMINI CRUSADER 6m
SEMI-RIGID INFLATABLE
6 PASSENGERS + KIT
AND FUEL

with an expedition totem were attached on either side of the vehicle. Held on by wing-nuts, these boards could be swung around in a few minutes in an emergency to reveal a large red cross on a white background. The second vehicle was nicknamed *Vulandlela*, a Zulu word for 'pathfinder' or 'one who opens the way'. Part-sponsored by Toyota, she was a tough little four-wheel-drive diesel Hilux. The Land Cruiser *Thirsty* would tow the big Gemini *QE2*, and *Vulandlela* would be responsible for little *Bathtub*. Mr Winch of Durban sponsored tough Warn winches, Continental the tyres. MNet, a South African TV station, would follow the expedition, along with a number of newspapers and magazines. We had certainly started to create enough of a buzz. Now we needed the action. Could we do it?

Pilgrims of adventure

News of our plans had spread like wildfire, and there were many young adventurers who wanted to join the expedition. We made the decision not to advertise, but rather to choose from family and friends. We were after a band of fellow adventurers who would be team players and make it happen through thick and thin. They would have to be our fellow pilgrims of adventure.

I explained to the eager young hopefuls that there would be no glory in this thing. 'Forget the destination. It will be the slow day-to-day grind of the journey that you will have to become one with: the constant pitching and striking of camp; the heat, rain and mosquitos; the living with a small group of pilgrims, day after day. Humour and goodwill will be key ingredients.' And so I made the difficult choice. The Afrika Odyssey team would total seven pilgrims of adventure – myself, my wife Gill, our son Ross, and four other strong young men whom we had got to know in some or other way: Nigel Hallowes, Rob Dodson, Warren Hulett and Jon Dahl. (The team is introduced in full colour on pages 26 and 27.)

Planning the route

We knew full well that we would have to move with the pace of Africa and face each problem as it arose. At this stage we did not know how war-torn Sudan would take to us putting our boats in the Nile. Would we be able to travel through Renamo territory down the Zambezi to the coast of Mozambique? No one had done it in 20 years. Whom does one write to and how does one plan? We decided that the best thing to do was to make the Afrika Odyssey Expedition as high profile as possible. We would carry a scroll of peace and goodwill from the Mayor of Cape Town to the Mayor of Cairo. This scroll would be endorsed throughout the journey by mayors, chiefs and VIPs, each with their own letterhead paper and stamp of approval. A letter of introduction from the South African Department of Foreign Affairs and an even more useful one from the African National Congress were added to our Afrika Odyssey Expedition scroll.

Mozambique sea trials

As South Africa started to wind down for the Christmas holidays of 1992, our convoy left for Mozambique. I had realized that we would need to do some pre-departure expedition trials, and what better way than to make them one of the chapters of the expedition. The boards on the side of *Thirsty* read 'The coast of Mozambique – Ilha da Inhaca, Santa Maria & Ilha dos Portugueses'. It would be an opportunity for us to unwind for the festive season, but, more importantly, to test boats, equipment and the team. Man, was I pleased finally to see our little convoy pulling out from Zinkwazi on the Natal North Coast.

Before things could begin I was to be given a quick lesson on African bureaucracy, as a teaser to what lay ahead. The port captain on Inhaca Island, who controlled nearby Portuguese Island, took one look at the branded boats, banners, radios and expedition equipment. It was 1992 and only a few travellers had visited the country since the recent end to the war. But now an entire expedition camped out on the Ilha dos Portugueses? *Nada!* No! So out came the paperwork, our letter of introduction and then a visit to the South African trade commission in Maputo. Hours became days. Finally we met again quietly and, with the help of an interpreter, we became friends. A lesson learnt – if we were to succeed in our expedition across Africa, the old rules would apply – lots of official paperwork, stamps, patience and big smiles. We would need to remember that, while the Swiss might have developed the clock, it's Africa who in fact owns the time!

And so, with the port captain on our side, we enjoyed our seaside playground. Warren and Jon certainly proved that they could keep us supplied with fish. We were all well aware of the sports fishing tag-and-release rule, but for much of our expedition, like the locals, we would be reliant on local food sources, which would more often than not be the rivers and lakes of Africa. We all learnt to handle the boats and equipment, and very soon were relaxed and tanned. Equally important as testing all the equipment was making sure that there were no real personality hang-ups that would spoil the expedition. Life's journeys have taught me that you can think you know somebody, but it's only once you've been together in the bush for a while that you truly get to know them. Fortunately, we had assembled a merry bunch of pilgrims. (My Swazi friend was right: Nkonkoni Rob's feet did stink.) Ross I could see was taking the expedition more seriously than the others were – after all, he had a family stake in it.

At night around the fire the talk always came around to 'Will it be possible? Will we make it?' With each day the excitement grew and soon the sunburnt, better-equipped team was making its way down to Cape Town for the launch of the Afrika Odyssey Expedition.

Cape of Storms

Cape Point

Cape Point is a place of history and adventure, of long-nurtured dreams of the sailors of old, of the Portuguese, the Dutch, the English and the French. For them this was the feared Cape of Storms, the Cabo Tormentoso, but also the Cabo da boa Esperanca, the Cape of Good Hope, representing the turning point of the southern seas as they voyaged east. For us it would mark the start of a turning point in our lives.

Friday 15 January

Today our humble armada arrived in Cape Town – two boats, two four-wheel drives and seven pilgrims of adventure. The pilgrims all have one thing in common – a thrilling sense of nervous anticipation. But a festive atmosphere accompanies our arrival as friends have come from across the country to celebrate the start of our madcap adventure. All this calls for a wild bout of merry-making that has Mashozi dancing on the table of a local restaurant. Back at the hotel, we end up in the Jacuzzi, and as I stumble off to bed I slur, 'Big day tomorrow – good night, chasps! *Lala kahle.*' As I go to bed I hear the wind howling outside. The Cape winds are notorious, and I just hope it won't be blowing a gale tomorrow. Right now you could blow the whole team down with a feather. They are young and tough, and I know that tomorrow morning they will be up and ready for the commencement of probably the greatest adventure challenge of their lives. I'm nervous as all hell.

Saturday 16 January

The Cape sun is shining strong and bright at the Victoria and Alfred Waterfront. The big day has finally come and the team are all neat and clean in their sponsored Afrika Odyssey Cape to Cairo T-shirts. Nkonkoni Rob is very talkative, a sure sign of a hangover. The expedition sponsors have set up their stalls and banners around the boats and vehicles, and we pitch our tents to give it all an 'into Africa' expedition feel.

The intrigued public bombards us with questions: Are you carrying guns? Where are you going to get food? How many African languages do you speak? What about malaria, wild animals, bandits and snakes? Are you crazy? Some ask for autographs, and the press, radio and TV news keep us on our toes. During the farewell speech and the handing over of a peace and goodwill message from the Mayor of Cape Town to the Mayor of Cairo a lump comes to my throat and I catch first Mashozi's and then Ross's eye. The rhythms of the marimbas and rawhide drums echo off the walls of this fine Western waterfront development. A Xhosa *sangoma* throws his bones and blesses our calabash and the boats with the swishing of his *nkonkoni* fly whisk – the tail of the wildebeest.

In a spray of champagne and with the flags flying, we launch our boats into the harbour, and the friendly lads from the National Sea Rescue Institute (NSRI) escort us out into a restless sea. The medical rescue helicopter roars overhead and behind us is silhouetted the unmistakable landmark of Cape Town – Table Mountain. The port captain reports winds of 10 knots and rising, and spray pelts us as the two tiny boats bounce out of the breakwater, passing Robben Island, the one-time captive home of Nelson Mandela who was released three years ago from Victor Verster Prison.

THE CAPE PENINSULA 'CABO DA BOA ESPERANCA'

ROBBEN ISLAND

CAPE TOWN. WE LAUNCH FROM THE V&A WATERFRONT ON SAT 16 JAN 1993 – CAIRO HERE WE COME!

HOUT BAY

KOMMETJIE

SEAL ISLAND

SIMON'S TOWN (YACHT CLUB)

HIGH WINDS AND ROUGH CONDITIONS. – HUGE WAVES BLOODY COLD FOR US NATAL BOYS!!

CAPE POINT

WE FILL OUR ZULU CALABASH WITH CAPE POINT SEAWATER AND TAKE AN ICY PLUNGE!

For us the Cape of Good Hope fast becomes the Cape of Storms. We hold on for dear life, riding high over a restless ocean buffeted by incessant winds from all quarters of the compass. The wind is demonic and the constant salt spray stings our eyes. The only way *Bathtub* can travel is by riding in the wake of *QE2*, and at times it is impossible to get on the plane as the boats wallow between the giant troughs. The adventure has truly begun!

Reaching the Point we nose into the forbidding swell and idle the Mariner Outboards. The traditional Zulu calabash decorated with glass beads is brought from the hatch, and I remove the hand-carved stopper. Amidst much applause from the fellow pilgrims I reach overboard and fill it with seawater. This water from Cape Point will be emptied into the Mediterranean at the mouth of the Nile – a simple and romantic gesture, celebrating the beginning and, I hope, the end of the Afrika Odyssey Expedition.

The seas are now mountainous, our two rubberducks bucking about as massive swells race beneath them to crash against the rock face of Cape Point. The calabash full, Warren leaps overboard into the icy grey water, followed by the other pilgrims one at a time. Everybody is determined to take the daredevil plunge, and as I hit the water I triumphantly shout 'Bamba!' In seconds I am pulled unceremoniously on board, much like a drunken walrus. I'm not as agile as the younger pilgrims, but I hope things will improve as I lose weight en route.

Leaving the heaving seas behind us, we head into False Bay where the sea flattens out and we take a breather. We have been at sea for nearly five hours and have successfully rounded the Cape. Gunning the Mariners, we high-tail it for the historic naval port of Simon's Town to spend the night there.

Gordon's Bay, 18 January 1993

Hi Debbie

Sawubona. We had a great farewell from Cape Town! You would have loved it. The rounding of Cape Point however was frightening and at times I was quite nervous. The NSRI accompanied us halfway and then had to turn back to rescue a fishing boat in distress, so we were on our own. This morning we bid farewell to friendly Simon's Town. Flat seas and good weather enabled us to spend a few hours photographing the thousands of seals on Seal Island. The beautiful creatures entertained us with great aplomb. But it's best to stay upwind! Man, do they stink.

The next chapter of the expedition is the Wild Coast of the Transkei. We'll pull the boats up the coast to East London. The plan is to do as much of the South African coast as possible, and to explore some of the bigger rivers and estuaries.

Mashozi and Ross send their love. We're all well! Please check on the dogs. Siyabonga - Kingsley

The Wild Coast

Hole in the Wall

Transkei's Wild Coast is truly magnificent with its long bays, sandy beaches, rocky cliffs and countless estuaries. Here the Xhosa and Pondo people augment their maize meal with crayfish, mussels, oysters and fish. Their conical thatched homes perch on the tops of the hills and cliffs with views of the rugged coast. Captain Cook, East London's Port Captain, tells us with a twinkle in his eye of freak waves off the Transkei coast capable of breaking ships in two – stories of monstrous winds, the continental shelf and the Agulhas current – and many a wreck! Glancing at our sea charts I notice the warning for tomorrow: 'Abnormal waves of up to 20 metres, preceded by a deep trough, may be encountered at the seaward edge of the continental shelf.'

Saturday 23 January

The Captain's weather forecast of a moderate south-wester proves to be correct, and we wake to find the wind pushing long swells towards our destination. Two tugs escort us out of the harbour, and with great excitement we push out into the surf and through the farewell spray of the tugs' fire hoses.

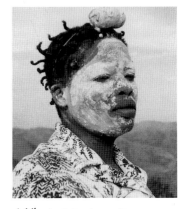

A Xhosa sangoma – may her prophecies be wiser than those of Nongqawuse.

Soon we're running with the wind to Kei Mouth, just on the plane and outboards at half throttle, shirts off and relishing the freedom. Dolphins and sea birds accompany us for much of the way. We've been warned about the hazardous presence of the Inniskilling Rocks at the river mouth, and it is with some trepidation that we cut inside them and race over the sandbar and into the Kei River. We are met by the dapper mayor who has come down to hand over written greetings and salutations from the village of Kei Mouth to be added to the Cape to Cairo scroll. We are humbled.

Sunday 24 January

We pull *QE2* and *Bathtub* off the beach as we've decided to explore inland. The somewhat rainy day starts off with Ruffus Hulley, a well-known trader and good friend, leading us along the rugged coastline to the exquisitely beautiful Nxara River, site of the kraal of Xhosa prophetess Nongqawuse. Overlooking this natural paradise we listen enthralled as Ruffus explains the circumstances that led to so much suffering among the Xhosa people.

One day in March 1856, 14-year-old Nongqawuse saw a vision of her ancestors in a river pool near the coast. The ancestors gave her a message, promising to free her people from the influence of the white settlers in the region if the Xhosa showed their faith by killing their cattle and burning their crops. Then the tribal heroes would rise from the dead, bringing with them wagons of treasures and herds of fat cattle. The grain pits of the believers would overflow, and their youth would be restored. Also, a mighty whirlwind would sweep all the white men into the sea.

The Xhosa slaughtered their cattle for 10 months, killing thousands of unfortunate beasts and burning their grain pits. But the ancestors failed to appear on the day that Nongqawuse had predicted and the young prophetess predicted a second day for the deliverance of the Xhosa nation. But the blood-red sun that she foretold did not rise on 18 February 1857, despite the 150,000 cattle that had been killed. Twenty-five thousand disillusioned people starved to death, while others were driven by hunger to work for the very people who they had believed would be swept into the sea.

After this story of tragedy we decide to explore another great river of the Xhosa people, the Kei. It is high spring tide and we are able to travel a good way up the river. Trumpeter hornbills herald our passage up this waterway, guarded by tall cycads standing like sentinels on the rocky cliff faces of the Transkei border. The southern bank forms a private game reserve and several kudu step out from the thick undergrowth to stare at our passing parade.

Monday 25 January - Through the Hole in the Wall

Launching out to sea in a strong south-westerly wind, *QE2* and *Bathtub* take four-and-a-half hours to reach one of nature's wonders – Hole in the Wall. The locals call it *Esikhaleni*, 'the place of the sound', describing how the sea thunders through the hole that it has bored through a detached cliff of stratified sandstone. Ross and Warren, the two skippers, glance at each other. Words aren't necessary and the throttles open, both boats leaping through this natural tunnel and into the calm bay beyond.

Going back through the hole takes even more daring. One wrong move and boat and crew will be smashed against the roof of the hole by the force of the incoming wave. How crazy too when you think of all the dangers that could lie ahead of us. But on expedition it's not just the destination that one thinks of; it's also the day-to-day challenge of the journey. So, while I feel it necessary to call Ross and Warren 'bloody crazy', I smile inwardly at their audacity.

FROM EAST LONDON TO PORT EDWARD - VERY ROUGH CONDITIONS UP THE WILD COAST SECTION!
WE STILL HAVE THE CALABASH.

Tuesday 26 January

For the first time on the expedition I feel we are developing a rhythm and a pace, and have allocated more specific duties to the team members. I am expedition leader and Warren is my assistant. He also skippers *QE2*, and is in charge of all mechanical duties. Gill, well travelled and practical, handles documentation, money and catering. Ross skippers and maintains the small boat. Jon is the medic, and, apart from being good with boats and fishing, he always keeps an even keel, and is good humoured and a great asset to the team. He enjoys a late night around the beer pots and he and Warren are old friends. Warren on the other hand is quick tempered, but I am sure he can look after himself in a sticky situation. I have every confidence in him and Ross as skippers. Nkonkoni Rob is enthusiastic and has a foreigner's excitement for a newly discovered continent. His and Nigel's job is to look after all camping equipment and to be responsible for the packing of the vehicles.

I'm feeling a lot fitter and am able to pull my belt in a notch, but with the constant pounding of the waves my kidneys are taking a hammering. The continual splashing of salt water is starting to infect our eyes.

High winds keep us battened down at the Murrays' cottage in Sinangwana for a few days, giving us time to explore on foot and by 4x4. Marijuana grows like a weed in these hills, making Nkonkoni Rob even jollier.

Monday 1 February

We wake early, having loaded the boats with enough fuel, food and equipment to get us through to the Mtamvuna River at Port Edward. We have learnt over the previous few days that trying to have the 4x4 vehicles meet the boats on a daily basis is almost impossible, as 30 minutes by sea can sometimes entail a five-hour drive.

The launch through the surf at Sinangwana is tough. The first attempt results in a cut motor, and *QE2* gets caught sideways by a giant curler that breaks over her as she sits, engines screaming, on a sandbank. Somehow she doesn't flip, but she's full of water. Out we jump, just in time to get her nose into the next wave. Warren hits the throttle, leaving some of us to swim for the shore. All the kit is wet, but Ross is fine in *Bathtub*. We regroup on the beach, and, after much excitement, finally make it out past the back line and head up the coast in rough seas past the Mgazana and the Mngazi mouths to Port St Johns and the Mzimvubu River.

The river is running chocolate brown and the swells are like blocks of flats racing in to crash onto the sandbank. We are in for a rough time. The earliest known shipwreck on the South African coast was that of the *São João*, stranded here on 5 June 1552, which gave Port St Johns its name. Now, over 450 years later, we attempt to make our way into the river mouth at Port St Johns.

As all ski-boaters know, coming into a river mouth on the back of a blockbuster is a somewhat frightening affair when you don't know where you're going or where the channel is. We send the small boat in ahead of us. They hit the tip of the sandbank and we find them tugging at the nose as they wave us into the channel. We are pleased to get away from the ever-present south-easterly and into the safe haven of the Mzimvubu, in Xhosa 'place or home of the hippopotamus'. After fuelling up, we travel as far as we can up this beautiful and historic river.

Launching back out to sea proves to be a nightmare. It takes us 15 adrenaline-filled minutes of circling, running and punching through the waves before we leave the brown waters of the Mzimvubu behind us. Flying over the crest of a giant wave, *QE2* becomes airborne. I lose my footing, tumbling over and ending up with my head stuck between the food box and a container of fuel, somehow unscathed. Jon drags me upright, but my aerial display remains the joke of the day.

The plan was to come in at Mntafufu, but the heavy sea is still running and it looks too dangerous, so on we go to Waterfall Bluff and Cathedral Rock. The Cathedral is a granite outcrop hollowed out from within by the waves. Because of the dangerous swells – Captain Cook's words still echo in my ears – we cannot get closer than about 50 metres to the rocks, and even that becomes dangerous as a wave nearly breaks on us. Today is not a day for taking chances, since Murphy seems to be travelling with us.

Having photographed the Cathedral and the Mfihlelo Falls plummeting 160 metres over a sandstone cliff directly into the sea, we move on to the mouth of the Lupatana where we hope to spend the night. When planning the expedition I imagined the boats at the base of the falls and the chance to spear fish and explore. But instead, here we are at the mercy of the wind and some of the biggest swells I've ever experienced. It is as if there is some great hand stirring the ocean from below.

Trying to land, our main problem remains the heavy surf and high waves. We get onto the back line for a better view of the shore, keeping a sharp eye on the massive swells racing towards the beach. I decide not to risk both boats through the surf – Ross and Jon in *Bathtub* will go and find the best way through, and then they will radio us. If we crash onto the rocks or roll the boats in the heavy surf, it will mean the end of the expedition.

Bathtub heads into the raging surf. We get the occasional glimpse of orange life-jackets and red boat and then they are gone. There's just the screaming of the wind and the roar of the waves. We wait anxiously, but no radio call. The light is now fading fast. '*QE2* for *Bathtub* – do you copy?' Repeated over and over. '*Squelch ... squelch.*' No reply. We travel nervously up and down the back line, balancing precariously on the fuel hatch to get a better view. Nothing! I imagine Ross and Jon upside down in the surf. I'm really concerned and we decide to go in regardless.

Just then, on some rocks to the south, we see a figure silhouetted against the sky. It's Ross furiously waving a life-jacket. We go closer and he motions for us to follow a deep channel that runs hard against the rocks. Riding on the back of a giant wave we open up the throttles and can soon see *Bathtub* high and dry on the beach. Ross and Jon sprint down to grab the nose, and using the power of each wave we pull *QE2* up the beach. Our radios hadn't worked because *Bathtub* had landed out of sight behind the rocks. Sopping wet, we remove our life-jackets, the adrenaline causing us all to chatter excitedly.

It's a memorable evening under the stars in an area that I first visited years before. The mangroves and reeds act as natural filters for the crystal clear river water. We gather driftwood for a fire and ease our sore bodies into the sand. This is the real reward of such an expedition. Eating well in the bush beats any restaurant meal, and supper consists of tomato soup, boiled mealies and a braai, washed down with Captain Morgan rum and strong, sweet tea served in heavy enamel mugs, now dented and chipped from the constant bouncing on high seas.

A Pondo woman by the name of Mahowdini looked after our camp at this spot some years ago. I am honoured when she comes up to me and, extending her hand, greets me by my Zulu name, Nondwayiza. She and her husband, aptly named Stanley, spend long hours talking around the fire. Mahowdini tells of the 11 head of cattle she is about to receive as bride wealth for one of her daughters, and of the new trading store that was recently opened just above her homestead. Very few people come to camp here nowadays and they miss the extra revenue, but the cattle are fat, the fish are biting, and crayfish and mussels are plentiful. However, the sea has been upside down for the week now. Don't we know it! Later, on hearing the weather report, we realize that we were getting the tail end of the cyclonic weather that has been hitting the Natal coast. It's bloody frightening!

Tuesday 2 February - Paradise up the Mtentu

In the early morning we're surrounded by a group of young Pondo boys who have arrived to gaze at our boats and equipment. Some of them have been hunting with dogs and have caught a spotted genet. They say they are going to eat the flesh and turn the skin into a tobacco pouch. Their reward for helping us push the boats over the sandbar is a ride in *QE2* – some are elated, others terrified.

The weather is calmer at last, but there are still big swells and a hint of a swing to a north-easter as we make our way up the coast and into the bay at Port Grosvenor. I'm travelling with Ross in *Bathtub* today and we decide to go in for a closer look. Once between the sets of waves we are committed and the next moment we're in shallow water. I do a sharp turn in an attempt to 'nose in' back out to sea, and hear that terrible grating sound of props meeting rock. We run *Bathtub* onto the beach for an inspection, and are impressed at the strength of the props and skegs, for very little damage has been done. It is going to be a difficult launch – the sets running too close together and the waves too high to punch through. I give the controls to Ross, and sit on the deck in the bow, facing backwards. Thanks to his good skippering, we do not emulate the fate of the 729-ton East Indiaman, the *Grosvenor*, that went down off this point in August 1782.

This unfortunate vessel, after a fair voyage from India, hit bad weather off the notorious south-east coast of Africa. In stormy darkness the ship was driven onto the rocks where all but 15 of the 150 passengers made it ashore. However, their troubles had only just started as they began the long journey down the coast towards the Cape, 1,000 kilometres distant. Two months after the ship went down, the first group of six seamen was found by white settlers near the Zwartkops River, 500 kilometres from the site of the wreck. The search party that was sent up the coast found only 12 more survivors of the *Grosvenor*.

We continue to the shores of the Mkambati Nature Reserve, where zebra and wildebeest graze on the green ledges above the rocky shoreline. The Mtentu River is the northern boundary of this game reserve, its sheer cliff faces, several hundred metres high, forming the ideal boundary to keep game in and poachers out. From the boats we can see the gap in the cliff face but nothing prepares us for the spectacular entrance to this river. It is neap tide and we have difficulty in getting through the shallow mouth, which is only just wide enough to allow the boats through and has rocks on the northern bank. We push through the shallows and in seconds are in a natural paradise of crystal water approximately 50 metres wide. The river is bordered on either side by steep cliffs and dense subtropical vegetation. The strident call of a fish eagle brings us back to reality and we move slowly up this wonderland. A few kilometres up the river, we turn into a heavily wooded creek that quickly becomes a dead end in the form of a high waterfall tumbling into the salty water of the estuary.

Back in the main river course, we travel for about 10 kilometres before coming to a large flat rock sticking out in midstream, looking much like the funnel of a sunken ship. We tie up the boats and use the rock as a lunchtime platform from which to view what must be one of the most beautiful river settings in Africa. Dwarf palms shine light green among the darker vegetation (I believe that this is one of the few places in the world where they are still found). The only other human we see on the river is a young Pondo lad with the English name of Lucky Boy. He is paddling along in half a canoe, sitting with the pointed end behind him, the open end kept just above the surface by an old piece of Styrofoam and a balsa log lashed on with a network of 'monkey rope'. Lucky Boy in his humble craft has managed to land a nice-sized rock cod and a few smaller fish. He is having difficulty in rowing against the wind so we load his canoe onto *QE2* and he jumps aboard *Bathtub*. He is delighted when we give him the opportunity to steer the boat back to his launching site. Leaving his half canoe, he disappears along an overgrown bush path to his thatched village on the krantzes above the Mtentu River.

A cascading waterfall is our shower, and we roll out our sleeping bags in a small forest clearing. Bushbabies cry out in the night and the firelight dances off the trees.

Wednesday 3 February

Being short of fuel, we wanted to be up and at sea by sunrise, to reach the mouth of the Mtamvuna before the north-easter came up. But man proposes and God disposes, and the sun is well up by the time we heave the boats over the sandbar. The sea is like glass and once again the dolphins frolic and swim alongside us. We realize that we have come to the end of the Wild Coast when we reach the Wild Coast Casino, standing like a shrine to man's gambling craze. But then we too have been gambling, not with cards and the roulette wheel, but with the elements of wind, sea, rain and tides. All we have to do now is travel up the Mtamvuna River, where the vehicles and the team who pulled the trailers from our camp at Sinangwana will meet us at the Old Pont.

These are interesting times in South Africa as the country wobbles towards democracy.

On arriving at the Mtamvuna we find the mouth barred by a sandbank. Ross drops me at the back line and I swim ashore to inspect the situation. I see a lone figure on the beach and approach him hoping that he might be able to tow us across the sandbar and into the river with his 4x4. I must look like an apparition coming out of the surf, or so his dogs think anyway, as they approach me warily. Mike Gregory turns out to be an absolute star – not only does he pull us over the sandbar (with the help of our inflatable rollers), but he also delivers a case of Castle lagers and some fresh bread upstream where we wait for the vehicles.

Mike joins us and we soon get round to toasting each other and the successful end to the Wild Coast. We've been travelling for nearly three weeks from Cape Town, and as the crow flies we are hardly closer to Cairo, but then our clear objective is to explore Africa's waterways. South Africa doesn't have a great river running north to south and so we've stuck to the coast. Cyclonic weather conditions have given us hell, but we've survived the tough sea journey. And, anyway, aren't these the stories that the Wild Coast is made of!

1 March 1993
Zinkwazi Beach

Hi Debbie

We've just completed our last stretch of South African coast, Maputaland. It was something special despite some bad weather. Our launch from Richards Bay was great. I was honoured to receive a very ornate letter from the mayor, and the brass band of the mostly Zulu 1st Battalion from nearby Mtubatuba played with great gusto as we raced out through the waves. It was rough going though with a howling south-easterly making things interesting, but once we got up the coast we had a great time. We camped at Cape Vidal - magnificent - with its high, forested dunes, some of the highest in the world apparently. The diving and fishing was excellent and Mashozi loved the turtle research station at Bhanga Nek. We went out one night with torches to watch thousands of baby turtles being released. I quite enjoyed the injomani - the local palm wine, which has quite a kick. Also up at Kosi Bay we got to explore the Thonga fish traps and cruise among the raffia palms trying to spot palmnut vultures. Lake Sibaya, SA's largest freshwater lake, and Lake St Lucia were heavenly. It is no wonder that this place is known as KwaZulu - 'place of heaven', home to the Zulu, the 'people of heaven'.

Last night the whole team, family and friends gathered at the Zulu Village of Shakaland for my 47th birthday and for a sendoff, as we leave SA tomorrow. A beast was slaughtered and the party continued well into the night. It is now a matter of cleaning and loading up the kit and final checks for the overland stretch to Botswana - there is no coming back. I can't wait and I know that I have a great team - tried and tested in the rough waters of the SA coast. The adventure begins!

Siyabonga, Kingsley
PS Please look after the dogs, especially Winston!

MOZAMBIQUE

KOSI BAY
BHANGA NEK
MAPUTALAND
LAKE SIBAYA
MKUZI RIVER
SODWANA BAY
CAPE VIDAL
LAKE ST LUCIA
Q EZ AND BATHTUB
UMHLATUZE RIVER
RICHARDS BAY

SHAKALAND - A FAREWELL TO SOUTH AFRICA 28/2/1993

MEDITERRANEAN SEA

CAIRO
EGYPT
NILE
LAKE NUBIA
NUBIAN DESERT
KHARTOUM   ERITREA
SUDAN
WHITE NILE
BLUE NILE
LAKE TANA   DJIBOUTI
ETHIOPIA
ADDIS ABABA
LAKE TURKANA
UGANDA   SOMALIA
LAKE ALBERT
KENYA
LAKE GEORGE   MASAI MARA
LAKE RWANDA   LAKE VICTORIA   NAIROBI
LAKE EDWARD   SERENGETI   LAMU ARCHIPELAGO
BURUNDI   MOMBASA
ZAÏRE   UJIJI   TANZANIA   PEMBA ISLAND
LAKE TANGANYIKA
LAKE RUKWA
LAKE MALAWI
ANGOLA   MALAWI
ZAMBIA   CAHORA BASSA
OKAVANGO R.   ZAMBEZI R.   LAKE KARIBA
VICTORIA FALLS   MOZAMBIQUE   CHINDE
OKAVANGO DELTA   ZIMBABWE
NAMIBIA   MAKGADIKGADI SALT PAN
BOTSWANA   KALAHARI DESERT
MAPUTO
SOUTH AFRICA   DURBAN
CAPE OF GOOD HOPE

ATLANTIC OCEAN

INDIAN OCEAN

ANTHONY RILEY '02

The traditional Zulu
igula calabash

Pilgrims of adventure

Kingsley (Nondwayiza)

At 47 I am the greybeard of the team. I am most often called by my Zulu name Nondwayiza, 'the African jacana' or 'lily trotter', the bird with the long legs and the big feet. Apart from being the figurehead, and I suppose the driving force behind the whole thing, I will attempt to keep some sort of an expedition journal. I want to record this historic South African-led expedition as the first of us going back into Africa after the restricting years of apartheid.

Kingsley (Nondwayiza)

Gill Holgate (Mashozi)

My adventurous wife Gill and I have spent a 'lifetime' adventuring together. We've lived rough and travelled rough. I met Gill (whom we all refer to endearingly as Mashozi – 'she who wears shorts') when I was a young man travelling the world. In Gill's words: 'I remember him when he was tall and thin. All he had was a short black beard and a rucksack of dirty clothes. I fell in love twice – firstly with Kingsley, and secondly with Africa, my newly adopted home.' Gill, originally from the UK, soon learnt Zulu. She ran safaris and documentary film shoots, a trading store and a Zulu beadwork project. Now 46, she is the mama of the expedition. The team will rely on her for food supplies and all finance and paperwork – everything from passports to vehicle papers and permissions. Gill is officially chosen as the expedition bursar.

Gill Holgate (Mashozi)

Ross Holgate

Ross Holgate

Ross and I are simply best mates. What a privilege – and those of you who are parents will know this – to be able to take off on a great African adventure with your son at your side. Ross is good with boats and engines, knows the bush and has a quiet, dry sense of humour. At only 20 years of age he is the youngest pilgrim. He ia tough and fit, and the girls like him. Ross will skipper Bathtub.

Warren Hulett and Jon Dahl

Both practical farm boys from Eshowe in Zululand, Warren and Jon are good sailors and expert spear fishermen, and to top it all, Warren is a diesel mechanic. Both have been in the army, and Jon, so as to secure the position as medic, made regular visits to the local hospital where he learnt basic first aid and how to inject, stitch and apply an IV drip. While it might be better to have a 'real doctor', no one can deny Jon's incredible enthusiasm. He turns out to be an absolute gem, but to this day I am relieved that he never had to stitch me up. Warren, an excellent skipper, will be in charge of QE2.

Jon Dahl

Warren Hulett

Rob Dodson (Nkonkoni)

Rob Dodson

A jolly Pom who came out to Swaziland on a working holiday, Rob fell in love with Africa. He has also hitch-hiked across East Africa and speaks a little Swahili. I asked a Swazi friend, whom Rob had worked for, for advice. 'Great lad, loves Africa, can fix things, but can't hold his booze and his feet stink. Knows restaurants and is a great cook.' And so I take a chance on Rob as expedition cook and driver. He proves to be as naughty as hell, sometimes difficult to handle, but great fun. He is soon christened Nkonkoni Rob, because of his habit of twitching his head like a wildebeest when he gets excited.

Nigel Hallowes

Nigel is not only the son of our dear old friends Paul and Liz Hallowes, but also Gill's godson. He has grown into a big, strong young man who loves Africa and is determined to join the expedition. Despite his large frame Nigel is a gentle, caring person. He is put in charge of back-up vehicles and supplies, and has remained a great friend – honest and reliable.

Nigel Hallowes

ABOVE: The team hams it up for a picture in the Cape Times. LEFT: Macece came with the Shakaland dance team (TOP RIGHT) to see us off. On the way down he fell asleep; waking as the vehicle emerged from a tunnel he decided that he was now 'overseas'! RIGHT: With flags flying we wave farewell to Cape Town. Cairo, here we come!

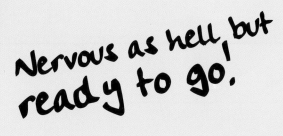
Nervous as hell, but ready to go!

Civic Centre
12 Hertzog Boulevard
P.O. Box 298
Cape Town 8000
Telex: 52-0966 CEECT SA
Fax: (021) 419-1129
Tel: (021) 400-2800

Burgersentrum
Hertzogboulevard 12
Posbus 298
Kaapstad 8000
Teleks: 52-0966 CEECT SA
Faks: (021) 419-1129
Tel: (021) 400-2800

OFFICE OF THE MAYO
CITY OF CAPE TOWN
KANTOOR VAN
DIE BURGEMEESTER
STAD KAAPSTAD

Ref: 6/2/6/1/1

1993-01-13

His Worship the Mayor of Cairo
Mayor's Parlour
City Hall
CAIRO
EGYPT

Dear Colleague

It gives me great pleasure to send to you and the citizens of Cairo warm and personal greetings from the Mother City of South Africa, by the hands of Kingsley Holgate, who has transversed Africa from South to North via its waterways.

In South Africa our struggle for a new and just political order is hopefully drawing to an end. It is, however, an exciting and challenging time in our country's history. Although it is sometimes frightening we have the prospect of a magnificent future of real democracy and peace. This year our ultimate goal is to establish tolerance and peace because without it we will not be able to secure a happy and peaceful future.

As Africans we must work together, and I am sure many problems will be solved. We need your support, understanding and encouragement to realise our dreams. Together we will have a great future.

Therefore it is a great opportunity for me to send to you, your Council and all the citizens of Cairo warm greetings of goodwill and peace. May you enjoy happiness and may your future endeavours be blessed with great success.

Yours sincerely

COUNCILLOR CLIVE KEEGAN
ACTING MAYOR

A COPY OF THE MAYORAL NOTE FROM THE CITIZENS OF CAPE TOWN — WILL THE ORIGINAL MAKE IT THROUGH TO CAIRO !?

ABOVE: AOE pilgrims and friends – Maputaland coast.
BELOW: Forever pushing and shoving – it's the nature
of the game. *RIGHT:* A Xhosa woman on the
Wild Coast. *BOTTOM RIGHT:* Thongaland
fishtraps are handed down from
generation to generation.

MAIN PICTURE: East London's town crier announces (he got our story a bit wrong and his breath smells of whisky – he's great fun!) our departure for the

Wild Coast and Maputaland

A journey through the jewel of the Kalahari

THIS PICTURE: The winding Okavango. INSET ABOVE: Nkwazi – the fish eagle. BELOW: Water in the usually dry Makgadikgadi Pan. BOTTOM RIGHT: At last – the mighty Zambezi. BOTTOM LEFT: The AOE team in their Robertsons' T-shirts (what would we do without those favourite stand-bys, Marmite and Aromat!). LEFT: Sunset at Katima Mulilo.

Salt Pans & Swamps

In 1849 David Livingstone discovered the Okavango, a 15,000-square-kilometre watery wilderness, home to lion, buffalo, crocodile and elephant. A place of hippo grass, waving beds of papyrus and crystal waters. He wrote: 'We found the water to be so clear, cold and soft, that the idea of melting snow was suggested to our mind.' The Okavango is not born from snow-covered peaks, but as summer rain from the highlands of Angola. Like Dr Livingstone, we too are going in search of these crystal waters that end their life as a delta set in a sea of Kalahari sand, the largest mantle of sand in the world. But first we must pay our respects to Makgadikgadi, once one of Africa's greatest lakes.

Friday 5 March

We arrive at the Tlokweng border post into Botswana, our vehicles heavily laden with everything we need to get us to Cairo: Castrol outboard oil, tents, spares, medical kit, camp chairs, food supplies, the braai grid and blackened camp kettle, and of course the three-legged old cast-iron pot. Initially we are refused entry, because of our boats and radios, but we produce our papers and eventually permission is granted.

We camp under the stars on the side of the Gaborone–Francistown road under a bright full moon and a heavy dew. Dry mopani logs spit sparks into the sky, and the flames light up our laughing faces. During the night the whistle of a distant train breaks the Kalahari silence. We are only a few kilometres from the Mafikeng–Victoria Falls railway line, a legacy of Cecil John Rhodes and his dream of a Cape to Cairo rail link.

Saturday 6 March

Sleeping bags hang on trees to dry and a lazy mood hangs over the pilgrims in Africa this morning. We set off at a nice slow pace, following the long ribbon of tar from Mahalapye to Palapye and finally to Francistown. A strong headwind has us averaging only about 75 kilometres an hour. Leaving Francistown we head due east to Dukwe and then down to Sua Pan. Sua and the Ntwetwe pans make up the giant Makgadikgadi salt pans that stretch for 12,000 square kilometres.

Travelling first through mopani woodland and then through short yellow Kalahari grass, we roll onto the largest salt pans on earth. What a sense of freedom, our vehicles racing across the pans against the giant yellow ball of the setting sun. Odyssey tradition prevails, and we whip out canvas chairs and open the bar for sundowners. Sunset over the pans is an unforgettable experience. For Ross and me it brings back memories of our great land yacht adventure a few years ago when we very nearly perished from thirst attempting to circumnavigate Sua Pan using only the power of the wind.

Tonight, as the sparks from our hardwood fire rise into the starlit sky, I gaze into the coals and imagine a time when this dry place was one of Africa's largest lakes, when one could hear the lapping of water on a lakeshore. Then there was a shift in the earth's crust, the rivers stopped visiting and the African sun turned the lake to salt. Yes, we've come to pay our respects to Makgadikgadi, once one of Africa's greatest lakes.

The hysterical cackle of a distant hyaena brings me back to my senses. Tomorrow we'll continue west into the sun, heading for the Okavango Delta.

Sunday 7 March - Sticking in Sua

A beautiful clear Kalahari day dawns on the Makgadikgadi, dust devils performing in front of a watery stage. The Nata River has flooded, filling just the top section of Sua Pan, and bringing with it thousands of pelicans and flamingos. In the shimmering heat we use distant baobabs as points of navigation. The Bushmen, or San, believe that God, in a fit of anger, hurled these giant trees from the skies, and they landed upside down, their roots in the air. To me they are like the elephants of the plant kingdom.

There is many a horror story about 4x4s having to be dismantled to get them out of Sua's sticky clutches. The pans have filled up to such an extent that we get caught between the veterinary cordon fence and one-and-a-half metres of water with a slippery bottom. But the spirit of the AOE carries us, and through we go, water coming over the bonnet and under the doors. Thank God for the winches – without them we would still be sitting in Sua Pan waiting for the water to recede. As it is, we emerge from the pans with gooey white Sua Pan mud clinging to the undercarriage of the vehicles like sticky toffee in your teeth.

Out from Sua we're onto the Makgadikgadi salt pan bar in Nata for a not-too-cold Castle and a fuel fill-up, and then on to the magical ilala palm belt west of Gweta. There is water everywhere and this normally arid area looks like a wonderland. We spend the night among the palm trees – a full moon, fish paella and the wind rustling the hundreds of palm fronds above us. No people, no officialdom, such is the magical Kalahari.

Monday 8 March

Maun has changed from just a dusty stopover for intrepid 4x4 travellers and big game hunters. Now it's a modern, bustling bush town. Some of the old character is still in place, however, and Land Cruisers and battered Land Rovers bear testimony to Maun still being the centre of a tourist and wildlife paradise.

I am introduced to the district commissioner who agrees to sign the Afrika Odyssey scroll. How Africa has changed: here I am sitting with my long beard looking somewhat 'bush happy', being interviewed by the black district commissioner, Miss Phophetsi. Not too many years ago I would have been talking to a khaki-clad British colonial civil servant, the picture of the former British protectorate of Bechuanaland completed by white-washed stones, old Bedfords, Land Rovers and the fluttering Union Jack.

The disease-control officials spray our boats to prevent the spread of water hyacinth, and as final preparations we get some ice blocks from the veterinary department and buy a huge pile of liver from the Greek butcher. We camp at Crocodile Camp, where a nearby village plays loud music throughout the night and the donkeys let rip with a constant braying of *aargh-phew, aargh-phew*.

Tuesday 9 March

Our adventure into the Delta starts today! We've decided to travel by road up the edge of the Delta to Sepupa, and then to work our way up and down from there.

A long, hot drive up the southern shoreline of the Okavango through Sehithwa, Tsau, Nokaneng and Gumare is rewarded when we arrive on the shores of the Okavango River, crystal clear and flowing swiftly from its source in Angola. We load up and launch downstream with our two guides, leaving the vehicles behind in the care of a local *madala*. We will return in three days' time.

Within minutes of launching, Jon and Rob both land tiger fish. This fish is a powerful hunter, with a mouth dominated by a vicious set of large conical teeth. Even poisonous snakes have been found in their stomachs.

We sight hippos and crocs as we travel downstream to our camp for the night – a beautiful spot on the south bank of the river under giant trees and guarded by a pair of fish eagles. I take one of the boats and travel upstream to observe the sunset in solitude, away from the bustle of setting up camp. Sitting on top of the boat console I can see beyond the walls of papyrus that stand on either side of the Okavango. I cut the motors and drift down the river. The sun disappears for another day, its departure heralded by the cry of the fish eagle. Soon the river is dark and overhead the stars begin their night vigil. Bird sounds are replaced by an orchestra of frogs, joined unfortunately by the whine of the mosquitos. As I head back downstream, the road of water is lit up by a brilliant full moon, which throws a yellow ribbon of light onto the river. A passing hippo grunts in the night. This is what I've come for!

Wednesday 10 March - Angry hippos

We awake to the sound of a thousand birdcalls – mourning doves, laughing doves, red-eyed doves, swamp boubous, grey loeries, white-rumped babblers, black-collared barbets and, of course, the sentinel cry of the fish eagle. Jon and Warren are up early fishing for tiger fish. Yesterday's catch of tigers has been left to steam all night, the succulent flesh falling from the bones and making excellent eating.

Our two guides are proving to be fine company. Ebe Kesietswe from nearby Etsala speaks brilliant English and has a good knowledge of birds. The dapper little fellow proudly wears a Zionist Christian Church badge on his leather jacket and is perfectly at home in this waterland. His companion, Aaron Motlakatshipi from Seronga, has been a guide and a tracker all his life and is a great strong man with an excellent knowledge of the Okavango Delta. Without these guides we could get completely lost.

The river in the panhandle is high and running swiftly, the water having come down from the Angolan highlands. It is amazing to think that it will take five months to reach Maun as it spreads slowly across the Delta.

We follow the river down to Seronga, fishing as we go, and enticing fish eagles to dive for their prey by tying bits of tiger fish up with papyrus and floating them downstream. You need only whistle to attract the attention of these magnificent birds of prey and then down they swoop, with a *whoosh* of speed, talons outstretched.

Seronga is a small, clean village of thatched huts inhabited by the Bayei and Bambukushu people. The decorated reeded walls around the homesteads show a pride in tradition, and the village has two schools and a small hospital. Seronga has had good crops and the cattle are fat. Aaron, who is from the area, takes us on a tour past the *khotlo*, the meeting place of the elders where tribal court is held. Then he leads us to the butchery, an area under a tree where a beast has been slaughtered. Some customers who do not have cash barter grain for meat. The entire beast will be sold today, piece by piece, in the unhurried way of Africa, with customers choosing their favourite cuts. We buy the whole fillet, string it onto a stick and cart it back to the boats like hunters returning with a trophy. We stop only for some millet beer being sold by some lovely old crones sitting under a reeded shelter.

At Seronga we leave the Okavango River to travel down a smaller river which is extremely narrow in parts, sometimes too narrow for the big boat, its sides brushing against the river's papyrus walls. On a bend in the river we are confronted by seven hippos. Aaron has previously had a bad experience with this unfriendly pod – one took a bite out of his boat – and he is reluctant to continue. A pair of fish eagles look down on the red-and-yellow inflatables, the occupants excitedly discussing what best to do. We decide to make a run for it.

Backing up, we gun the Mariners and charge. The hippos sound and I think we're through. Next moment we hit something with both motors. At full throttle the motors click up into shallow drive, screaming as they cavitate. We think we've run into a hippo and are caught on its back, but quickly realize that we're actually on a mudbank – a highly dangerous situation when surrounded by angry hippos. Keeping the throttles wide open we plough through the bank, into deep water and out of danger. The big boat shoots past us at full speed, touching bottom as it goes.

Our destination is Guma Lagoon, and after travelling for many miles along the narrow channels we are relieved to arrive in this massive open lagoon surrounded by huge trees. We back-track up the narrows and find an incredibly beautiful island on which to camp, sharing our evening paradise with a colony of hadeda ibis that heralds our arrival and the setting of the sun with raucous cries. Large enamel mugs of chilled wine set the tone for a pleasant evening and a fillet-of-steak feast.

Thursday 11 March

We load the boats for our trip back up to the Seronga junction, hoping the hippos are in a better mood. The river seems to be flowing more strongly, with small islands of papyrus being swept downstream. There is no doubt that the floods have reached the panhandle. We've been in the delta for a week, and after our morning's journey we pitch camp early and relax on terra firma. During the night I lie awake listening to the night sounds: jackals cry in the distance, hippos grunt, the fly-sheet flaps in the breeze. I hear a rustling noise and get up to check on the boats. Animal eyes shine in the torchlight and then disappear. I'm relieved not to find outboard engine thieves!

Friday 12 March

Waking, I hear the *swish swish* of a fly rod – and then a cry of dismay. Warren has got his rod and line stuck in a thorn tree. No amount of tugging can free it, and he has to climb the tree to rescue his gear. The entire camp gathers to give advice, none of which helps Warren, as the branch he is standing on breaks and he is left a clinging captive to a thousand thorns. Finally rescuing his gear, he declares fly-fishing a thorny issue.

By the time we reach Sepupa our fuel supply is low, and we decide to take the big boat out of the water. Mashozi, Ross, Aaron, Nkonkoni Rob and I continue upstream to Shakawe, another five long hours of winding river. The vehicles and other pilgrims take the dirt road to meet us at Shakawe Fishing Camp, and by the time we arrive they are firmly ensconced in the bar. We were warned when we appointed Nkonkoni Rob that he can't hold his booze. To date he's been a great Odyssey pilgrim, but this evening he's giggling hysterically and telling the filthiest jokes, invariably forgetting the punchline. He is trying to impress two American Peace Corps ladies who, I can tell, are getting very irritated. But the worst comes when we're standing around the communal braai. He decides that the most practical way of extinguishing the high flames would be to pull out 'Percy'. We manage to stop him just in time, but the guests are now thoroughly

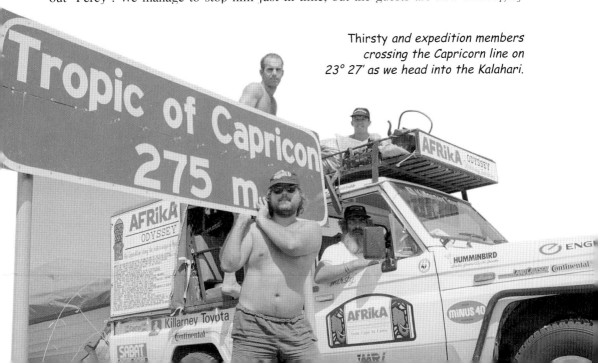

Thirsty and expedition members crossing the Capricorn line on 23° 27' as we head into the Kalahari.

Updating the expedition journal with Mashozi.

disgusted. While I can see the funny side of the situation, this is not the way for a member of an expedition of peace and goodwill to behave! I send him to his tent, and tell him in no uncertain terms that he no longer has a place in the expedition. He's fired and will have to make his own way home.

Saturday 13 March – The Tsodilo Hills

A shadow falls across the front of my tent. It's Nkonkoni Rob, red-eyed and sheepish. He hands me a note of apology. It will never happen again. And please, I must understand that it was the demon drink! This expedition is the most important thing in his life. The note ends with the words: 'Please, Kingsley, I need a second chance. Forgive me!' I call him back to my tent and give him a warning, explaining that if in the future he needs to let off steam he should go off somewhere on his own. An expedition such as ours is also a diplomatic mission. We shake hands and he thanks me profusely. He's a great lad!

We decide to have a break from boats and rivers and invite Rob Caskie, whom we met last night, to join us on a detour to the Tsodilo Hills, the ancient place of the Bushmen. Rob, a Natal boy, is a ball of fire. He has a love for the bush and photography, and is working in the area for a well-known wildlife film-maker and photographer.

A few hours of grinding and bouncing through soft Kalahari sand finally brings us to the hills – giant rocky outcrops standing guard over hundreds of Bushman paintings. None of us has been here before and we are all captivated by the mysterious aura of the place. We pitch camp in an open area between the higher 'male' and somewhat lower 'female' hill, as they are known by the Bushmen. Our backdrop is a giant cave and the ever-changing colours of the rock faces, lit up by the setting sun.

Ross, Nigel and I brave some stinging nettles to climb onto a rocky perch. How many Bushmen have sat on this same ledge, clicking away in their strange tongue, their love and understanding for wild things clearly shown in the hundreds of paintings that provide modern man with a glimpse into the past? Being the eternal romantic, I can feel the spirits of these people around me and, as the evening breeze fans the leadwood coals of our campfire, I feel a strange peace and connection with the past.

Sunday 14 March

We awake to the mournful call of the emerald-spotted wood dove. We try whenever possible not to travel at all on Sundays, or at least as little as possible. Today we will relax in this ancient place and travel back to Shakawe later this afternoon.

High up on top of a rocky ledge, overlooking a never-ending stretch of Kalahari, nature has carved out a perfectly symmetrical Jacuzzi. This round pool is fed by rainwater from a sculptured hole in the rocks above – a natural rainwater gutter – and is deep enough for two or three people to sit in. I climb up there to spend some time on my own. Stripped naked and sitting in the pool, I gaze over a massive expanse of Kalahari, now green and flush after the best rains in many years.

The sandy track back to Shakawe is only about 40 kilometres long, but it takes us almost three hours of back-breaking bouncing and grinding through soft sand to get there. We begin to dream of ice-cold beer long before we actually reach the pub at Shakawe Fishing Camp.

15-16 March - Popa Falls

The Namibian border post officials are extremely friendly as we head through to the Caprivi Strip, welcoming us to their country with broad smiles. The gravel road from Mahembo is excellent, and we are camped back on the Kavango River (as the Okavango is known in Namibia) at Popa Falls by the time the sun sets. We sing happy birthday to Nigel while having a sundowner sitting in the rapids at Popa Falls.

The Popa Falls area is so beautiful and the facilities so good that we call a rest day. Everybody relishes the idea of an opportunity to wash clothes, read and rest. I sit on the banks of the Kavango, writing my journal, the river's gurgling creating a wonderfully relaxed feel. The shade of several giant trees shelters me from the noonday sun and in the distance rain clouds are gathering to the command of rumbling thunder.

I am increasingly finding that by spending time in the wilderness I am truly able to unwind. It's a privilege to have my family with me on the Odyssey. Earlier this morning Ross and I wandered up the rapids, just the two of us sitting out there in the middle of the river discussing the adventure. Would it be safe to do the Mozambican leg of the Zambezi? How would we get across southern Sudan? Would the boats and motors stand the pace? On crossing the rapids I slipped and fell into the current. He extended a hand, and the 27-year age gap between us meant nothing as we both laughed at my clumsiness.

A loud clap of thunder finally summons the rain, and I race for shelter – the journal under my arm and a camp chair over my head. We're almost past the rainy season now, but I'm sure that occasional thunderstorms will continue to visit us as we go. What a relief after the years of severe drought that have crippled southern Africa. At one time we feared that, with the rivers so low and the drought so bad, we might have had to call off our crazy Afrika Odyssey.

But the Kavango River is running strongly, and to the north of us the mighty Zambezi has risen. This year, for the first time, we will be present to witness the Kuomboko ceremony, which failed to take place last year because of the drought. This 300-year-old celebration marks the rising of the waters on the great Zambezi floodplain. In a loud and colourful procession, the *litunga*, the Lozi king, will be paddled to his wet-season palace to escape the rising floodwaters. Tomorrow we leave for Katima Mulilo and the commencement of the Zambezi leg of our expedition. So much to look forward to!

The Zambezi –
Livingstone's River
of God

The Nalikwanda, the Lozi royal barge

Dr David Livingstone believed that the only way to stop slavery was to find navigable routes into the African interior so as to promote Christianity, civilization and commerce. His arrival on the Zambezi in 1851 was a turning point in his life. He was moved to tears by the sight of this great river, calling it the 'River of God'. It was to change him from missionary to explorer.

Armed with a tattered Bible and a sextant, he set off with his porters to travel on foot and by dugout canoe from Luanda on the Angolan coast to Quelimane in Mozambique, a distance of some 4,300 kilometres, which included almost the entire length of the Zambezi River.

Wednesday 17 March

We meet the Rundu–Katima Mulilo road at Mohembo and turn right, running along a dusty, dead-straight road for over 300 kilometres. The white dust is like talcum powder; beards and hair turn white and we age a hundred years. This is the Caprivi, a narrow strip of Namibia wedged between Botswana, Angola and Zambia, its history going back to the time of the 'scramble for Africa', when the continent was carved up like a cake to be distributed among the European powers. This thin strip of land gave Germany access to the Zambezi from South West Africa (now Namibia).

Here too, the rains have turned the area into a lush wilderness, the elephant grass sometimes standing higher than the vehicles. We stop on the bridge over the Kavango River to pay our last respects to this swollen ribbon of water that has been our host for the past week or so.

In Katima we meet with Dr Andries Gouws (Dr Dries), the local doctor and, fortunately for us, an authority on the Zambezi River and Zambia where he has hunted for many years. Sitting us all down – a map of Zambia spread out in front of us – he gives us a full rundown of the area. Our timing is spot on, and the water has risen sufficiently to allow us to travel unhindered on the mighty Zambezi River.

'All very well,' says Dr Dries, fixing us all with a stare, 'but at least one of you will certainly get malaria. We have roughly 20 cases a day of chloroquine-resistant malaria – and it can be fatal.' He warns us to take precautions, to treat any symptoms immediately with chloroquine, and, if there is no improvement after 24 hours, to treat with quinine tablets and/or quinine intravenously. He suggests that Jon meet with him the next morning to go through the treatment in more detail and to mark all landing strips and mission stations on the map. He offers to fly us out in the case of an emergency, and I must say I feel more confident knowing that we have such valuable back-up. Crocodiles, he warns us, are also a serious problem on certain parts of the river.

Our camp for the night is the delightful Hippo Lodge overlooking the great Zambezi River. It consists of a pleasantly converted old South African Defence Force camp. But now, where once there were bunkers, guns, khaki and camouflage, there are only fishermen, fellow adventurers and the odd Katima resident enjoying a sundowner.

Thursday 18 March

Katima Mulilo is a colourful little town, its name meaning 'to quench or put out the fire' in Silozi. One explanation has it that people travelling the river often used to carry live coals in the dugouts to be used for making fires when they came ashore at night. Very often the rapids at Katima would cause the coals to be quenched as water washed into the boat. Another story goes that young men wading across the river to visit their girlfriends on the opposite bank would often have the flames of their desire quenched by the icy, waist-deep Zambezi waters.

As a courtesy we call on the governor – a genial chap who agrees to give us a goodwill letter for our scroll. We then drive to the Zambian border a few kilometres upstream to try to find out when the Kuomboko will be taking place. At the border the friendly Zambian Customs officials in their crisp white shirts and dark trousers are sitting in the shade of a tree outside the Customs office. They explain that they are unsure of the exact date, but believe it will be on the second, third and fourth of April. I am determined not to miss the Kuomboko, one of Africa's greatest ceremonies, and we decide that we must get up to Mongu as soon as possible.

Back at Hippo Lodge we find Jon taking his job of medic quite seriously. He is practising giving an intravenous drip on Warren, who, suffering from a giant hangover, is quite happy to have a saline drip attached to his arm, the drip dangling from an overhanging thorn tree. The hangover is the result of a serious bout of drinking, brought on by a telephone call made to South Africa. It appears that things with his lovely blonde fiancée are not going that well back home, and he is struggling with the long-distance relationship. Despite the drip,

Jon practises his skills on a hungover Warren.

several aspirin, and the luxury of a bacon-and-egg breakfast, his mood remains low.

Hippo Lodge has a planked area that juts out over the Zambezi, and we sit on the chairs provided under a canopy of thatch and mopani poles, spectators to a magnificent sunset over the river. This is the beginning of a dream come true – a chance to travel almost the entire length of this legendary waterway. Going to bed, I feel the first signs of a fever coming on.

Friday 19 March

Having sweated through the night, I wake up with the symptoms of malaria. Jon immediately treats me with chloroquine tablets that make me feel quite nauseous. At an emergency discussion with the pilgrims, we agree to stay on at Hippo Lodge to monitor my condition. Fortunately, we are close to a hospital, although Dr Dries has taken off for a few days and will only be returning on Sunday.

While I am sweating out the malaria in bed, I read *Zambezi: Journey of a*

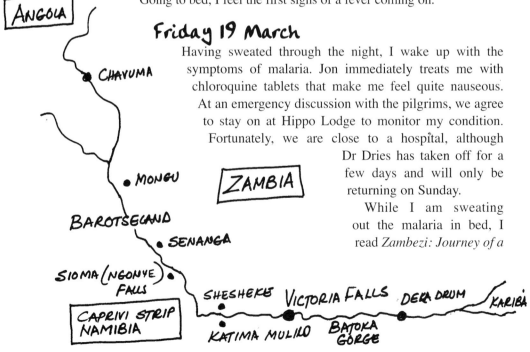

River by Mike Main. His chapter on the Kuomboko ceremony and the Lozi people quickens my desire to reach the floodplains in time to be a spectator at the event that 30,000 people are expected to attend, with buses laid on from all over Zambia.

Saturday 20 March
Still in bed – the fever persists and I am feeling weak. If my condition does not improve, we will seek medical help tomorrow.

Sunday 21 March
The chloroquine seems to be working. I'm feeling a little stronger today. In the afternoon we visit the home of Dr Daide, an Egyptian doctor who works at Katima Mulilo hospital. He is extremely helpful, treats me with Fansidar (used in treating chloroquine-resistant malaria) and passes me as fit to continue with the expedition.

Monday 22 March – Sioma Falls
I am still feeling ill and, after all the spook stories, I am a little nervous to travel on. But, being optimists, we pack up and leave Katima. At the border post we meet a colourful local who warns us to be careful when crossing the Zambezi on the Senanga ferry. According to him the ferry is 'buggered', the rusted rivets on the bottom causing it to leak. 'Be sure,' he says, 'to check that the team of women who bale the water out with buckets first do their job before you load the vehicles.' Good advice no doubt.

Once we are in Zambia, it is as if time has stood still. A rutted sandy track leads west, following the mighty Zambezi. Friendly villagers smile and wave as we pass. I don't think too many vehicles come this way.

We have heard that the Ngonye or Sioma Falls, the first of the breached dykes that mark the southern end of the Barotse floodplain, are, next to Victoria Falls, the most beautiful place on the river. We are not disappointed.

A buffalo skull marks the turnoff to the local Department of Wildlife office, where we meet Alfred Ilumbela, the ranger in charge. He points out a camping spot near the falls and, with the help of four-wheel drive and the winch, we find ourselves under some trees with a spectacular view of the water roaring over the falls. The floodwaters, he tells us, are almost at their highest. There are no hotels and no amenities, merely a massive expanse of Africa.

The local kids are amazed at our circus and come in droves to view these strange-looking adventurers. Alfred arranges for two game scouts to guard our camp at night. Not that it is unsafe, he says, but we are close to the Angolan border and he just wants to make sure that nothing goes missing.

Francis Mseteka and Oscar Mukule of the National Parks and Wildlife Services arrive with a shotgun and a .30-06. They drink coffee with us and tell us of the problems they sometimes have with Angolan poachers in nearby Sioma Ngwezi National Park. While most of the poaching is minor, they sometimes have to shoot on sight when poachers are armed. These scouts do their training in the Kafue and the Luangwa national parks and are committed to conservation. Theirs is a tough life patrolling the park on foot, sleeping in the bush for two weeks at a time. They earn only about R200 a month, but are proud to be employed at a time when jobs are scarce. They talk of the relative riches in South Africa, and of the days when their fathers worked on the gold mines there. I admire their dedication to duty. Elephant, buffalo, giraffe, sable and roan antelope and other species abound in Sioma Ngwezi, a somewhat unknown game reserve.

Tuesday 23 March

I am still suffering from malaria and am now getting a bit nervous. If I do not improve within the next 24 hours, I will have to get urgent medical help from one of the mission hospitals in the area. Today, however, I spend sitting quietly on the banks of the Zambezi. The water flowing through the volcanic rocks has formed plenty of beautiful bathing pools, and the pilgrims, eager for adventure, put on life-jackets and jump into the river below the falls. They get more than they bargain for, and are sucked under and tumbled down the rapids for well over a kilometre. Warren and Nigel end up on the opposite river bank, and have to walk a good way downstream to where the river smooths out and they can swim across. Nigel, not being the most athletic of fellows, arrives back at camp several hours later with tales of having stared death in the face and lived.

Wednesday 24 March - Senanga ferry crossing

It is with great relief that we find the Senanga ferry is operational, albeit leaking and operating on only one engine. The river at this point is about 300 metres wide and flowing swiftly, so it is with a certain amount of trepidation that we drive our vehicles and boats onto the pontoon. Taking off with a roar, it runs backwards, with the current, to arrive safely at the opposite shore somewhat downstream from where we launched. This is obviously intentional, as there is a landing point and a sandy track that takes off across the floodplains to Senanga.

Our first view of this Barotse floodplain is truly amazing: a vast expanse of clear blue water surrounded by green grass and occasional outcrops of trees, interspersed with the conical roofs of the Barotse villages and the silhouettes of long dugout canoes.

On arrival at Senanga I go to visit a Dutch aid doctor at the hospital. I have started my own treatment of tetracycline (antibiotics), but the fever is now in its fifth day. Friendly Doctor Joep examines me, and a blood test proves to be positive for malaria. He prescribes a course of quinine tablets. Once again his advice is to be careful: malaria kills!

Thursday 25 March

We meet a delightful old Barotse gentleman in Senanga. Born in about 1905, he was educated at a mission school, his tutor a Yorkshireman, which no doubt explains his keen sense of humour. In the early days, before there were roads, he used to paddle in a dugout from Senanga to Livingstone in 17 days. And here we think we are big shots with our inflatable boats and outboard motors! He also once had the honour of rowing in the royal barge at the Kuomboko ceremony. The old fellow takes us to the district office to meet the district chairman who readily agrees to give us a 'piece of paper' from Senanga for our Afrika Odyssey Expedition scroll.

At Mongu we are joined by a film crew and Getaway magazine, all with news from home.

On the way out of Senanga we pop in to see Mr and Mrs Harrington. Mr Harrington is the son of Arthur Harrington and a 'local lady'. His late dad was one of the great pioneering characters of the area, who, legend has it, often walked into the local pub demanding credit, meaningfully lifting his pet leopard onto the bar counter. After consuming large quantities of grog, he would fire his revolver through the screen of the open-air cinema in Livingstone in protest at the on-screen antics. He was also the one who built the royal barge used in the Kuomboko.

Mr Harrington is, like his father, a famous boat builder. He explains how, in the early days, they built flat wooden barges that they used to transport goods from Senanga to Livingstone and back. Eighteen paddlers would paddle on contract at R10 per return trip. Oxen would pull the barges round the rapids, and at Sioma Falls the barges would be let down on thick, woven bark ropes, the goods being carried round. Paddling back against the current must have been a test of body and soul.

With Mr Harrington

The people of Senanga will proudly tell you that the road to Mongu is the finest tarred road in the whole of Zambia. It passes through beautiful woodlands, with stacks of firewood for sale at the roadside – a commodity not readily available on the Barotse floodplains. We camp at the back of the hotel in Mongu, our tents under a giant mukwa tree. The sun sets behind Lealui, from where the Kuomboko will set off next week. During

the night the Barotse xylophones sound across the floodplain, as the excitement surrounding the ceremony builds.

A development aid consultant with the Dutch government, whom we met in Senanga, organized me a treatment of Larium, the new wonder drug for treating malaria. I gave myself the full dose before leaving Senanga in the hope that the confounded parasite will bugger off. I am still feeling rotten, however, and am getting pretty desperate!

Long-horned Barotse cattle grazing on islands in the floodplain.

Friday 26 March

The fever lingers on, and I spend the day lying under a giant mukwa tree, watching the cattle being herded across the floodplain, the herders on dugouts, their cattle chest-deep in water. How the early pioneers must have suffered from malaria, especially when the waters rose on the floodplain, a massive breeding ground for mosquitos. Here I am, feeling sorry for myself, but at least I have the use of modern medicine. I just wish it would hurry up and work.

The pilgrims spend the day at the market and at the museum at Limilunga. Everybody, they say, has Kuomboko fever. As they return to camp the heavens open, an almost daily occurrence in Mongu at this time of the year. As it's Friday, Ross, Jon and Nkonkoni Rob hit the Mongu nightspots. They obviously have a good time, *Thirsty* only getting in at first light. But I worry through the night – I have been unable to insure the vehicles, and Land Cruiser theft is a national pastime in Zambia.

Saturday 27 March

Feeling terrible, I consult a Dutch doctor in Mongu. She tells me that the side effects of Larium can be dizziness and nausea, and that it can affect one's blood pressure. My pulse and blood pressure seem to be OK, and I will have to have a blood slide on Monday. She explains that we should take chloroquine at the very first sign of fever and I should take an added dose because of my above-average 105-kilogram weight – we learn as we go. I feel better now that I've had the nausea and dizziness explained. I was considering having myself airlifted this morning, but decide to wait and see.

Mongu is in a state of genteel decay, the tarred road through the centre of town so potholed that everybody drives on the dirt at the side of it. Shops have delightful names such as 'A Touch of the Year 2000' (ironic since time appears to have stood still since the 1950s). The tiny street market stalls sell everything from mopani worms, dried mushrooms, *vetkoek*, vegetables, fruit and fish eggs, to hand-hewn planks, bark rope, second-hand clothes from Europe and America, colourful cloth from the East, hand-made tin pots, fish, woven mats, baskets, and fish traps. The vendors stand up as you reach their stall with the words 'Hello, customer'. Good humour and friendliness prevail. There are hoots of laughter from the maize porridge and meat vendors, who are all keen to feed my already large frame, which with my beard is a constant source of amusement to them. It is a society frozen in a past colonial time, with a delightful use of English. A Land Rover with no wheels and no engine is either 'buggered' or 'has developed a temporary fault'. The police we are told are 'dormant', and any question not understood gets the enthusiastic response of 'yes please!'

Little thatched shacks, dugout and plank canoes, a dredger, the temporarily buggered post boat and a canal disappearing into the floodplain comprise the Mongu dockside. The dredged canal meets with the main Zambezi course some 20 kilometres away.

We go to have a look at Limilunga, the *litunga*'s summer palace, where the Kuomboko ceremony will end. Even the curator of the little museum can't give us the exact date for the ceremony, but it is still rumoured to be next weekend.

Sunday 28 March

I write a note to the *litunga*, respectfully requesting a meeting with his Royal Majesty to sign our scroll of peace and goodwill. The pilgrims deliver it to Lealui, the winter palace.

In the afternoon the heavens open and we huddle around the stew pot under a tarpaulin. Even with the rain, the malaria and the indecision regarding the Kuomboko date, it is still a great adventure to be here in the heart of the Barotseland floodplain. The *indunas*, we are told, have only just returned from Lusaka and will decide on the Kuomboko date tomorrow. Remember, Africa owns the time!

Monday 29 March - A royal visit

Launching *QE2* and *Bathtub* from the little Mongu harbour creates a stir. The local fishermen are amazed by the expedition boats and new outboard engines, and everybody wants a ride and the chance to try the controls.

On arriving at the island of Lealui we are granted an audience with the *litunga*. He has received our letter and is expecting us. We wait for quite some time in the Prime Minister's council chambers where he and his *indunas* are holding court. This is interspersed with much handclapping, a means of greeting and of emphasizing a point. The Prime Minister, an elderly man with a very dignified bearing despite the lens-less, horn-rimmed spectacles perched upside-down on his nose, has a twinkle in his eyes. But this twinkle does not prevent them from closing as he nods off to sleep from time to time. This only encourages the *indunas* to talk and clap more loudly in the hope that he is still listening.

Finally the moment comes, and, in the presence of a senior *induna,* we are ushered through to the palace by way of a reeded courtyard. Mashozi, the only woman in the party, has to enter through a side entrance. The palace was built in the 1920s and has a Polynesian flavour, its steeply pitched thatched roof supported by high wooden beams. Clapping our traditional greeting, we all kneel in front of the palace entrance. The *litunga*'s menservants invite us in. It's like something out of *Raiders of the Lost Ark*.

Our eyes gradually become accustomed to the semi-darkness as we all kneel in front of the *litunga*. I expected to find him dressed in leopard skins and ostrich feathers, with tanned skins, grass mats and beer pots on an earthenware floor. No, his majesty the *litunga* is dressed in an old colonial-style safari suit in a room furnished with large, over-stuffed armchairs and a low table on which lies his delicately carved ivory-handled fly whisk. I explain the purpose of the expedition and the honour in which we hold this visit. He responds in a clipped Oxford accent and in perfect English, 'Anyone for tea and biscuits? Do take a seat.' And so the royal menservants serve us tea and biscuits, kneeling as they do so. Africa is never as you expect it!

I wonder how many previous adventurers have been here with requests for mineral and hunting rights, requests to build mission stations and convert heathen souls. His majesty agrees to sign our scroll, which we will pick up at a later date. Then comes the crucial question: 'When is the Kuomboko likely to take place?' Such is the secrecy of the event that the king turns to his senior *induna* and asks whether there is even going to be a Kuomboko this year.

Heading for our boats, we notice that the carpenters have already begun to repair the royal barges. The *Nalikwanda* is a flat-bottomed boat capable of carrying 120 paddlers plus the king and his royal entourage, who sit amidship under a giant canopy topped by the model of an elephant. Pulling on a rope makes the elephant's ears flap to the beat of a large royal drum, which keeps time for the paddlers. A careless paddler will get thrown overboard if he does not paddle correctly.

It is late afternoon by the time we leave the island of Lealui, and, with a local Lozi to guide us, we finally cross the Zambezi and make our way up the Luanginga River. We aim to cross the floodplain from Mongu to Kalabo, a distance of approximately 100 kilometres. No words can convey the size and beauty of the Barotse floodplain as the setting sun chases us onto an island where we camp for the night.

Unfortunately we are not the only occupants of the floodplain looking for a dry place to camp – so are thousands of red ants, which at 4 am decide that the warmth of our tent is the place to be. We hot-foot it over to Ross's tent, but this refuge is short-lived as the red ones seek us out. They bite like hell and no place is sacred, not even one's nether regions. There is much swearing, shouting and slapping, and we are all forced to vacate our tents and dismally huddle around the campfire, eagerly waiting for the sun to rise.

Tuesday 30 March

Not too many craft such as ours make their way up the Luanginga River judging by the way the locals rush down to gawk and wave at the passing flotilla. Travelling at what must seem like a furious rate of knots, our guide gets lost from time to time. The poor fellow is used to paddling the river in a dugout canoe, with ample time to take his bearings. When asking how far to the next village we are told, 'Oh, with such a balloon boat, she is close.'

We are all impressed by the extreme friendliness of the people. We slow down for passing dugout canoes loaded to the hilt with trade goods, fish, mealie meal, mangoes and the occasional bicycle. It is considered bad form to race past in high-powered boats, and we have to slow down to prevent our wake from flooding them. The locals indicate their appreciation with smiles and shouts of greeting, and sometimes open-mouthed amazement.

It of great pleasure to have the privilege of meeting Members of
Africa Odyssey Expedition from Cape Town to Cairo.

I feel excited, because it is quite rare for God's people of this kind
to take the trouble and visit us at Kalabo — which is far across the
Zambezi and Luanginga Rivers.

Therefore on behalf of the Local Community and workers, and of course
on my own behalf I accord a message of peace and goodwill to the
participants in this expedition so that they can successfully accomplish
their Mission.

Part of the letter from Kalabo's district secretary

At Kalabo we tie up under a large tree and go off to the local government rest-house in search of some cold Mosi beers. Kalabo used to do a lot of trade with Angola but now most of the shops along the dusty main road stand empty. A number of these enterprises were once white-owned, but were subsequently nationalized. The government is offering businesses back to the original owners, but who'd want to come back to memories, malaria and a civil war across the border?

A village constable calls us away from the rest-house, demanding that we report immediately to the district secretary. We take off half-heartedly, fearing we may be held up by some unnecessary officialdom. We are ushered into a decaying office, where the small, smartly dressed district secretary can hardly reach across his massive well-worn desk to shake hands warmly with each of us. He explains that Kalabo has not had visitors in many years. Would we be so kind as to sign the visitors' book, and would we accept the freedom of Kalabo? Do we need anything and how can he best be of assistance? We are given a place to camp and offered the use of a nearby government house. A letter for our scroll of peace and goodwill is immediately typed up on an old-fashioned typewriter and presented to us with more smiles and handshakes. We are honoured and humbled by it all.

Late that afternoon, Ross and I take *Bathtub* some distance up a man-made canal that joins Kalabo with the Angolan border. The canal crosses the Lua Flats, still rich in game and birdlife, a sea of green floodplain stretching into the horizon.

Wednesday 31 March - Friday 9 April

Once back in Mongu, we decide to head north, to the upper reaches of the Zambezi. MNet sends in Duncan McNeillie and cameraman Lourens van Rensburg to cover the story. Patrick Wagner of *Getaway* magazine, who becomes a great friend, also joins us along with our old friends Barry Leitch and Lloyd and Hella Balcomb. We journey up the river past Lukulu, and finally up to the falls at Chavuma, located on the border between Angola and Zambia.

It's wonderful to have fresh faces and new conversation around the campfire at night, and we live off bananas, mealie meal porridge and fish, one night even roasting a goat

49

on the fire, using *Thirsty*'s long spare wheel lever as a spit. It's full moon and we travel the Zambezi at night, the boats leaving a silvery wake on the moonlit water. On our way back to Mongu we pass the only bridge across the Zambezi between the Angolan border and the Victoria Falls. The incredible suspension footbridge, built by local missionary folk, spans the river at Chinyingi, its old cables begged from the copper mines.

Finally we make it back to our base camp at Mongu, but there is still no Kuomboko. The delays are costing us time and money, and we are no closer to Cairo. It is time we get moving.

We really must get it right – it's the boats that go in the water!

Saturday 10 April

It's good to be back in Mongu at the expedition base camp. It feels like home and we are treated like locals. We head for our favourite place, the post boat at the harbour, where we enjoy a couple of cheap beers as we watch the cattle being driven back to land by dugout at sunset.

A thundering downpour sends us running to peg down our fly-sheets. We huddle around the *jikos*, small charcoal stoves made from tin, to get dry. Exhausted from our river journey we are all soon in bed, and the downpour continues throughout the night. During the early hours of the morning I hear the familiar creak of the food box lid ... a hungry pilgrim, I think, as I snuggle down deeper into my sleeping bag.

Sunday 11 April

I wake to the shout of Warren crying blue murder. He was in charge of security and went to bed with a loaded spear gun next to him – but to no avail. With the rain pouring down onto our tents we didn't hear anything and have been ripped off good and solid. The thieves' muddy tracks form a path from our camp to the fence where everything must have been loaded onto donkeys to be transported down to the harbour. Thousands of rands' worth of equipment gone – outboard engine spares, propellers, fuel containers, a toolbox and an entire trunk of vehicle spares. This is a disaster for the expedition! We race off to the police station to make a lengthy statement, but I'm sure our kit is halfway to Angola by now, on a boat that is probably being driven by our fuel. The police blame it on Angolan refugees. For us it is an irreplaceable loss. Still, no one was hurt and we are safe. But it is a lesson learnt: when you stay too long in one place, people get to know your camp and what's in it, and have time to plan.

To make matters worse, the royal drums have not yet started and there is no sign of a date for the Kuomboko, or any guarantee that it will even happen at all. Sadly we decide to leave the great adventure of Barotseland and head downstream, our destination *Mosi oa Tunya* – 'the smoke that thunders'. Greatest waterfall of them all!

Vic Falls
15 April 1993

Hi Debbie

Just a short note to let you know that we've arrived safely at Vic Falls. Can you believe it's taken us 4 months from Cape Town! Our journey from Barotseland included yet another waterway, a section of the Kafue River and the Itezhi-tezhi Dam, an area that will always be remembered for its incredible beauty and the all-Africa tsetse fly record! We slapped ourselves black and blue and Mashozi is still covered in bumps, although both she and Ross are otherwise well. I've been struggling with bloody malaria, which has at least helped me to lose a bit of weight.

Unfortunately Warren has decided to go back to Zululand. He's been a real gentleman about it all, explaining that he desperately needs to get back to his fiancée. We've been expecting this for some weeks now. Ross is going to take over from him as skipper of QE2 and I will take over Bathtub from Ross.

We're all really getting into expedition life and one day runs into the next. We just camp wherever we end up, invariably on some beautiful sandbank with crocs and hippos as constant companions. It's quite scary when I think of how far we still have to go and the many obstacles. I've found that the best thing is not to get caught up in the destination, but rather to work at completing and enjoying each day - maybe it's a lesson in life!

Nigel is a bit homesick, Jon is just like the Zambezi - he goes with the flow. Nkonkoni Rob is delightful but naughty (he's out on the town at the moment). And Mashozi and Ross are the backbone of the expedition. No fireside grub tonight - we'll hit a restaurant in Vic Falls. I can already taste the succulent steak, egg and chips!

Siyabonga - say hi to the dogs.

Kingsley

Thursday 15 April

Sindibisi Island is paradise. Our hut is almost in the river, and from the bed one can gaze across at it raging in full flood, the whole of the Barotse floodplain draining down past us towards the Victoria Falls.

Will of Tongabezi Lodge offers to guide us downstream, past the old boat club, to Livingstone Island, which sits right on the edge of the Victoria Falls. With a certain amount of trepidation we roar over the rapids and down to the lip of the falls. Suddenly the props cavitate and we lose power as the motors are tilted up on shallow drive because of the rocks. I panic as the current takes us towards the very lip of the falls. Will, at the unfamiliar controls, hesitates. I lunge across and knock the levers into neutral, allowing Ross to leap to the motors

Looking upstream into the Victoria Falls

and drop them down. The props take, and with our hearts in our throats we throw the anchor onto Livingstone Island, to walk in the footsteps of David Livingstone.

In 1851 Livingstone first heard of the great waterfall, but it was only in 1855 that he set out to visit it. He spent the night at Kalai Island a few kilometres upstream from here, having come down the river bank on foot. The next morning he set out by dugout canoe to approach the 'smoke that thunders' and landed here, on Livingstone Island, from where he had his first view of the falls. In his journal he wrote: *'Creeping with awe to the verge, I peered down into a large rent which had been made from bank to bank on the broad Zambezi, and saw that a stream of a thousand yards broad leapt down a hundred feet and became suddenly compressed into a space of fifteen to twenty yards. It is the most wonderful sight I had ever witnessed in Africa.'* Of the surrounding area he wrote: *'No one can imagine the view from anything witnessed in England ... it had never been seen before by European eyes, but scenes so lovely must have been gazed upon by angels in their flight.'* And here we are, 138 years later, equally enthralled by the incredible beauty of the Falls.

Drenched in spray we walk out to the edge of the falls, to hug and shake hands.

Saturday 17 April

Our cottage at the municipal campsite in Victoria Falls makes a practical base camp and gives us a chance to clean our equipment. The pilgrims are finding the town extremely sociable, with plenty of foreign travellers, known by the locals as 'black feet' (referring to their dusty feet and sandals). Some are hitch-hiking, others have their own vehicles, and the rest are a part of the happy, hippy band of overlanders in the massive 4x4 Bedfords and MAN diesels trundling across Africa. The number of times you've been robbed, bought a carving for an old T-shirt, got goofed, had malaria and been stuck in the mud is all part of the storytelling at the Vic Falls campsite. The town, with its bungee jumping, white-water rafting, photographic safaris, canoeing, and the constant flights over the falls, attracts thousands of visitors. Dr Livingstone must be turning in his grave!

Nigel spends a good deal of time in the public phone booth, phoning his family and friends. He comes back to camp full of news and I immediately sense that he is becoming extremely homesick. Suddenly he's realizing that Cairo is still many months away and the journey is tough, with constant loading and unloading, the responsibilities of the vehicles, no discos or clubs; just hard work and the magic of Africa. Such an expedition is not just fun and games. I feel sorry for him. He's very loyal, but I know he's missing home and the buzz of city life.

Tomorrow we pack up for Deka further down the Zambezi, and the Kariba stretch of the great Afrika Odyssey Expedition. I'm keen to get back into the bush again.

Sunday 18 & Monday 19 April

Navigating the road from Vic Falls down to Hwange and then back down to the Zambezi below Vic Falls with its fearful gorges takes the better part of the afternoon. At the Deka Drum Fishing Camp, Jock the manager makes us most welcome at the rustic bar, which is propped up by some colourful Zimbabwean gold miners.

The Zambezi is hurtling past Deka. Considering the danger of the rocks and rapids, and in an effort to save fuel, Jon, Nkonkoni Rob and I launch into the river in *Bathtub*, leaving the rest of the pilgrims to drive round to Milibizi. Heading downstream we soon reach Devil's Gorge. This stretch of the river is very moody with steep rocky banks on both sides, massive baobabs silhouetted against the skyline, and numerous rocky inlets leading off to unknown destinations. In the gorge I can imagine great monsters working beneath the water's surface.

A pod of hippo aren't too keen to have us travel up the Gwaai, a brown snake of a river that slides down between steep rocks to join the Zambezi. We meet up with the rest of the expedition and after the hustle and bustle of Vic Falls it's good to be on our own again. Now, with Warren gone it is just Mashozi, Ross, Nigel, Jon, Nkonkoni Rob, the calabash (padded and tied up in its old blue plastic coolbox) and myself.

Tuesday 20 & Wednesday 21 April

We awake to the call of the fish eagle and gaze out across Lake Kariba. The Batonga people refer to the Zambezi River as 'Kasambabezi', which means 'those who know wash here' (in other words, if you know the river you can wash without being attacked by crocodiles). But, in more recent times, the greatest threat to these people has not been the crocs, but the arrival of white men with their 20th-century technology and their plans for a mighty dam.

In 1955 it was decided to build a dam here in the Kariba Gorge. A gargantuan scheme was envisaged, a massive concrete arch to be thrown across the Zambezi, so forming a lake of over 5,000 square kilometres. It would be the largest man-made lake on earth, putting upon the earth's crust a weight of 177 billion tons.

The Batonga believed that the lair of their river god, Nyaminyami, was below the dark waters of the Kariba Gorge. Was the white man insane? Did they think they could put a great wall across Nyaminyami's lair? He would destroy their foolish dream and tear it to shreds. The engineers laughingly dismissed the Nyaminyami myth and work began. But by early March 1957 it became apparent that Nyaminyami was planning an attack. An enormous volume of water was descending towards the dam site, and, as the floodwaters hit the Kariba Gorge, the Zambezi rose 5.5 metres in just one day. But incredibly the workings were not entirely washed away. The coffer dam was pumped dry and work on the main wall began in earnest. Then came the unbelievable news: Nyaminyami was licking his wounds and plotting a fearful revenge.

On 16 February 1958 the coffer dam succumbed to the raging Zambezi. The river continued to rise, the engineers recording a torrent that reached 33.5 metres above low water level. There were waves of nearly five metres. The damage was severe and work was put on hold for months, but in December 1958 the last opening in the wall was finally sealed. Behind the Kariba wall the lake grew to nearly 322 kilometres in length and 32 kilometres at its widest point. A massive sheet of water bisected the traditional lands of the Batonga – their lives had changed forever. Operation Noah was launched to rescue and relocate the many animals that were trapped on the fast-diminishing islands of high land, but, even so, many animals drowned in the dam's rising waters.

Possibly our presence is reviving the spirit of Nyaminyami – the level of the lake has dropped considerably over the last few years, but now it is rising by the hour as a result of the floodwaters.

Lake Kariba can develop quite a chop and our boat ride down to Binga is bumpy as we meet the oncoming wind nose on. I try to take most of the strain off my back by bending my knees and bracing my thighs. Short, untidy waves break over the bow of *Bathtub* and soon I'm forced to ride in the wake of *QE2*. We travel just on the plane,

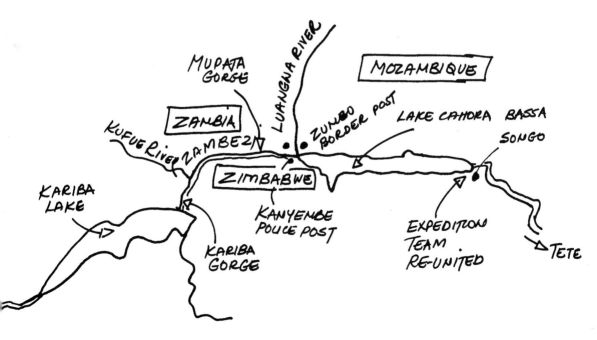

conserving fuel wherever possible. Nkonkoni Rob is travelling with me, and Mashozi is with Ross in *QE2*. Nigel and Jon have taken the vehicles round to Binga.

The inner harbour at Binga is fed by a natural opening in the cliffs, and it's a treat to get out of rough water. Because of the wind we decide to take our boats out of the water and go round to Bumi Hills by road. This gives us the opportunity to observe Batonga lifestyle and to spend a night on the Chizarira escarpment, which must have one of the best views in Africa. Nature puts on a great sunset, fringed by tropical storms.

Ross finally gets it right: drawing smoke through the water-filled calabash.

The drive down the escarpment to Bumi Hills is beautiful, especially after such excellent rains, and we visit several friendly Batonga villages. The old women in the villages are great pipe smokers, their water pipes consisting of a calabash with a long stem. The bowl of the pipe is fashioned from clay and the tobacco or dagga is drawn through maize or millet with hot coals on top of it, the smoke then passing through the calabash filled with water. Under the old Rhodesian colonial government these were the only people who were still legally allowed to continue their 'dope-smoking' tradition.

Reaching the shoreline of Lake Kariba – opposite the Ume River and the Matusadona Game Reserve – we camp on an open plain graced by elephants, buffaloes, waterbuck and impala. Lions roar during the evening and the partially submerged dead trees stand out like pale ghosts in the moonlight. It is heavenly.

But during the night the malaria sweat and fever return.

Thursday 22 April

We decide to leave our trailers and vehicles at the Bumi Hills Museum and spend a few days on the lake. This is an opportunity to have all the pilgrims on the boats and to view game from the water. We take a local young Batonga with us as a guide and camp help. Zazo Virhiringane is good company and a new face around the fire. Wherever possible we invite the people of the area to join our expedition. This way we all get to know local customs, folklore and history.

Setting off from Bumi we camp on a small island. The bloody malaria has got to Nigel and me, so we sleep it off among the reeds while the others go game-viewing off the Matusadona mainland. It is almost dark by the time *Bathtub* gets back to camp, the pilgrims delighted by what they have seen. The sunset turns the water to golden yellow, and there is hardly a ripple, just the tranquillity of Africa. We break open a precious bottle of Captain Morgan rum and toast the sunset and our odyssey.

Ian Adamson is young, wiry and tough. With his wispy red beard, tatty shorts, velskoene and old felt hat, he certainly looks the Zimbo part. Although he is the smallest of the pilgrims we soon nickname him Mahlafuna - a Nguni word for 'forever eating' - as he makes a huge dent in the grub box and loves drinking. The river-rat knows the river and its moods, and he comes aboard as the official bush mechanic.

Friday 23 April

No sooner do we get into the mouth of the Ume River than we see a massive bull elephant, who, on spotting us, climbs up onto a rocky ledge and, turning his backside towards us, promptly empties his bowels. We are able to get both boats to within a few metres of him and his two mates. There is plenty of wildlife and the mandatory fish eagles calling from the dry trees. We travel up the Ume as far as we can, being extra cautious on account of the thousands of dry trees, some of which are lurking just under the surface of the water, waiting to rip open the pontoons of unsuspecting rubberducks. But Nyaminyami, the river god, is on our side, and the boats get through intact. We spend the heat of the day resting, and that afternoon as we travel upstream past Bumi we see a herd of around 300 buffaloes and elephants, waterbuck, impala, warthog and zebra. Our camp for the night is a deserted island on the Kota Kota Narrows.

Our plans to spend another day here change when a kapenta fisherman pops by and warns us that it is illegal to camp on the island. The real danger we are told is of being shot as a poacher. It is not uncommon for poachers to come across from Zambia, and the Zimbabwean anti-poaching unit shoots on sight. Bearing this in mind we pack up camp and travel back to Bumi.

We then head across the lake in both boats, Nigel, who is still battling malaria, driving the one and Ross the other. Jon and Nkonkoni Rob in the meantime drive round from Bumi via Karoi and down to Kariba. It is a nine-hour journey as opposed to one-and-a-half hours by boat.

24 April - 10 May - Kariba Town

What a wonderful buzz Kariba town has – friendly pubs, houseboats by the score, hunters, fishermen, safari operators and a shop that sells great pies. It's paradise after the months of travel. Soon everybody knows about our adventure and we set up a base at Kariba Breezes Hotel with its hot showers, bacon-and-egg breakfasts and gin-and-tonic sundowners.

As we were expecting, Nigel, somewhat weakened by malaria, decides to leave the expedition. He has been a great help and we're sad to see him go, but we wish him luck, understanding that his time has come.

We meet Ian Adamson, a local Zambezi River Guide, in a pub. He is a trained mechanic and is prepared to drop everything and join our expedition. Ross, Jon and Nkonkoni

Rob like him and within a short while of Nigel leaving us we have a new pilgrim. He's somewhat taciturn, but loves Africa. I think he'll do us proud. We throw a party to welcome him aboard officially.

From Kariba it's decided that the group will do a nine-day canoe safari from below the dam wall down to Kanyembe. Powerboats are not allowed and it is the finest way to view this section of the Zambezi. Wildlife is plentiful and the river here astonishingly beautiful.

But on the eve of our planned departure Mashozi and I both go down with a bad bout of malaria. Ian Adamson knows the river well and we urge the others to continue. And so for financial reasons our expedition base camp is moved from Kariba Breezes back under canvas at nearby Mopani Bay. Mashozi and I enjoy the opportunity to be on our own and no doubt the young pilgrims feel the same way. I notice that my seat on the canoe has been taken by a pretty Kariba girl by the name of Tonya. She and Ross have hit it off, and she's a real honey.

Tuesday 11 May

Although still a little weak, Mashozi and I are over the malaria at last. The pilgrims had a fascinating time on their Zambezi journey down to Kanyembe – lions in their camp, constant brushes with hippos and a hair-raising experience with a bull elephant. Everybody looks sun-tanned and fit, and I'm pleased that we're all safely back together again.

Wednesday 12 May

It is with a certain amount of sadness that we leave Kariba today, heading for Kanyembe and the Mozambique border. It's good to be in the convoy again, *Thirsty* groaning in second gear as we follow *Vulandlela* and *Bathtub* up and out of the Zambezi Valley to Makuti. From Karoi via Mwami we snake back down into the valley and enter the Chemore Safari area. Our home for the night is a derelict hunting camp in the reserve. Hyaenas cackle incessantly throughout the night, accompanied by the agitated screams of baboons.

Thursday 13 May

Back on the narrow track to Kanyembe we pass through an area where thatched villages nestle among giant baobabs. The bush, stretching hundreds of kilometres across the Zambezi Valley, is changing from shades of green to autumn's yellows and browns, and there are plenty of elephant and buffalo tracks across the sandy road.

Kanyembe is Zimbabwe's last outpost on the Zambezi, a place seldom visited. Ross, Mashozi and I bid farewell to Nkonkoni Rob, Jon and Ian. They will drive via Harare to Mozambique to set up camp as close to the Cahora Bassa dam wall as possible. If we do not get there by noon in four days' time, we will set off a flare at 3 pm. Flare or not they should then come and search for us along the south bank. We will hang an article of clothing from a tree and light a smoke fire on the shore of the lake just in case there's a radio breakdown. It's 1993 and the upper reaches of the Cahora Bassa are wild and untravelled. Our real concern is not the natural dangers, but rather armed bandits or poachers. Once again there's that delightful flutter of nervousness in the pit of my stomach. I know that Mashozi and Ross feel it too.

At Kanyembe we launch at the old DC Camps slipway. Here we meet Nkonkoni Rob, who is waiting for Chris Hougaard, the owner of the Cahora Bassa Fishing Camp and Kafukudzi Hunting Camp. We have heard a lot about the two Hougaard brothers – Peter and Chris – two wild characters who pioneered the upper reaches of Cahora Bassa, establishing a hunting camp there in the mid-eighties among Renamo, local poachers and 10,000 kilometres of wild African bush. I am even more excited to learn that Steve Edwards is also in residence there. Steve canoed the Zambezi in the early seventies and is the author of the book *Zambezi Odyssey*, which we used when planning *our* odyssey.

We ask Rob to let them know to expect us, requesting that we be allowed to camp there tonight. I feel a lot easier as I don't know what to expect in this lawless part of Mozambique, and before travelling down Cahora Bassa I need to check out the security situation with people in the know. It has been extremely difficult to get any information about this area, since for nearly 20 years no one has travelled it.

Before leaving Kanyembe, Mashozi, Ross and I travel up into the magnificent Mupata Gorge, sighting hippos and crocodiles, the surrounding hills decorated with giant baobabs. *Bathtub* copes easily with the fast water and rapids of the gorge and we race the motors, wanting to make sure they're running perfectly prior to committing to Mozambique.

Back down the gorge we exit Zimbabwe from the friendly police post at Kanyembe. We cross to the old Zambian trading post of Feira which sits at the confluence of the Luangwa and Zambezi rivers. Well, Zambia is the same even in this wild and remote corner. The music at the rest-house on the river bank is at full volume, and we are greeted with broad smiles and Zambian English washed down with cold Mosis. Leaving our passports with customs we shop for last-minute supplies at the market overlooking the Luangwa River.

Zumbo border post is everything I expected. A sombre Portuguese-style building stands on a rise over the river; a tattered Mozambican flag flutters lethargically from a flagpole. The customs officials look at us in amazement – travellers arriving by rubberduck are indeed a rarity.

Customs wants $20 from each of us, which we refuse to pay as we already have visas. They have no English, we no Portuguese, but we work it out. Imitating the firing of an automatic weapon I ask if we can expect any trouble from bandits. Their grins and energetic shaking of heads seem to indicate that all will be well. On asking directions to the Hougaards' camp we get the typical rural African hand signals, which mean somewhere downstream within the next few hours or so, depending on whether you are walking or going by dugout canoe, but, in this red 'balloon boat' with two engines, who can possibly tell how long it will take. We launch onto the river, leaving this sad, deserted place with much handshaking and many *obrigados*.

Jumping into a river crawling with crocodiles seems like madness, but what else can we do when we're repeatedly getting stuck on sandbanks. Then all of a sudden we're into deep water, and we break all world speed records to leap aboard, pouring water all over the kit as we do so. And so we make our way downstream, not knowing where the hell we are. The sun sets behind us over Zimbabwe, Zambia and a corner of the wild country of Mozambique, which will host us for nearly a thousand kilometres of lake and river.

In the unhurried way of Africa, I explain our objectives and ask the locals for advice.

Kafukudzi is situated on the south bank, its thatched huts overlooking the river. Expecting just a place to camp, we are surprised by a long and fascinating night of old-world hospitality so often found in remote parts of Africa. We are taken to our bush camp huts which have clean sheets, hot showers and mosquito nets. Supper at the hunting camp follows, and then the opportunity to meet with owner Chris Hougaard, as well as Steve Edwards, professional hunters and staff. What a great bunch of buggers – rough, tough men of the bush. It is a late night of good humour and bantering at the well-stocked bar.

Steve Edwards is fascinated by what we are doing. He is a fit, wiry fellow and great adventurer who has travelled along many other rivers since his great Zambezi odyssey. His main objective now is to stamp out poaching in 'their' area of Mozambique. They have been funded in their efforts by the returns from buffalo and leopard hunts (leopards are plentiful in the wild hills and valleys) but are losing the battle. Officials, they say, are lethargic and do not have the infrastructure and funds to cope with the problem. Steve has obtained tape-recorded confessions from a number of the poachers who openly admit to being lent guns and ammunition by government officials in return for skins, meat and ivory. Two poachers are in custody at the camp. This is the Wild West.

Friday 14 May

After breakfast we are presented with a packed lunch and an extra 25 litres of fuel. Wind, we are told, could become our number one enemy because the axis of the lake is into the prevailing wind. Our rough and ready hosts wave from the river bank.

Later we get caught up in a mass of water hyacinth, and then the wind starts picking up. What if the wind really comes up and blockages from weeds cause lengthy and costly detours? We could be stuck in this wild place for weeks. The wind becomes too strong to continue, and we are forced to pull off at midday, camping in a half-built hut.

Here we meet Izak Tempo – self-confessed poacher, hunter and fisherman of repute. He joins us for a simple meal and, after a few beers, tells us that he sells leopard skins to a white man who comes from Zimbabwe, and that occasionally he shoots an elephant, but the tusks are small. And yes, he hires an AK47 from the police at Zumbo and repays them in meat. Leopards are plentiful and he catches them in a trap.

The wind continues unabated and we have to spend the night in this desolate place. Izak Tempo bids us farewell and takes off into the night. I recorded our conversation on my pocket tape recorder, and Mashozi is terrified that he might later realize he should not have shared his secrets with me and return to do us in with his hired AK. We sleep as close as possible to *Bathtub*, tying down all the equipment. Every sound wakes me up and I have a restless night. It's an eerie place.

Saturday 15 May

We try to beat the wind by getting up at 4 am. If we do not make at least 100 kilometres today we are going to be late for our noon rendezvous with the pilgrims tomorrow. We have only an hour of calm water, and then we are back into the chop and wind. It is bumpy and rough – almost scary.

The pounding of the wind eventually forces us to stop in an area shown on our map as The Narrows. Here the fishing villagers speak only Portuguese and Madema, the local language. By using our map and pointing to various rivers and getting them to repeat their names, we are able to approximate our position. Enormous tiger fish and bream are in abundance at this very basic fishing camp, where the cooking is done in clay vessels. The people tell us that no white people come this way and there are no shops, clinics or schools. A bar of soap or a handful of salt buys a big pile of fish.

We push on against the strong headwind. It is hard going, and we are very worried about the fuel we are guzzling against the wind. But luck is with us – as we get into the wider section of the lake it becomes calmer, the water clearer. This calls for a swig of Captain Morgan rum, and our mood starts picking up. Still, we feel very alone, the three Holgates in a tiny open boat in the middle of the African nowhere. We ask fishermen for directions as we go, but we can't understand each other and it's all desperate hand signals. Then, in the distance, we see our first motorized fish-trading boat. We follow it through the narrow gap out of the vast bay. This part of the lake, with its white rocky islands and clear light green water, is wild and beautiful.

We've been told to look out for a white house, and we soon spot the landmark, the only First World structure on this part of the lake. It is occupied by a Zimbabwean involved in a kapenta project. We anchor *Bathtub* and go up to the house to ask for directions, and are assured that we are on course for the Cahora Bassa dam wall.

Back in *Bathtub* fuel is extremely low. The headwinds have eaten into our supply and we are left with under 30 litres for both motors. Thank goodness for the fuel from the Kafukudzi Hunting Camp. But at least the wind has stopped and we streak across a sheet of glass, heading east. Soon we're in an area of high, smooth rock islands and a deep, steep-sided gorge. We continue travelling until sunset and then pull *Bathtub* onto an eggshell-coloured rock island. We huddle around the yellow flames of a small fire, the firelight dancing off the rocks. Mashozi cooks up a simple stew, and I play my harmonica. Sunburnt, stiff, sore and tired, we go to bed early. I hope that the young pilgrims are safe.

Sunday 16 May

It's a perfect morning, but there is no grunting of hippos as there was on Kariba. From a passing fisherman we learn that it's about 25 kilometres to the dam wall, but that security will not allow us to land there. We could get shot up, so we should go to a small craft harbour some way to the south of the wall and down a side channel. But how do we tell our land party who are expecting us at the wall? At about 11.30 am we hear Nkonkoni Rob's excited voice – '*Thirsty* to *Vulandlela*.' We instantly perk up, make contact and meet at 12.05 after four days and an adventure that will be long remembered.

We camp at the Frelimo army base with a great view up the gorge, eating on the level top of an old Portuguese bunker, with *Cardosa and Luis 1/2/70 01/1972* inscribed in the concrete. We've made it!

Our trip down the Cahora Bassa has taught me that to travel further down the Zambezi in Mozambique without an interpreter and guide would be madness. The area is still volatile, and we need to be able to talk to locals. How else will we learn the ways of the country? We discuss our problem with one of the locals, and soon have Roy Nkomo standing to attention in front of us, carrying a change of clothes and a blanket. Roy's mother is of Portuguese extraction and his father was a Zulu. So now we've got an interpreter and guide who speaks English, Zulu, Portuguese and the local dialects. The poor fellow is desperate. He's been working on a local fishing boat for five months, but hasn't seen a cent. We agree on a daily rate and leave a deposit with his mum.

Monday 17 May

The road out of Cahora Bassa is extremely scenic with views over the dam into the terrifying gorge below the wall. Dr Livingstone called it 'that damned gorge', for on his transcontinental journey from Luanda to Quelimane he had detoured around it, failing to listen to Portuguese accounts of great rapids and fierce waters. It was a mistake that was to cost him dearly.

The road to Tete is good tar, and the villages along it all have full granaries. Famine brought the war and the country to its knees, and it was almost impossible to deliver food into the war-torn rural areas. But there have been excellent rains and crops, which have arrived at the same time as the peace talks.

Tete is chock-a-block with UN forces. Lorries are travelling the Tete corridor at night and the bridge over the Zambezi at Tete has a constant flow of traffic. The nightclub/ restaurant down on the river, next to the bridge, allows us to camp in an open yard alongside them. We have been warned *not* to make too much of a fuss with the bureaucrats, but the owner of the restaurant insists that we go and see the governor of Tete Province to get clearance through what could be a very sensitive area. This is a mistake. The governor demands written authority from Maputo or an end to our trip along the Zambezi. This is typical of this country where everybody is too afraid to make a decision and bureaucratic snarl-ups are part of everyday life. I do some phoning to friends in Maputo, but in the meantime I decide that come what may we are going to Chinde at the mouth of the Zambezi, and if push comes to shove we will put the small boat in the river and go for it.

Tuesday 18 May

We've unwittingly camped behind a hedge next to a fowl run shared by turkeys and ducks, which all strike up at 4 am. If this isn't bad enough, the security guard who's stomped his feet all night outside our tent lets rip with his AK47, which has us all diving for cover. No choice but to be up early. He claims he was scaring off a thief.

I manage to get hold of John Morrison in Beira who agrees to fly in 200 litres of fuel to Marromeu on Friday. This means that the expedition to Chinde can happen, thanks to Food for the Hungry and their daily relief flights from Beira to Marromeu. John must be a kindred spirit, as he is prepared to put 200 litres of fuel on an old Russian aircraft for a total stranger!

Roelof van Tonder from the SA Trade Mission phoned last night from Maputo to say that he had not been able to speak to the governor personally but had sent a fax. I decide not to go back to the governor's office for fear of being turned back. I ask what time the governor takes his siesta, and from the pub below the Zambezi bridge I learn there are no gunboats patrolling the Zambezi, the helicopters are buggered and there is no radio network downstream. This helps me make my decision – we will take a gamble.

At 12.30 pm – which is the start of the governor's midday siesta break – we put *Bathtub* into the Zambezi for the journey to the Indian Ocean. On board are Mashozi, Roy (our new guide and interpreter), Ian, Jon and I plus supplies and 175 litres of fuel for 300 kilometres. Ross, Nkonkoni Rob and Geoffrey Blythe, an old Kariba friend, are going to travel to Nsanje in the south of Malawi with both vehicles and *QE2*, and then by boat down the Shire River to meet us in three days' time at its confluence with the Zambezi. Let's hope they make it through the sandbanks and Mozambican officialdom to the confluence, or we'll be in a jam.

The wonderful feeling of freedom is back on this wide, fast-flowing river. The Cahora Bassa sluice gates have been opened and the river is flowing at about eight kilometres an hour and rising. This means limited sandbanks and speedy, easy travel. There are a few isolated villages along the river bank, but it is amazingly wild only a few kilometres outside the hustle and bustle of Tete.

The vegetation is thick and unspoilt, although the rising river is eating into the sandy banks and uprooting some big trees. We are delighted to see pods of hippos along the way. Massive, incredibly aggressive crocs up to six metres long plunge into the water and make a beeline for the boat. Their heads and backs exposed, they make amazing speed through the water. It is quite terrifying, even for Ian Adamson who has canoed the middle Zambezi as a safari operator for two years. The hippos are also behaving strangely, running along the sandbanks and plunging into the water in a most undignified fashion. No doubt we are spoiling the peace and tranquillity of a river that has not been used since the Portuguese left.

We were warned by the United Nations guys in Tete to keep a low profile and to favour the south bank, as things are still a bit risky in Zambezia Province. Once again we find that no one can give us real information. But the general feeling is that peace is on its way and that the Renamo forces are honouring the agreement. Maybe this is the ideal time for our adventure, with the euphoria of peace that follows a protracted war. Hopefully a bunch of mad *abelungu* in a brightly coloured boat will look like another peace-keeping or famine relief organization, and will be seen as further proof that things are improving. Or so we hope anyway as the villagers gape at us with amazement.

About an hour downstream from Tete we arrive at Lupata Gorge, an event that I have dreamt of for many months. For me this is a significant milestone in the Zambezi journey. Livingstone first entered the Lupata Gorge in a dugout on 24 April 1856. That night he slept on Mozambique Island, something he was to do several times again.

This historic gorge proves to have a character all of its own, with its sheer towering cliffs funnelling us along its swift, deep water and into its spectacular entrance, in the centre of which stands Mozambique Island, rising steeply like a giant plum pudding. Little or nothing has changed here since Livingstone's time. This is how he must have seen it when he steamed upriver in September 1858 in his paddle steamer, the *Ma Roberts*, which was so slow that Livingstone complained her engines would have been more suitable for grinding coffee.

I imagine the *Ma Roberts* as it wheezed asthmatically through the Lupata Gorge at a pace somewhat slower than a dugout canoe, the crew cutting trees as they went to feed the boilers. And then Livingstone's disappointment at the next great gorge (what is today the Cahora Bassa) where he finally realized that this part of the Zambezi was unnavigable – so ruining any chances of travelling from Chinde to the Victoria Falls by boat. There were rocks in God's highway.

Mozambique Island is 200 metres long and 100 metres wide, and we tie up the boat at the bottom end. This is a strange place with its thick grass, needle-like and dangerously sharp aloes, euphorbias, and grey, elephant trunk-like creepers up to 20 centimetres thick that have wrapped themselves around tree trunks and stones, like giant pythons constricting their prey.

We inscribe an old broken pot with *18/5/93 Afrika Odyssey Expedition*. This pot is hidden in a giant baobab growing above a level bank (an ideal camping site) on the southern shore of the

Grogan had this to say about his journey from Chinde by barge up the Zambezi: 'It's a dreary, hot, monotonous journey, the only excitement getting on and off sandbanks when the boys on board pole for their lives, and thirty or forty others in the water pull and push the barges, making a meal for a crocodile ... There are many crocodiles which slimed noiselessly into the water before one could get a decent shot, and dropped quietly out of sight without making a ripple.'

island. If any traveller ventures this way, please leave an inscription on the pot, to keep the spirit of adventure alive. Above this spot we find a number of broken pots and enamel plates, all of which have been slit through the centre with an axe. According to Roy it is a gravesite, so, despite the fact that like Livingstone I wanted to camp here for the night, we decide not to interfere with the spirits of a forgotten people.

The sun is sinking behind us as we continue down this spectacular gorge. We camp close to its exit on a bank of clean white sand, with some resident hippos. I struggle to sleep, my thoughts with my only son Ross.

Wednesday 19 May

We have close on 200 kilometres to do before 3 pm today if we are to meet with *QE2* at Mutara for plan A of our rough schedule. Only the Afrika Odyssey Expedition could be doing this remote section of the river with no detailed map. We requested maps from Maputo some months back, but, as with so many things in this country, they just didn't materialize. So it is a case of asking as we go. Thank God we have an interpreter.

Mutara is easily recognizable by the railway bridge spanning the river between Sena and Mutara. The bridge is several kilometres long and very impressive; it has over 30 sections, two of which have been dropped into the water by Renamo explosives. Mutara itself is in a state of disrepair. Crocodiles are plentiful and attacks frequent; people living on the river banks have to use long poles with a container tied to the end to get water out of the river.

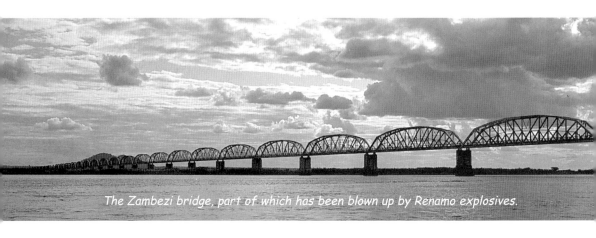

The Zambezi bridge, part of which has been blown up by Renamo explosives.

By 3 pm *QE2* has not arrived. We leave two notes with the locals and push on down towards the confluence with the Shire River as is the plan. As yet we have not seen or heard another motorized boat on the river. The only craft are dugout canoes and as always people are amazed to see us. One delightful old codger in a massive dugout loaded with maize, on seeing us, promptly stands bolt upright in his canoe and snaps off a smart military salute. What a credit to these people that they can still remain so polite and cheerful after so much deprivation. Their saving grace is that, provided it rains and they have crops, they can survive in the bush, unlike their counterparts living in refugee camps in Malawi.

Thursday 20 May

Awakening to a cold wind and eerily thick mist, we are in no rush, reckoning we only have about 40 kilometres to go to reach the Shire confluence, where we are to meet *QE2* at 2 pm. Our arrangement is that we will camp at the confluence and wait till 10 am tomorrow, after which we will go up the Shire in search of them. These pre-arranged meetings in the bush always have to have a plan A, B and C.

I'm concerned for Ross's safety and will only relax when we're together. But I'm also extremely confident in his youthful ability. He's developed a real love for Africa and has a maturity beyond his years. Still, I feel guilty sending him off into the unknown as I have. I'll never forgive myself if something happens.

We finally locate the confluence with the help of a proud Renamo soldier, who explains he is pleased that peace has come at last and that they can continue their daily lives without interruption. 'But we have not handed our guns back yet,' he informs us with a big grin. He goes on to assure us that we are at the only Shire confluence with the Zambezi, one used by all canoes travelling down from Nsanje in Malawi. The water, he tells us, is very deep. There are no blockages, bureaucratic or otherwise, and no sandbanks. I breathe a sigh of relief.

Hearing all this good news, and being a few hours ahead of schedule, we cruise up the Shire that flows deep and wide, apparently out of distant blue mountains. There is a belt of thick reeds on either side. The bottom reaches of the Shire seem sluggish as it winds its way out of Lake Malawi to join forces with the swift-flowing Zambezi.

A few kilometres up the Shire we stop at a village that boasts some huge mango trees. From the shade beneath them we have a good view up the river. We boil up a pot of tea and prepare to wait. At one minute to 2 pm we hear, much to our relief, the sound of outboards in the distance. Nkonkoni Rob, Ross and Geoff arrive, handing out ice-cold Malawi Greens (the local nickname for Carlsberg beers) with a flourish. We all hug and shake hands like long-lost friends, 'Bugsy' Geoff dog-barking with excitement, very relieved that everything has gone according to plan in this remote part of Africa.

We stop at an acacia belt to gather firewood, and our camp is another pristine sandbank. The spread of water in front of us is guarded by a pod of hippos, who noisily announce our arrival to a flock of African skimmers, gracefully skimming the mauve sunset waters of Livingstone's 'river of God'.

We are awakened during the night by a loud crash! Wide-eyed, we leap up, thinking we must be under attack. But it was only a collapsing sandbank and the constant crashing of the high caving sandbanks continues throughout the night.

Friday 21 May

Today we will head down to Marromeu where we hope to get fuel. The bends in the river and the winding to avoid the sandbanks are costing us a lot of extra fuel, so much so that we might be forced to leave *QE2* in Marromeu and continue in *Bathtub* as best we can.

We stop to talk to some fishermen on a sandbank, who have set up just the simplest of structures as a rudimentary camp. Their nets and dugout canoes are spread out on the sand to dry on a mat of grass, along with the previous night's catch of about 75 fish:

Wildlife

(from Tete to Chinde)

African skimmers
Fish eagles
Egyptian geese
White-crowned plovers
Saddle-billed storks
Goliath herons
Open-billed storks
Pied kingfishers
Pelicans
Spur-wing geese
White-faced whistlers
Great white herons
Grey-headed gulls
Water dikkop
Malachite kingfisher
Burchell's cuckoo

Hippos 118 (up to
Shire confluence)
Crocs 24 (NB crocs
very aggressive)

How simple life can be –
a fire, a pot, a boat and
a mosquito net!

tiger fish, chessa, and mudsuckers averaging close to a pound each in weight. They tell us that they make a living selling the fish in Quelimane, where the people from upcountry enjoy the freshwater fish. For the past six years they have been unable to fish this section, as the territory was in the hands of Renamo and anything moving on the river was 'shot up'.

Nothing could have prepared us for our arrival in Marromeu. Standing on the river bank, its smokestacks silhouetted against the sky, is the wreck of a giant sugar mill. It was operational until 10 years ago when Renamo attacks closed everything down. The sugar estate homes of Portuguese colonial vintage are mostly still intact, but some of their windows are broken, and they are badly in need of a coat of paint. Even the massive toolboxes at the sugar mill remain full of tools, long unused, although nature has moved in with rust and decay.

Shops stand open for business, with one trading store offering six bottles of orange juice, two tins of fish and a few empty grain bags. The only place with good stocks is a little shack where we purchase Black Label beers, South African export quality. Once again it is the informal sector that keeps things going. As we walk back to our boats through the market – followed pied-piper-like by dozens of kids – we observe the limited buying power of the locals: cooking oil is sold by the tablespoon, sugar by the bottle top and diesel by the beer can. Tobacco is cut off a roll and lit from a taper, sold complete with a scrap of paper to roll one's own. Life carries on thanks to the amazing adaptability of Africa.

The centre for the Food for the Hungry is in an old sugar estate house, and we are extremely relieved to find a dented 200-litre drum labelled *Kingsley Holgate A/O/E. Pay $200 or 600,000 mets*. It is good value when you think it has been flown in from Beira in an old Russian transporter. To us it is an absolute lifesaver. I speak to John Morrison of Food for the Hungry on the radio, and he agrees to fly us in yet another drum, which means we can take both boats to the coast.

The sun is setting over the distant palm trees just downstream from Marromeu by the time we pitch camp on a suitable sandbank. We now have an extra member on the AOE in the form of Dickens, a little guinea pig that Mashozi purchased with its cage at the local market. She couldn't bear the thought of it ending up in a cooking pot. During the night we hear gunshots and the rhythmic beating of drums.

Saturday 22 May

Mashozi releases Dickens back into the bush and after toast and coffee we set off for Chinde and the coast. To be on the delta is extremely enjoyable. The bush gives way to grassland and palm trees, and passing Luabo we see another wrecked sugar mill sticking out above the trees, and then, at Beno, gardens of coconut palms, mango trees and bananas. We are welcomed with great enthusiasm, people on the banks waving with both hands, others giving thumbs up.

Birdlife on the sandbanks is increasing, and on one sandbank alone there are well over 500 open-billed storks, which take off in a massive black cloud as the boat disturbs them.

Unfortunately some of the new petrol has water in it and we spend an hour drifting down the Zambezi as Ross and Ian clean out the carbs and fuel system.

The Rio Chinde, one of the fingers of the Zambezi's delta, is a rich brown, and the first few kilometres of its banks are thick with banana plantations, which give way to grasslands and coconut palms. We are about 50 kilometres from the coast, and one can already feel a large tidal difference. It is obviously low tide as mudbanks and sandbanks are well exposed. Fishermen in their dugouts are plentiful, as are the fish that they are holding up for sale.

At 1 pm on 22 May 1993, after 67 days on the river, we round a sweep in the Chinde River and see Chinde – graveyard to paddle steamers, sugar barges and tugs, their jagged black metal sticking out like sharks' teeth above the water, ready to tear our rubberducks apart. Beyond them are a few ships off-loading relief maize, and beyond that the Indian Ocean. We are overjoyed at finally reaching our destination on this mighty river.

Friendly locals mob the boats and, leaving Roy to look after the vessels, we walk up through the village to the Food for the Hungry organization's office where we radio to confirm our safe arrival. John Morrison speaks to his staff in Chinde and organizes us chickens, rice and incredibly tasty mud crabs, all washed down with cold Castles as we sit on bags of not-for-sale US maize. Until recently we were the enemy as South African-backed Renamo fought for control of this Frelimo outpost. Now here we are sharing a meal – chewing a tough chicken and sucking the flesh from giant mud crabs.

Sunday 23 May

There is so much to see and do here and we start off by interviewing an old Chinde resident who worked on the river for many years as a crew member on a stern-wheeler which travelled upstream as far as Tete. He explains that some of the old corrugated-iron dwellings in Chinde are in fact British, and that the previous Chinde is actually underwater, claimed by the sea in an area constantly being eroded by sea and river. In the second half of the 19th century Chinde was a swampy, 10-hectare British enclave, leased to them by the Portuguese. It provided the British with a transport link to Central Africa and Nyasaland (present-day Malawi). A fleet of hardworking paddle steamers made the trip from the coast up the Zambezi and then on up the Shire to Malawi or on to Tete. But Chinde's days as a bustling port were numbered, especially when the railway linked Beira to the interior of the continent. One fearsome cyclone in 1922 sent 10 of the ships to their rusty graves, and the cost of replacing them and fighting the ever-eroding sandbanks became too much for the British, who abandoned the port in 1923.

Friendly, peaceful and charming, the town once had several clubs, a hotel, electric lights, tarred roads and even a tennis court. It was a good life for the early colonists, judging by the grand homes and large gardens. Prawns, plenty of fish, fruit and coconuts make for a fairly easy life in a town that has not suffered unduly during the war.

Senhor Carlos, the maritime administrator of Chinde, in his spotlessly white officer's uniform, poses for photographs with the team and hands over a letter which will be the Mozambican part of the Afrika Odyssey scroll. He even accompanies us out to sea for our end of the Zambezi chapter, which we celebrate by all leaping off the boat and clinging onto a buoy far out in the Indian Ocean. An exciting end to a river we will never forget.

An afternoon walk with Carlos around the old Chinde wrecks is fascinating – especially the *Majingo*, built in England in 1926. This once beautiful stern-wheeler was the personal 'houseboat' for the manager of Sena Sugar, and is now used as a ferry up and down the river. The pilot gives us a tour of his vessel, which, like most things here, is 'under repair'.

It has been disturbing to see no game on the river as we have come closer to the coast, and to be offered leopard and game skins together with ivory at Chinde. But we have done a game and bird count on the river from Tete down to the Indian Ocean and are amazed by the number of crocs and hippos still to be found. Birdlife too is plentiful with graceful flocks of over 50 African skimmers often seen.

At the war-ravaged mission station of Shupanga we locate Mary Livingstone's grave.

Monday 24 May

Today we head back up the Chinde and the Zambezi and on to the Shire and Malawi. Once again the gawkers are back in full force, looking over the low wall and into our campsite. Early morning gawkers we call sparrow farts. Some are habitual gawkers who have been with us for three days now. We also have dugout gawkers, water-carrying gawkers – who almost lose their load from gawking – and then of course there are the ever-present pied-piper gawkers who follow us from place to place. For many of these little ones we must be the strangest *abelungu* they have ever seen.

QE2 runs out of fuel just short of Marromeu and *Bathtub* makes it with only a teaspoon to spare. Unfortunately, one of the drums of petrol waiting for us has over 40 litres of water in it. The second drum is fine, however, and once again we're saved by Food for the Hungry, who provide petrol for the empty and grog for the thirsty – a case of Black Label is also waiting for us.

With all the fuel problems we only get away from Marromeu at last light to make camp on a mosquito-infested sandbank. We have no firewood, so we sit around a few candles, enjoying a merry sing-a-long and getting stuck into the Black Labels.

Tuesday 25 May – Mary Livingstone's grave

Once the thick mist lifts we take off to Shupanga about 20 kilometres upriver, where Mary Livingstone is buried. Shupanga is totally overgrown, and we push our boats through the thick reeds and then through shoulder-high elephant grass. There is not a soul in sight, but I see a church steeple in the distance. Eventually we come across two little kids, but we have no one to translate as Roy did a bunk this morning. We waited, revved the outboard motors and shouted for him – but he was gone.

By drawing the sign of a cross, then drawing a finger across the throat as a sign of death and then indicating someone sleeping, we try to get the message across. They lead us down a path and through dense undergrowth to the walled cemetery still with its gate. We are drawn on by excited shouts of 'Here it is' from Nkonkoni Rob and Jon, and there, in thick undergrowth, is a headstone about 1.5 metres high and standing above a cement plinth, one side of which is still chained off.

The gravestone is intact, other than for a small chip out of the top corner. The solid cast-iron cross above the gravestone is removable and has been knocked from its place, apparently by automatic gunfire. We place it back on top of the gravestone. Standing next to the grave and looking over the cemetery wall one can clearly see the Zambezi in the distance, the river that played such a part in David Livingstone's life. One wonders what sort of life this brave woman lived, the hardship, trials and tribulations. She died at the age of 41 from malaria. We take off our hats and stand in silence. The church next to the graveyard is desecrated, as is the large Shupanga House and many outbuildings. This must have been a sizable mission station until the Portuguese departed.

The sun is fierce in the afternoon as we finally make it to the confluence with the Shire. Camped on a sandbank opposite the confluence, we experience our last sunset on the Zambezi. It is a windless night, and swarms of mosquitos chase us under nets and into tents for an early night.

The Shire & the

A ferry boat on the Lake of Stars

It was on New Year's Day 1859 that Dr Livingstone nosed the Ma Roberts out of the Zambezi and into the deep, winding Shire River – a river that would finally lead him to discover Lake Nyasa, the Lake of Stars, on 16 September 1859. In later years the Shire brought other explorers, missionaries, hunters, traders and adventurers from Chinde on the Indian Ocean into central Africa. Malaria and the horrific slave trade were early obstacles to travellers on the river. Now, as we make our way up the Shire, the old riverboat steamers and the Portuguese have long since gone, and the slave trade has passed, but sickness, malaria and the aftermath of the bloody civil war remain.

Lake of Stars

Wednesday 26 May

Mist prevents us from leaving as early as planned. Ian is feeling ill, and Jon thinks it might be heatstroke. We also have a fuel problem – *QE2*, the big guzzler, has been swallowing it against the current. We will carry on as far as possible together, and then *Bathtub* will have to go on ahead to pick up more fuel in Malawi.

As the sun becomes hotter the wooded hills start to throw off their blankets of mist, revealing range after range of astonishingly lovely hills and peaks. The constant bends and twists in the river are trebling the distance as the crow flies, and I can tell that we will soon run short of fuel. Off to the north-east of the river is Mount Morumbala, but such are the river's twists and turns that we never seem to get closer to it.

We are waved ashore at a well-kept reeded village where I decide to have a look around. I immediately regret it. Pictures of Alphonso Dlakama, the leader of Renamo, are attached to reed walls, telling me that this is a Renamo stronghold. A gang of unruly young men, most of whom are quite drunk, greet me with smiles, handshakes and *Bon dia*'s. I 'saunter' back to the boats. Ross sees the look in my eyes and quickly fires up *QE2*'s engines. A young man lurches towards the boat and tries to climb aboard, at which point an older 'soldier' grabs him and kicks him in the face. In a flash everybody is kicking and throwing punches. Fortunately, *Bathtub*'s outboards start on the first pull. Another drunk lurches for the boat and narrowly misses getting caught in the props as we roar upstream. They're obviously mixing something with their palm wine!

Ian's condition has worsened considerably, and he is suffering from severe headaches and diarrhoea. I am so busy concentrating on avoiding an old pont that I drive the boat at full throttle into thick reed and Kariba weed, much to the mirth of the onlookers both on the banks and in two passing dugouts. To their amazement Ian lurches towards the back of the boat, and, without any thought for the spectators, his shorts around his knees, in absolute agony and totally out of control, empties his liquid bowel into the Shire River. We dose him up on antibiotics and keep him drinking rehydrate. But nothing seems to help and he's getting progressively weaker.

Renamo leader
Alphonso Dlakama

We soon come across *QE2* which was ahead of us and has run out of fuel close to Mount Morumbala. We are still an estimated four hours from Nsanje, and it will take about three hours with the current to get back here again from Nsanje. So, leaving Nkonkoni Rob and Jon with *QE2*, meagre rations and their sleeping kit, I set off in the small boat with Mashozi, Ross, a desperately sick Ian and as much gear as we can carry. Ian lies corpse-like on top of the kit up front in the bow. We need to get him urgent medical attention or he'll die.

When *Bon dia*'s change to *Hello*'s and the relics of old Portuguese homes and stores are left behind, we realize that at last we are in Malawi, the 'warm heart of Africa'. What a relief! Down in these lowlands it certainly is very warm, with midday and early afternoon temperatures hardly bearable.

At Nsanje, the old Port Herald, we leave the boat in the care of the smartly clad river police unit, who are amazed that we've made it. We arrange a shady place for Ian to sleep, then rush off in search of medical help and a bank to change some cash into Malawian kwachas. The plan is that Ross will go back down-stream immediately, sleep on the river with the others and come back tomorrow.

We go to chat to *Médecins Sans Frontières*, the French medical relief agency. They begin treating Ian immediately for dysentery and dehydration. The commercial bank does not operate every day and is closed. The nearest bank is about 100 kilometres away and will only be open tomorrow morning. We try to change money at the Red Cross and UN – no luck. Eventually we go back to the French who by nightfall have helped us out with our money problem. But it is now too late to fetch the others, and they will just have to spend a night alone in Mozambique.

Strangely enough, now that I am in the safety of Malawi I am more concerned for their security, especially as all the relief agencies we have been speaking to are amazed at what we have achieved. None of them have been operating inside Mozambique. I guess that for them the stories heard in the refugee camps around Nsanje (350,000 refugees) have been enough. So yes, I guess that to a degree we have rushed in where angels fear to tread, but certainly our brazen trip down the Zambezi and back up the Shire has only brought cries of delight and greetings from all we saw. No doubt we were seen in a positive light, a sign of the return to peace, and at no time did we feel threatened.

We pitch camp in front of a delapidated house occupied by *Médecins Sans Frontières* next to the old Beira railway line, Ian tucked up and being cared for by Mashozi. Ross is looking a bit grim, and chances are he is coming down with Big M. We agree that if he can't make it tomorrow then I will go back down the river alone.

Thursday 27 May

This morning Ross is looking extremely ill, Ian is getting weaker and I've got the squitters. Happiness in Africa is indeed a dry fart! I take off alone with plenty of Mazoe Orange juice and four Greens to meet the lads on the river. I meander through the reed beds, villagers rushing down to the water's edge to stare at the bearded monster, this time going downstream. The sun beats down and I begin to feel weaker and weaker. Soon I'm so weak that I can no longer stand at the control console and I make a seat from the fuel containers. The glare on the water is killing me and the hot dry fever and headaches begin. I'm alone on the river, back inside Mozambique and the malaria is hitting me, this time with a vengeance. I open up the throttles and snake through the bends at high speed, shamefully flooding the occasional dugout. But the fever is really bad and I must keep going. I find *QE2* and the pilgrims where we left them below Morumbula Mountain, low lying, swampy and hot. I sit in the shade of a tree and gulp down as much water as I can.

The pilgrims have had an interesting time. They traded fish-hooks for fish, which they roasted on the coals. A young Renamo soldier arrived in camp and Rob asked to inspect his AK47. But when he cocked it the little kids ran off screaming into the bush. What atrocities must have been committed to cause such a reaction.

We fuel up *QE2* and head back towards Nsanje. I lie sweating in the shade of *QE2*'s canopy. Tying up again at the Nsanje river police post we get the news that Ross is down with malaria. Mashozi has wisely treated him immediately with Larium and he is out for the count. Ian needs attention, and Nkonkoni Rob, I forgot to mention, treated himself with chloroquine last night for malaria and is not feeling too good either. And I have headaches and diarrhoea again. Was it really worth it? We made it to the mouth of the Zambezi, and had a wonderful and exciting adventure, but at what price to our health? My biggest fear is always of severe illness – cerebral malaria, snake bite, serious injury.

But we are fortunate once again, as malaria has struck close to a good mission hospital and a friendly Dutch couple are able to treat us, as do the doctors and nurses of *Médecins Sans Frontières* who provide a simple room for the Afrika Odyssey Expedition patients. So it is in a relatively safe environment that I too go down with malaria, suffering a very heavy fever and delirium for the third time in under three months.

Saturday 29 May

Last night a burglar cut open our tent and gently removed Mashozi's moneybag with about R5,000 in cash in it. What a blow! Mashozi heard a light scratching on the fly-sheet and the meow of a cat. Hmm, a true 'cat burglar'. He slit open the tent with a knife and put his hand in to take the money just inches from her head!

My condition deteriorated to such an extent on Thursday that Medical Rescue International were contacted and emergency plans put together through them and the South African Embassy to airlift me out of this remote corner of Malawi. But thanks to quinine, that age-old drug, this is not necessary. I'm being treated with a full seven-day course, which they say will get the bug out of my system. It makes me quite nauseous and deaf. But it is most definitely an improvement on being an inmate at the Nsanje cemetery, as interesting as it may be to lie next to the old settlers.

Ross, owing to his youth and Larium, is off partying after 24 hours. I take a full three days to recover and lose over five kilos in that time. I'm weak with the ringing of quinine in my ears. But I'm alive, and so are Ian and the rest of the team.

Hi Debs

I'm sorry about all the confusion with Mashozi and Ross wanting to airlift me out of Nsanje. It appears I was on my last legs but I am now 100% OK. Lake Malawi has been simply idyllic, a paradise after the testing time on the Zambezi and Shire rivers. From Blantyre our journey took us by road to Zomba, the old administrative capital established here in 1891, so that, among other things, the Brits could monitor the slave caravans that passed here en route to the lake and then overland to Zanzibar. How those desperate souls must have suffered with fewer than half of them ever reaching the coast, chained like animals, beaten and whipped, or if too weak simply clubbed to death.

From Zomba we explored Lake Chilwa and then went on to Mangoche, the old Fort Johnson, a former stronghold for British troops. Near the town's clock tower a naval gun off the HMS Gwendolin still stands. The boat's captain Commander EL Rhodes earned a place in history when he captured the German gunboat the Herman von Wissman. This British victory was the very first naval battle of World War 1, fought on this virtually unknown lake in Central Africa in 1914. But the story does have a humorous side to it. Prior to this Captain Rhodes had an excellent drinking relationship with the captain of the German vessel, which he found laid up out of the water on the German East African side of the lake. On sighting the enemy the crew of HMS Gwendolin opened fire and eventually scored a hit. The enraged German captain rowed out in a dinghy to demand an explanation for his friend's behaviour, only to find that Germany was at war with Britain. They really should have let them know!

We set up our first expedition base camp on Lake Malawi at Cape Maclear near Monkey Bay. Lake Malawi is one of Africa's most beautiful and fascinating Rift Valley lakes, which Livingstone named Lake Nyasa, Lake of Stars. It is an inland sea, 575 kilometres long and

58 kilometres at its widest point, occupying one fifth of Malawi's total land area. It's fed by 14 rivers and drained by only one, the Shire, which flows from the lake's southernmost tip. With our tents pitched under shady trees, QE2 and Bathtub pulled up on a sandy beach and with the services of John Engine, a local cook and boatman, this was paradise. We dived into the clear waters of the lake, Otto Point and the islands, and visited the ruins of the old Cape Maclear Hotel.

Built in 1948, it played host to passengers travelling with the BOAC that provided the flying boat service from England to South Africa. Sitting among the ruins of the old hotel I could imagine those delightful days of air travel with just 28 passengers and eight crew in a slow four-engined flying boat. Landing on the Nile, Lake Navaisha in Kenya, swooping low over the vast herds of game and landing here, on what was then Lake Nyasa. White dresses, hats against the sun, the roar of its engines as it takes off to land again on the Zambezi just up from the Victoria Falls at Jungle Junction.

One can't travel through this respectable country without being reminded of the horrors of the East Coast slave trade. Further up the lake we stopped to visit Nkhotakota. A sea of thatched roofs, this is said to be the largest traditional village in Central and southern Africa. It was also the largest Arab slave-trading depot on the lake and by 1870 approximately 10,000 slaves were said to pass through the town annually.

Our next camp on the lake was at Kande Beach, 13 kilometres south of the village of Chinteche. Just a little pub, a few long drops and a camping site, a great place to relax, swim to the nearby island, observe the villagers and their dugouts, and prop up the bamboo bar, with beers being brought in by wheelbarrow from the local supplier. Here once again vehicle and boat party all met up. Our logistics in Malawi are so easy with the good support roads and English spoken everywhere.

At present we're at Chikale Beach just south of Nkata Bay. We've made a delightful camp here, and this will be our base camp from which we will explore Likoma Island and the north of the lake. We leave tomorrow!

Keep well! All our love
Kingsley and the Afrika Odyssey team

Monday 14 June

We launch into a rough lake in the direction of Likoma Island. With us we have dear old friends Ann and Don Balmer from Zululand. Soon the waves are building high from the south and I'm forced to ride in the wake of QE2. It's tough going with the wind coming from the direction of the Mozambique shoreline opposite. Likoma and its smaller sister island Chizumulu are entirely in Mozambican waters, but for some reason when the Portuguese and British split up the southern part of the lake in the 1950s these two islands were allocated as Malawian territory.

In about 1886 missionaries Lucil Johnson and Chauncy Maples decided Likoma should be the HQ of the Anglican Church in Nyasaland. On this small island they initiated the building of a cathedral that would be a replica of Winchester Cathedral in England, and be constructed using only local materials. The baked mud-brick church, St Peter's, complete with stained glass windows, was built on the spot where suspected witches were once burnt alive. When in 1895 Chauncy Maples went to London to be consecrated Bishop of Likoma he couldn't wait to return. Finally back in Nyasaland, he took a small boat and headed for his dear Likoma. In the darkness the boat capsized in a squall and

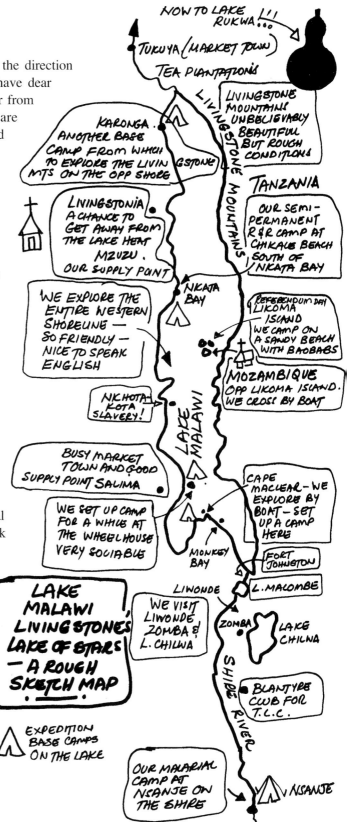

NOW TO LAKE RUKWA !!!

TUKUYA (MARKET TOWN)
TEA PLANTATIONS

LIVINGSTONE MOUNTAINS UNBELIEVABLY BEAUTIFUL BUT ROUGH CONDITIONS

KARONGA. ANOTHER BASE CAMP FROM WHICH TO EXPLORE THE LIVINGSTONE MTS ON THE OPP SHORE

TANZANIA

LIVINGSTONIA A CHANCE TO GET AWAY FROM THE LAKE HEAT MZUZU. OUR SUPPLY POINT

OUR SEMI-PERMANENT R&R CAMP AT CHIKALE BEACH SOUTH OF NKATA BAY

NKATA BAY

WE EXPLORE THE ENTIRE WESTERN SHORELINE — SO FRIENDLY — NICE TO SPEAK ENGLISH

REFERENDUM DAY LIKOMA ISLAND WE CAMP ON A SANDY BEACH WITH BAOBABS

MOZAMBIQUE OPP LIKOMA ISLAND. WE CROSS BY BOAT

NKHOTAKOTA SLAVERY!

LAKE MALAWI

BUSY MARKET TOWN AND GOOD SUPPLY POINT SALIMA

CAPE MACLEAR—WE EXPLORE BY BOAT—SET UP A CAMP HERE

WE SET UP CAMP FOR A WHILE AT THE WHEELHOUSE VERY SOCIABLE

FORT JOHNSTON

MONKEY BAY

LIWONDE

L. MALOMBE

LAKE MALAWI LIVINGSTONE'S LAKE OF STARS — A ROUGH SKETCH MAP

WE VISIT LIWONDE ZOMBA & L. CHILWA

ZOMBA

LAKE CHILWA

SHIRE RIVER

BLANTYRE CLUB FOR T.L.C.

EXPEDITION BASE CAMPS ON THE LAKE

OUR MALARIAL CAMP AT NSANJE ON THE SHIRE

NSANJE

despite the close proximity to land he refused to leave the boat and swim to shore. The crew begged, but over the storm they heard his shout: 'I feel my hour to die has come.' Presently all the survivors could hear were his groans and prayers and repeated cries of, 'I am a miserable sinner!' Soon the water choked him and he sank. Two weeks later the Bishop's body was washed up on the lakeshore, recognizable by his cassock shroud. We are amazed at the beauty of his legacy, St Peter's Cathedral, that still stands.

Likoma's rocky outcrops are polished smooth by wind and water. The massive rocks are white with cormorant droppings, and huge baobabs stand like sentinels on isolated sandy white beaches. An island paradise! Today is referendum day and feelings are running high. The general belief is that most people will vote multiparty. The island's results will be announced this afternoon from under the great baobab tree in the market square. We leave the crowds, buy a goat and make a camp on a sand spit surrounded by baobabs and boulders, purchasing our firewood from Mozambicans in dugouts. (Mozambique is just a few kilometres across the water from our camp – thousands of kilometres of unspoilt country.) Our curried goat stew is delicious and a cold wind blows throughout the night.

Tuesday 15 June

The referendum results are hailed out under the baobab: Registered voters 3,367. Number for the multiparty Lantern party, 1,470. Number for the one-party Cock, 257.

I meet with Arthur, the local headman, who offers me a choice of scenic sites on the lakeshore, requesting that I come back and build a safari camp. One such place is absolutely exquisite, with 10 or so mature baobab trees standing in a cluster on a secluded beach. A tempting thought for the future.

Wednesday 16 June – Monday 5 July

Early morning we wake up to the throb of engines across the lake. It's the old lake steamer, the *Chauncy Maples*, chugging off to distant Nkhotakota.

In *QE2* and *Bathtub* we make our way across a lake that is as smooth as oil, and soon we are back at Chikale Beach. It's like coming home. One day runs into the next, and it's becoming increasingly difficult to leave, especially for the rest of the pilgrims. They've even created a volleyball net and are entertaining all and sundry. I too am enjoying having a base camp from which to explore and watch the clouds of black lake flies gather in the distance. We spend the next two weeks exploring the surrounding lake and the area. Our exploration includes a jaunt to the old 1894 Livingstonia Mission high up in the foothills of the Nyika Plateau, a visit to the Manchewe Falls on the Chitimba River and some small safaris up to Mzuzu to buy fuel, get ice and on one occasion even to watch rugby on a snowy screen. We'd better move – we're getting soft!

Tuesday 6 July

We have a great send-off from Nkata Bay. John Engine, the cook and camp hand we hired at Cape Maclear, is sad to see us go. Worried that all the kwachas we've paid him might be stolen on the bus, he stuffs them down his underpants and into his shoes. It is people like John Engine who have made our stay here so pleasant.

FORESTED CLIFF FACE

PLANK FOOTBRIDGE

GAWKING ROCKS

SANDY BEACH

MASSIVE ROCKS

CLEAR MOUNTAIN STREAM FLOWING INTO THE LAKE COMPLETE WITH WATERFALL AND BATHING POOLS

LAKE MALAWI

QE2 & BATHTUB

(A CAMP SO BEAUTIFUL – I SCRIBBLED A SKETCH IN THE JOURNAL.)

On the road to Karonga, we come across the eccentric house of Mr Solomon Ngoma who has dressed his home with car parts and other scrap, transforming it into a den of make-believe. Outside is his prepared grave and an office with a toy telephone and hundreds of gadgets made from junk. From here he makes a call to the ancestors below. Upstairs in the den is his coffin, which has soap and fresh linen inside it. There is also a mortuary, a chapel, and a room where his body will be guarded as it lies in waiting. An old gramophone with tired batteries will play the funeral dirge from crackly speakers throughout the house. A funnel linked to a tube allows one to urinate from the top floor, but the stench of urine is so strong that one can only doubt the efficiency of Mr Ngoma's plumbing! We bid farewell to the old crank who has prepared himself so well for death.

To us this northern shoreline of the lake is certainly the most beautiful. Steep slopes plunge down into the lake with little villages nestling against white beaches, rocky shorelines and giant baobabs. Our camp just north of Ruarwa is idyllic. The small sandy beach lies below a waterfall, and is a natural sanctuary, with 'gawking rocks' at a safe distance. A thickly wooded cliff face forms the backdrop and a plank bridge across a little river takes pedestrians further along the footpath from Nkata Bay to Karonga. In the evening two guys walk through camp with flaming torches, off to night school.

Wednesday 7 July

After breakfast and an icy early morning swim we continue north past Deep Bay and on to Florence Bay, where in 1946, the year of my birth, a frightful accident happened below Mount Waller. We stop *QE2* and *Bathtub* and gaze into the depths where the lake steamer, the *Vipye*, went down with 200 or more passengers, of whom only 49 survived.

Dr David Livingstone's expedition here refers to the great waves on Lake Malawi as follows: *'The waves we most dreaded rushed upon us in threes, one after the other in rapid succession. Then a few minutes of calm and another charge of three perpendicular-sided, enraged masses.'* It was these freak trios that capsized the *Vipye*, and it took just a few minutes for her to be lying on the lake bed in 60 fathoms of water.

We too experienced the giant threes on our way to Likoma, but today a gentle swell carries us north to Karonga where the shoreline starts to flatten out into a lakeshore plain dotted with baobabs. We spoil ourselves and take rooms at Cleopatra's Beach Chamber Motel at Kabwe just north of Karonga Town. It's the ideal base from which to launch our boat safari to the Livingstone Mountains that beckon us from the opposite shoreline.

Thursday 8 July - The Livingstone Mountains

Jon is down with malaria. We treat him with Fansidar, and Ian offers to look after him while we take off across the lake for the Livingstone Mountains. The crossing is a little bumpy, but worth every bump and every splash. By late afternoon we arrive below the towering peaks and cliffs. There are no sandy beaches on this side; just steep pebble beaches with dugouts pulled up high above the crashing waves. Little huts cling to the high sides of the mountains and people grow cassava in patches on the hillsides.

The wind picks up and it is almost dark before we finally select our pebble beach. We land the equipment through the surf, then turn the boats' bows into the waves. Soon everyone is drenched. The anchors will not hold on the pebble bottom of this section of the lake, and we're forced to anchor the boats to a submerged rock and a pinnacle just off the beach. I'm concerned that the boats might break loose in the night. In this wind the fibreglass hulls will smash if they end up on the rocky beach, the waves pounding into them.

Our chosen spot is a sinister place with its high cliffs, deserted huts above us, broken pots, a grain stamper and buffalo beans. These grow in the thick bush and the thousands of tiny hairs on the outside of the pod make one sting and itch like crazy, leaving painful welts and bumps. A singsong around a lonely fire and then off to sleep, our sleeping bags stretched out for a lumpy night on the beach. Ross sleeps close to the night line, armed with a torch and a knife to cut the ropes if the boats end up in a tangle on the beach. The onshore wind continues to blow.

2 am: My worst fears are realized! All hell breaks loose as one anchor rope breaks and the boats end up being pounded onto the beach, *Bathtub* on top of *QE2*, props against pontoons. There is much shouting as ropes are cut. We're all in deep water, wrestling with the boats and ropes, waves breaking over our heads. I just hope there are no crocs. It's dangerous as, barefoot, we slip and slide on the pebbles. Finally we push both boats back out through the waves. Ross and Nkonkoni Rob will have to spend the rest of the night on the boats a kilometre or two out into the lake. They take a bottle of Captain Morgan rum with them against the cold. Soon their song and laughter drift across the water on the wind.

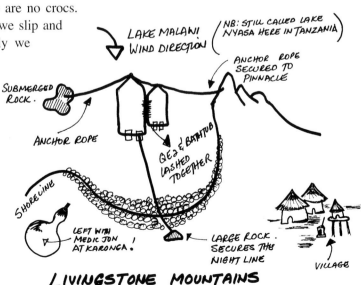

LIVINGSTONE MOUNTAINS

Friday 9 July

Sunrise brings with it calm waters and a canoe that arrives at our beach bearing a huge clay pot for brewing millet beer. Behind the canoe and paddler, walking along the beach, are little children all carrying bundles. People are moving into the empty village close to where we have slept, and immediately the strange feeling of the previous night leaves us. No longer are we at a deserted village site, but among friendly strangers who are truly amazed to find us here on the day they have chosen to move into their homes. They greet us warmly in Swahili, and we feel like first-time explorers in a strange and foreign place.

The wind has stopped and the swell subsides. After breakfast we carry our kit on our heads through water to the boats, which have returned from the sojourn out on the lake. We are off to explore the Livingstone Mountains further; view after view unfolds as we pass waterfalls tumbling hundreds of metres into this magnificent Rift Valley lake.

As we make our way to the top end of the lake, the shoreline becomes more populated. Sheltering under some giant mango trees are a few huts with handcrafted pots stacked up against their walls under the wide, thatched eaves. This tempts us to go ashore. What friendliness and enthusiasm we find there. Charles Donald becomes our instant guide as he, in his colourful pidgin English, gives us a run-down of traditional life in this delightful area.

The huts are spotlessly clean inside, with maize cob designs pressed into the white clay floors. A thick reed mat provides a ceiling and a loft above the rafters. There is no furniture inside, only clay pots for cooking. It is the true Africa of old. We are given a full-on pottery display, chairs first being pulled out as we are made to sit like early colonials under a thatched area. Charles's mother lectures in Swahili, Charles providing excellent translations on the various stages of the age-old craft. Clay pots are shipped from here across to the markets.

Finally the pots that we have purchased are put on a dugout and taken out to the rubberducks. Then 'Father himself' (that's me!) has to be ferried out by dugout, as he is seen as old and dignified – the greybeard could not possibly be allowed to swim. With some oranges as a final gift, together with much handshaking and waving, we are off – strangers in a land that without hesitation opened its arms to us.

Sunday 11 July

Jon is on the mend but is still very weak. We will have to monitor his progress very carefully. The crossing into Tanzania goes smoothly, but across the border the road deteriorates badly – potholes and boat trailers don't go down well together. As we climb out of Malawi and up to the highland area towards Mbeya, we stop from time to time to look back over this vast Rift Valley lake and the towering heights of the Livingstone Mountains that bid us farewell over many kilometres.

Our camp for the night is in a tea plantation that covers the landscape like a soft, green carpet. To the west the sun sets over distant hills. No sooner have we camped and lit our customary fire than the gawkers arrive. This is our first experience of Swahili gawkers who stay on well after dark, but at least they keep at a respectful distance.

Municipal Council of Livingstone

AFRIKA ODESSEY EXPEDITION

With profound joy, thanks and gratitude, I salute and welcome to Livingstone the legendary Afrika Odessey Expedition team and its adventurous team leader Kingsley Holgate. Great is this rare privilege to meet these humane nature lovers and visioneries who as scholars and messengers, I dare say, by virtue of their mission, are greater than the senders of the message. May the expedition's noble mission to explore and study the waterways of Africa and related enviroment and its quest to engender and promote peace and goodwill amongst people of Africa attain abundant fruition and prosper.

Livingstone, established in 1904 by the British South African Company as a village at the old drift along the Mighty Zambezi River, is named after a Scotish explorer and Missionery, Dr. David Livingstone, who was the first european to see "The smoke that Thunders" – (Musi-oa-Tunya in the local vernacular) on November 16, 1855 , which he named Victoria Falls, after Queen Victoria. It is the oldest Municipality in the Country and was the capital of the then Northern Rhodesia (now Zambia) from 1907 to 1935 when the seat of Government was moved to Lusaka, a more central locality. Musi-oa-Tunya or Victoria Falls is a top natural wonder of the world and chief tourist attraction in this part of Africa, and has earned Livingstone the famous tag of 'Tourist Capital of Zambia'.

Its natural beauty and virgin environment is an open and enticing invitation to the whole world's humanity to be generous tolerant and to seek accommodation for and from each other for mutual benefit and esteem. It is my firm belief that man's endeavours to further and better the knowledge of this environment and develop should be harnessed for the good of all humankind. As a continent experiencing positive sound and conducive political and economic change a cordinated approach to development in peace and harmony is of cardinal importance. Just like there cannot be tangible positive socio-economic development without peace, there can be no meaningfully positive development in isolation. We all need the concerted collective effort counsel support and encourage-ment to overcome backwardsness and lessen human suffering.

As I bid farewell to these courageous explorers and bearers of the Scroll of Peace and Goodwill, I wish to on behalf of all the Councillors and the residents of Livingstone Municipality, and indeed on my own behalf, send greetings and brotherly endearments to His Worship the Mayor of Cairo, his Councillors and residents of that city and all the civic leaders and people along the expedition's route.

Humanity is one and so is our destiny.

"Bon voyage."

ABOVE: A pontoon crossing in Zambia as we head for Chavuma and the Angolan border. LEFT: The Mayor of Livingstone added these words to our scroll of peace and goodwill.

CHAVUMA DISTRICT COUNCIL
P.O. Box 99
CHAVUMA

Our Ref: CDC.../32/1/PMC

Your Ref:

Date 7th April, 93.

It is of great pleasure to have the privilege of meeting members of the Africa Odyssey expedition from Cape Town to Cairo.

I feel very proud for, it is very rare to meet people of this kind who can spend their time and money to take trouble of coming to visit us at Chavuma, where there is a big falls on the might Zambezi River. The falls is intended to put up a Hydro Electricity there. which would supply Electricity even to other Districts in the North-Western Province.

On behalf of the people of Chavuma District including the workers, and indeed on my own behalf, wish them a successful journey up to the accomplish of their Mission.

With love.

Patson M. Chiseso
SENIOR ADMINISTRATIVE OFFICER IN CHARGE
C H A V U M A.

LEFT: A note from the Angolan border town for our scroll. INSET BELOW: On the Zambezi life moves at the speed of a dugout – and the current. RIGHT: In colonial times locals pushed guests from Livingstone to Vic Falls.

MAIN PICTURE: Cahora Bassa Gorge – the rocks in God's Highway that halted Livingstone's Zambezi expedition. RIGHT: A Batonga woman smoking her traditional calabash pipe. LEFT: Elephants on the Chobe, a tributary of the Zambezi.

THIS PICTURE: 'I named this place of great wonder the Victoria Falls after my regent queen ...' Dr David Livingstone

ABOVE: Friendly gawkers are a fact of life on expedition. BELOW: Forever asking directions, and always getting unusual answers.

THIS PICTURE: Launching QE2 near Nkata Bay. RIGHT: The local people are fascinated by our red and yellow 'balloon boats'.

MAIN PICTURE: Livingstone called Lake Nyasa the Lake of Stars - to us it is definitely the warm heart of Africa.

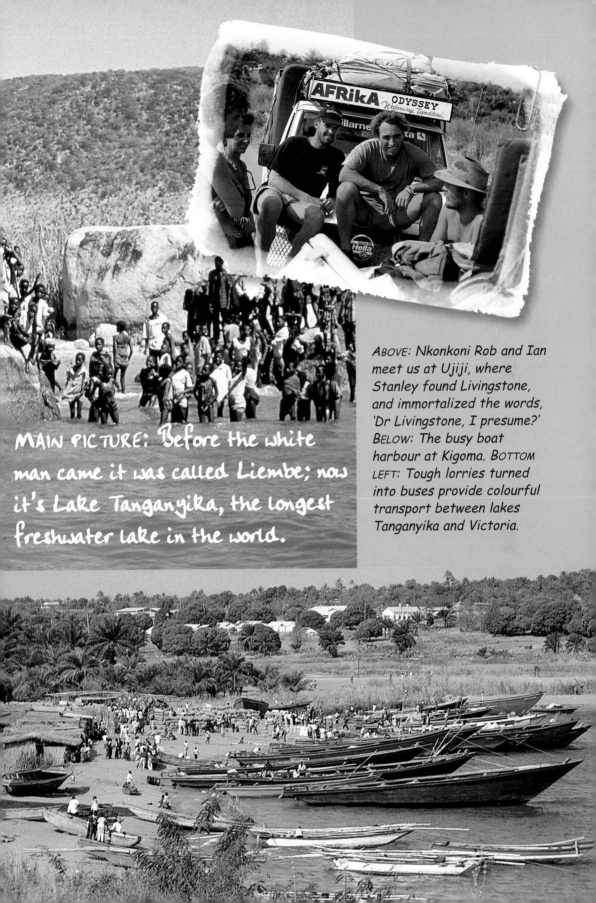

MAIN PICTURE: Before the white man came it was called Liembe; now it's Lake Tanganyika, the longest freshwater lake in the world.

ABOVE: Nkonkoni Rob and Ian meet us at Ujiji, where Stanley found Livingstone, and immortalized the words, 'Dr Livingstone, I presume?' *BELOW:* The busy boat harbour at Kigoma. *BOTTOM LEFT:* Tough lorries turned into buses provide colourful transport between lakes Tanganyika and Victoria.

Rukwa, Africa's

MAIN PICTURE: Rukwa, a forgotten jewel in the necklace of Great African Rift Valley lakes.

TOP INSET: At night local fishermen use lamps to attract fish. LEFT: A fisherman with his catch. ABOVE: Rising Rukwa water levels create a minefield of submerged stumps – murder on inflatables. RIGHT: Pumping fuel: sometimes it's dirty or has water in it – it's always bloody expensive!

forgotten lake

Lake Rukwa simply doesn't exist on tourist maps or in guide books. When we asked for information, people in Mbeya raised their eyebrows in disbelief. One friendly government official warned us about the fierce Lake Rukwa crocodiles: 'You know, sir, we had so many reports of people having been killed that we sent a Land Rover full of government officials down there to investigate the situation, and, can you believe it, two of them were eaten! Don't go, please don't go.'

Monday 12 July

The road up to Tukuya is rough and potholed. The town itself is a real outback town, dusty and dry, its unpainted buildings topped by corrugated-iron roofs. The market is extremely colourful, and, much to the delight of all, we share some tea, buns and meatballs with the locals. An East African atmosphere prevails, with the *mutato*-type taxis, brightly coloured and overloaded, driving like crazy. Large handcarts loaded with bananas, charcoal, red tomatoes and firewood are being pushed in every direction.

Mbeya is much bigger than anticipated – a sprawling Wild West town, with a bustling market stocked with great vegetables. We overnight at a local mission and the wonderful meal of fresh vegetables, chips and fried eggs is bloody luxury.

Tuesday 13 July

The guys at the German mission's trade school in Mbeya are only too pleased to help service our vehicles before we do a major fuel-up of both boats and vehicles that costs thousands of Tanzanian shillings – we need a shoebox of money to pay for it. But the fuel should be sufficient for Lake Rukwa and beyond.

As we leave Mbeya, Jon goes down badly again and is sick on the side of the road. The Fansidar seemed to have cured him, but now, six days later, things are looking worse than ever. He's taking great strain and I'm *very* worried. There is a Mormon mission station at Mbozi and we turn off to it down a narrow track in search of immediate help.

By the time we reach the hospital Jon is delirious. Dr Thomas, the German doctor, is in Europe, but we are taken to his wife Teliza, a lovely lady from Rwanda, who directs us to their home. Without hesitation, Telly gives up her bedroom for Jon. We do a blood test (positive) and put Jon on a course of quinine straight away. We take out the drip set so that we can give quinine intravenously if necessary. Luckily we don't have to use it: after a few tense hours the quinine starts to work and he improves slightly. We make our camp in the grounds of Telly's house – the boats, vehicles and trailers cluttering her backyard. Telly and her friends join us round our little fire for a bottle of Zimbabwean wine and a chat. We are the first South Africans she has ever met. Before meeting us, she confesses, she did not even want to visit Malawi in case she bumped into South African tourists! Fortunately we get on well, and I hope that this initial South African–Rwandan contact will help to improve the poor image of white South Africans – a legacy of apartheid.

Wednesday 14 July

The quinine has worked, thank God! Jon is much better. If only we could all be on the newly developed Larium all the time, we could prevent these costly delays to the expedition, but it's new on the market and very expensive. Jon is OK, but what would have happened had it been cerebral malaria? He is our medic, the one who has trained to keep the rest of us in shape. We will need to spend the day here to give Jon more time to rest. Tomorrow we will set off to Rukwa if he is strong enough.

Isn't it amazing that we still resort to using quinine as the last-resort cure? Unlike so many other early missionaries, explorers and hunters, Dr Livingstone survived in Africa because of his ability to control and cure malaria with quinine. His specially made pills known as 'Livingstone Rousers' consisted of jalap, calomel, quinine, rhubarb and a little opium. In typical Livingstone fashion he wrote, 'Take quinine in 4–6 grain doses every 2–3 hours till the ears ring and deafness ensues.' And so even today, more than a century later, here we are still taking quinine to survive.

11 am: Change of plan. Jon has improved so much that we're off to Sumbawanga, about six hours from here. To get there we turn off at Tunduma near the Zambian border, narrowly avoiding a collision with some daredevils on an out-of-control handcart loaded with charcoal. The road from Tunduma to Sumbawanga winds its way over a bleak, almost treeless landscape, peppered every 10 kilometres or so with small, huddled villages. As we reach the brow of one of the thousands of small hills, Sumbawanga comes into view, sprawling across the brown land, its church a central pinnacle.

Thursday 15 July

Everyone we pass, young and old, seems to be working. A man sits sewing on his humble veranda – a masculine occupation in Tanzania. His neighbour is setting up a neat reed fence around her vegetable garden. Right next door, a young girl with a baby secured to her side with a colourful wrap is pumping water from the communal pump. She takes off with a large bucket of water on her head – baby and all. Who knows how many kilometres it is to her home? The women here are dressed so colourfully, with an elegant wrap around their waists and another, sometimes of the same design, over their shoulders and heads.

While in Mbeya we briefly met local missionary Ken Kemper. I asked him about Lake Rukwa and the roads, and, as is the way in Africa, he scrawled his name on a piece of paper and said: 'You'll have to go through Sumbawanga – if you need help come and see us. Rukwa is fascinating, but you'll need good directions. It's really wild.'

We really need help in Sumbawanga – Jon is still weak and looks like a ghost. He's going through hell, and being on the move isn't helping. After getting hand-waving directions from the locals, we eventually find Ken and his wife Cathy at their home. The Kempers have two guests – another missionary, Bev, and an American nurse, Dawn – all in Africa to serve God. Thank God for them. They provide a sanctuary for us (especially Jon who really needs medical help) and missionary hospitality. We camp in the garden and have a feast of buffalo meat, rice, gravy, carrots, ice cream and American cookies.

Friday 16 July

At 2 pm we leave from Ken's place minus poor old Jon who has been left behind with Dawn and Bev. He is ashen and gaunt, but at this stage is out of danger. He is terribly disappointed, for, of all the waterways we will traverse, Rukwa is possibly the most remote and least known, and he has been so looking forward to it.

The dusty drive from Sumbawanga over the escarpment and down into the Great African Rift Valley is extremely steep and twisty. We have to engage first gear low ratio over holes and stones, not ideal for towing *Bathtub* laden with fuel and supplies. The views over Lake Rukwa are incredible, but are unfortunately barely visible as a result of the countless winter bush fires burning across this giant and exciting piece of Africa.

We finally make it down to the village of Muzi where there is quite a dense population along the fertile lakeshore – wild-looking people who stare in amazement. The crops have been good and in every village giant pots of *pombe* are on the boil, and if that doesn't suit your taste there is banana beer on offer. It's late afternoon and groups of brightly dressed people have gathered under their favourite tree to indulge in the ancient ritual of sundowners. The Sumbawanga missionary influence doesn't seem to have reached down into the depths of this part of the Great African Rift Valley.

We try taking a track down to the lake itself, but it has washed away. With the sun setting behind the Rift Valley Escarpment, now towering above us, we have to admit that once again Rukwa has eluded us. We make camp on a lonely airstrip once used for red locust control. The place has a mysterious feel, and soon the rhythmic beating of rawhide drums, high-pitched singing and occasional screams drown out the night's bush noises.

Saturday 17 July

We are escorted to the lake by a flock of pelicans and a lone fish eagle via some rickety pole bridges. The many fish lying to dry outside the handful of fishing villages are proof of the good fishing. We come across a hunting party, one of them offering to be our guide on the lake. Henry Chise is a wiry little fellow who speaks good English. The hunting party is making its way across to the opposite shore and will follow us in a wooden boat.

We leave *Thirsty* and everything we own with one of the fellows in the village against payment of 5,000 shillings if all is fine on our return. By noon we are ready to launch. The wind is blowing fairly strongly from the south, and our guide warns us to be careful of the many crocs. Launching from the thick, oozy, black mud, we push our way out into the lake through the glistening green reed beds. The dry trees sticking out above the surface of this lake show that it is slowly but constantly rising.

A mass of people are present to see us off, the rubberduck creating quite a buzz. Heavily loaded, and with the added weight of our guide, *Bathtub* has difficulty getting on the plane, especially as there are some rather large waves. A prop change on one motor improves things, and we are on our way again across the soapy grey water of Rukwa with the Rift Valley Escarpment running along the length of the lake.

Our plan is to cross the lake to the northern shore, an area that is said to be less inhabited, with plenty of wildlife. Our first attempt to land at the fishing camp of Ithumba is unsuccessful – the hundreds of trees sticking through the water are a potential minefield for *Bathtub*'s inflatable pontoons – and we are forced to move on again.

The next village is Kambuangombe. Raising the Mariners to shallow drive and moving slowly through the stumps, we get into a narrow channel between the reeds. The props churn their way through the thick mud and are helped along by our two stout Zambezi river paddles. Nobody is too keen to jump into the water to help push on account of the large crocodile population. Fishermen in dugouts point excitedly through the trees with their paddles, warning us that some of the channels are shallower than others.

When you travel as we are doing, always be prepared for anything. Be prepared for the journey to be your master. Things will never be as imagined. I mistakenly thought we would camp on deserted sandy beaches, as on Lake Malawi. But no. As we pull *Bathtub* through the black ooze between dugout canoes, the fishermen of Kambuangombe come pouring out of their rustic reeded huts to gaze in amazement at 'Holgate's Circus'. The people are very hospitable and we are introduced to Dalah Njui, the courteous 'secretary' of the fishing camp, who speaks good English and immediately takes us on a guided tour.

The village is a documentary in the making, inhabited by roughly 150 fishermen who work for several small co-operatives, which own the nets and dugouts required to harvest this bountiful lake. What a privilege to camp here and be part of their timeless way of living. We sit around the fires listening to stories of great fish and crocodiles, and other local folklore in this remote part of Lake Rukwa.

Sunday 18 July

We awake to the cry of the fish eagle. Our plans to go hunting for buffalo with the hunting party don't materialize as the party doesn't arrive. Instead we go out on foot across impressive game country, seeing ostrich and impala, but not much else other than the remains of a dead buffalo – shot by poachers we are told. The shoreline of Rukwa below the escarpment is becoming very populated. People and cattle are moving in and there are fires everywhere as land is cleared for *shambas*.

On getting back from our walk we find that officialdom is playing a hand. It appears that we need a permit from Parks and Wildlife to be here. The camp is here with their permission, and the camp's committee is afraid to continue hosting us unless we return from Sumbawanga with the necessary permit. Dalah is doing his best, but the committee – left over from socialist times – is still obsessed with paperwork. This is all discussed at a committee meeting, the door left open for all to hear, as everyone has a say regarding the fate of these strange *wazungus*. We decide to leave that afternoon, after thanking our hosts and the committee, and promising to call in at the Parks' office in Sumbawanga. I leave a letter as security that I will do so. The committee and fishermen all turn out to see us off, and we make our way out into the lake, with dugout paddlers riding in our wake.

There is a reasonable swell and we take a quick refreshing plunge, keeping the motors running to frighten the crocs. We dodge the fishing nets as we go, the shadows lengthening as we head back towards the steep Rift Valley Escarpment.

Monday 19 July

Having driven back over the escarpment to Sumbawanga, we stop in at the game post at Muzi to report our presence when Henry says he could be arrested for taking us to Kambuangombe. I decide on the 'temper trick', putting on an act of being really angry and threatening to go to the head of department in Dar es Salaam if I have any more trouble.

At Sumbawanga we are happy to find that Jon has fully recovered from malaria and is in good spirits. Nkonkoni Rob, Ross, Henry and I take off to the game department to 'clear our name'. The main guy is away and his assistant battles with his English, so we get passed on to a man in forestry. *Hakuna mutata*. At least we have honoured our commitment and made peace with the authorities, so absolving the Kambuangombe fishing camp from 'harbouring South African bandits'. We write off directly to Kambuangombe to let them know that all was well.

Tuesday 20 July

Johann Boytler, a missionary from Kipili on the shores of Lake Tanganyika, whom we met at the Kempers, gave us an excellent route to take from Sumbawanga to the lake. Travelling through savanna grasslands dotted with large acacia trees, a seemingly endless sandy track brings us to the village of Nyamarera. From there we drop over the escarpment through woodlands of tall hardwood trees. The dusty track begins to descend sharply as the sun sets, and we make camp in the trees.

It's a normal evening – vehicles and boats parked, tents and mozzie nets up, a small fire, kettle and pots, camp chairs and food boxes, the pilgrims chatting excitedly about Lake Tanganyika. Suddenly I notice Mashozi is missing. I find her sitting alone in the forest. She's wild-eyed and uncommunicative. Wondering if we've had some domestic tiff that I don't know about, I leave her be. Later I find her in our tent, all dressed up in jeans and a sweater, clothes scattered everywhere. She's sobbing her heart out, spluttering that she's missed a jump and lost her horse! She seems to be back in her childhood – a kid at a riding school in England. Hysteria sets in and I get scared. I chuck a bucket of ice-cold water over her, and this brings her back to her senses. The camp is all whispers, thinking the 'old farts' are having a fight. I get out the medical kit and give her pills to calm her down. We have a bad night and the next day Mashozi is nauseous and still suffering from dizziness, depression and severe headaches. It's so out of character, as she's normally the toughest of the lot of us. Then we realise that it must be the side effects of the Larium, which she's been on for several months. She stops taking it immediately. To add to her discomfort she's all swollen with bloody tsetse fly bites. Sometimes I wonder if we should really be putting ourselves through this! Would I ever be able to forgive myself if Ross or Mashozi didn't make it back? Africa is riddled with the graves of those who haven't.

Tanganyika, the lake

Hand-crafted lake boats

'All the lakes you have seen are different from Liembe. They are blind lakes, asleep. In the rain Liembe sleeps but, when the clouds dissolve and the night wind dies down before daylight, Tanganyika awakes to look at the moon and the stars, and the lake is full of eyes.' These were the words of an old African to a British zoologist about Lake Tanganyika, originally called Liembe. The 'eyes' were the millions of freshwater jellyfish that are found in this vast inland sea. It was on the shores of this lake at Ujiji on November 1871 that Henry Morton Stanley found Livingstone and greeted him with the most famous line in the annals of exploration.

with eyes

Wednesday 21 July - Dam to Kipili

From our campsite on the side of the Rift Valley Escarpment, the road drops sharply into a valley and brings us finally to Lake Tanganyika and the isolated village of Kipili. Stretching for 677 kilometres, this Great African Rift Valley lake is the longest fresh-water lake in the world, its waters lapping Zambia, Zaïre, Tanzania and Burundi, and reaching depths of 1,433 metres. It holds one-sixth of the world's fresh water.

Besides the Boytler homestead perched above Kipili, we see little modern Western influence. The inhabitants of this protected harbour make a living by fishing from plank canoes with reed nets at night, using paraffin pressure lamps to attract the fish. They survive on fish, rice, maize and cassava.

Johann Boytler, a likeable Moravian missionary from Denmark, built the mud-brick missionary station from scratch. He's not the Bible-punching type, but a practical man with a dry sense of humour, who understands the people's needs. He has provided the village with a hammer mill, is building a school, and his next project is to build a mobile 'boat clinic' to service the villages along the lakeshore. Only then will he build the church.

The family really makes us welcome. Johann sits round the table with us and we map out the best route to take on what promises to be a fascinating lake. We decide we'll use Kipili as a base from which to explore the shoreline to the south, which Johann assures us is one of the loveliest parts of the lake.

Thursday 22 July

Johann, an adventurer at heart, is fascinated by our journey and offers to show us round the islands just off Kipili. We decide to leave for our trip south tomorrow. The lake is incredibly beautiful, with its sandy beaches and palm-fronded fishing villages. At one of these villages we visit an old master boat builder. An ancient hand-drill (driven by the quick to-and-fro movements of a string bow), wooden mallets, an assortment of chisels made from old car springs, a variety of adzes and an old handsaw make up his collection of well-used rudimentary tools. There are no drawings – it's all in his head. Soon another of his master-pieces will ply the shores of Lake Tanganyika, carrying fish, charcoal, fruit, vegetables and probably a bit of contraband to and from the distant hills of Zaïre and Zambia.

Johann has another fundi building a boat for his clinic down on the lakeshore. The ribs are suitably shaped trees and branches, and the planks made of a close-grained hardwood that grows in abundance in Tanzania. These are not rough-hewn Arab dhows, but sleek long craft, capable of carrying up to 50 people. The planks are 'corked' with cotton waste soaked in palmnut oil. Unlike the dhows of the East African coast, they don't use sails, as the lake's high winds and massive waves make outboard engines preferable.

Friday 23 July

As always there's that exciting feeling in the pit of our stomachs as we launch into a new and, for us, undiscovered waterway. We take with us two guides. Simon Mwantake, an immigration officer from Kipili, acts as our official interpreter. The other fellow, Sosoliso, speaks no English, but having grown up on the lake has a great deal of

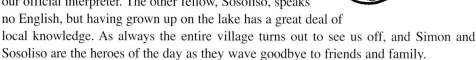

WE LEAVE CALABASH AT KIPILI FOR SAFE-KEEPING!

local knowledge. As always the entire village turns out to see us off, and Simon and Sosoliso are the heroes of the day as they wave goodbye to friends and family.

Once out of the bay we head straight into the *Kusi* – the seasonal south wind. Conditions are such that we have difficulty in getting *Bathtub* on the plane. The last time we had such huge swells was in the Indian Ocean. But these are worse: unlike the long rollercoasters at sea, these are so close together that the boats crash into each oncoming swell.

The coastline is fairly barren apart from a few isolated fishing villages situated on sandy beaches between rocky outcrops. It is magnificent – wilder and more rugged than most of Lake Malawi. A delightful bay with the name of Mongwe N'suwi serves as a camp for the night and a haven from the *Kusi*. Too tired to put up our tents, we sleep under the stars, despite the massive *mamba* (Swahili for 'crocodile') gliding up and down in front of our camp.

Saturday 24 July

The Odyssey members are all bad at rising early, and I move from one sleeping bag to the next pulling at toes to get a sleepy reaction and the odd muttered curse. None of us has been eaten by the cruising *mamba*, but by morning we have all moved our bedding a little further away from the water's edge. Mashozi, who is well again, even took the precaution of packing some luggage around the foot of her sleeping bag. The locals tell us that this particular *mamba* is in the habit of coming ashore at night to eat the *daaga* – tiny kapenta-like fish left out on the beach to dry.

Despite our efforts to beat the *Kusi* by being up early, when we get on the water the swell is already up – it is going to be a bumpy ride south. In *QE2* Ross is at the helm with Mashozi and Jon standing facing forward on either side of the steering console. Simon, our guide, sits on the fuel hatch in the centre, strapped into his life-jacket and hanging on for dear life. He thinks we're crazy. Local boats don't go out in weather like this! Ian is at the back of the boat. I'm standing at the steering wheel of *Bathtub*, feet firmly in the straps, Nkonkoni Rob to one side and Sosoliso on the other. Our kit is tied down under a waterproof tarpaulin. Our noses are smeared with block-out, and sunburnt, cracked lips with Lip Ice. Soon we are all drenched from the constant spray, but at least it's not salt water and is easier on the eyes.

Just past Kala we find an enticing lagoon. Sosoliso guides us through its narrow entrance and on to Kasola village, which we name Sosoliso's Camp. Once again we watch the sun set over the distant hills of Zaïre and then settle down for a cold, dewy night under a starlit sky, well fed on Nkonkoni Rob's chicken stew. Because of the heavy *Kusi,* we will have to find more fuel or start setting back for Kipili.

It's been a long road and the pilgrims are starting to feel the pace. The normal humour level has dropped off a bit. We've been living in boats, vehicles and tents for seven months now. We have a great team, but I guess that what we need is a good blow-out – new faces and a whole lot of socializing. Nairobi, I'm sure, will be the place.

Sunday 25 July

The *Kusi* has dropped today, and the water is smoother but still running a swell. We follow the narrow, crystal clear Lwazi River. It takes us off the lake and into the Kipanga ('palmnut vulture' in Swahili) traditional palmnut-growing villages. Here people make a living from fishing, growing cassava and rice, and more importantly the making of palmnut oil. We spot scores of the vultures, sought after by birdwatchers on other parts of the continent, where they are a rarity. At Mbita, one of the villages, the locals perform a wonderful *ingoma* dance for us, with giant wooden drums, handclapping and traditional songs. Suddenly the chairman of the village arrives. He has not been informed of these goings on, and not even Sosoliso can save the day. Without warning the pilgrims, I put on

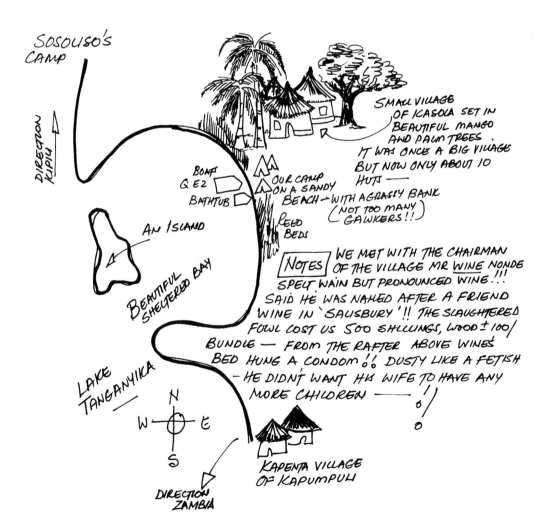

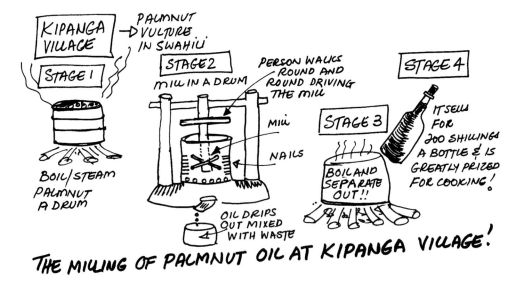

THE MILLING OF PALMNUT OIL AT KIPANGA VILLAGE!

my most wide-eyed, maniacal look (it comes easy these days) and go into my best stu-stut-stuttering act. Unable to deal with me, and still mad as a snake, the chairman marches off to his hut, leaving us to make our way down the Lwazi back to Lake Tanganyika.

We overnight just south of Musi at a beach where Lorenzo Riccardi's Rainbow Expedition camped. Musi's immigration man, Godlove Tsipepepma, hosts us in his simple home, offering us some most welcome Primus beer from Zaïre. The village has a football club, the Victoria Rangers, who are desperately in need of a new ball, but unfortunately we are unable to help them on this count.

Monday 26 July

It is another wonderful morning, and Ross and I go out for a swim/bath, first making sure there are no *mambas*. Instead, a water cobra has us beating a hasty retreat out of the water.

After breakfast we go on to the ruins of the German fort of Bismarck. The fort is extremely well placed on a flat promontory that sticks out like a spatula into the lake. For the German colonial government this was the perfect location from which to guard the southern shore of Lake Tanganyika. Straight lines of mango trees on either side of the entrance reflect the German attention to orderliness. But the fort is a lifeless ruin and, where the German bugle once sounded, now there is just the wind.

Sitting in the boats in the shadow of the fort wall we have an urgent discussion. Owing to the tearing winds we have been battling against, we are desperately short of fuel. At the very best if we turn around now we might get one boat back to our base camp at Kipili, and even there fuel is in short supply. We decide that Mashozi, Simon, and I will take *Bathtub* and the empty fuel containers and run south to the Zambian port of Mpulungu in the south-east corner of Lake Tanganyika. Ross, Ian, Jon, Nkonkoni Rob and Sosoliso (who's sadly out of *pombe*) will continue south to Tokulungo ('place of little stones') where our guides tell us some *wazungu* live. When we come to join them we are to look for a couple of white-washed buildings.

And so we head off into the unknown with little *Bathtub*. The wind has dropped and we ride just on the plane, the two Mariners rattling along. It's market day at the Zambian port and we pull up among the wooden lake taxis on the beach. Among the hive of activity I spot a white face – the local priest. We've been shown such kindness from local missionaries that I don't hesitate to introduce myself and request help. Leaving Simon to look after *Bathtub* we're soon bouncing along in the front of the Catholic Father's beaten-up truck. It's late afternoon by the time he delivers us back to the boat, loaded up with fuel and supplies. Mashozi can't believe that we even found some fresh cheese! Simon is thrilled to see us, worried that we might have fallen foul of Customs and Immigration. We fuel up and wave goodbye to the friendly Father. The water is like glass and we open up the taps in a race against the setting sun, the late afternoon wind in our faces, the water turning to orange and gold, the now familiar feeling of freedom.

It's dark by the time we reach Tokulungo, but the lamps are lit and there's noisy chatter. Our delightful Zimbabwean hosts have set up a fascinating industry here, teaching the local fishermen to dive for tropical fish, the unique cichlids, which they catch and then export overseas. Imagine: a little brightly coloured cichlid in a fishtank in some German home comes from this lonely settlement on the shores of paradise.

Tuesday 27 July - Kalambo Falls

Getting away from the boats for the day is a pleasant change, and we make our way up to the top of the escarpment in search of the Kalambo Falls. As we climb through *miombo* and *chipya* woodland, the treetops provide a shady cover from the hot sun. This is the type of vegetation on which the indigenous population practise the *chitimene* (slash-and-burn). The attitude is that the woodlands stretch forever and that they are an unending resource. Areas close to any road are being destroyed for charcoal, the hardwood trees being cut at an alarming rate. I understand that people need to survive, but what about the future of the forests? There is an urgent need for strict conservation and education.

The hard, steep climb from the lakeshore has everybody puffing, the sweat and last night's heavy tequila intake flowing from our bodies. Thank God for full water bottles.

The Kalambo Falls are one of the unforgettable sights of Africa. The Falls and the gorge are obscured from the Kalambo Basin by the ridge of hills forming its western boundary, and we don't see the falls to their full advantage until we reach the flanks of the gorge. Here the water falls 221 metres over a bar of hard quartzite rock in a single unbroken drop into the gorge below. Sir Charles Dundas, a former acting governor, described this spot as the 'dizziest place I have ever seen in my life'. In the dry season the river at the top of the falls is barely more than 3.5 metres wide, but in flood it must be as much as 18 metres wide, perhaps more. Nkonkoni Rob and Ross take a swim in the river at the edge of the falls. This is the river that marks the boundary between Zambia in the south and Tanzania in the north.

We climb down onto the ledges of the vertical walls on either side. One slip and you're a goner! These ledges, formed by the jointing of the quartzites, provide resting places for the marabou storks. If this was America or Europe there would be tourist kiosks, hotels and a cable car – here fortunately the only sound is that of water roaring over the falls and into distant Lake Tanganyika.

It is not known who the first European was to visit the Kalambo Falls, but they were first measured in 1913, by Messrs Lionel Smith and Chris Draper from Abercorn, in what is now Zambia. Lionel climbed down into the gorge by crossing the lip of the falls and scrambling down the cliff face on the north side. Draper, at the top, tied a piece of calico onto a stone and lowered the stone on a long string held over the gorge with a raffia palm pole. Smith, at water level at the bottom of the gorge, fired a shot from his rifle as the stone and calico touched the water.

It's time to go back and the pilgrims race ahead. When Mashozi and I finally reach the lakeshore, we get lost in the bush and only reach the white-washed camp thanks to a lift in a passing dugout canoe. It has been a hard but fascinating day.

Wednesday 28 July

Conditions are absolutely ideal, the lake smooth with a slight *Kusi* behind us. It seems that the heavy winds are over for a few days, and it is much better now that we are heading north. We decide to make directly for Kipili, a six-hour run if we travel fast. On the

Legend has it that once a mother and her children threw themselves off the edge of the Kalambo Falls, choosing to die rather than be captured by slave traders.

way down, battling against the heavy *Kusi,* we missed some of the beauty of this stretch. Apart from the skippers who had to concentrate through each wave, the passengers also had to hold on for dear life and balance against each oncoming swell. Now we stop off along the way to relive the charm of this lake: fishermen pulling in their nets; thatched villages, each with their own sandy beach, nestling among palm trees. The area from Lupata through to Kipili is incredible with its tiny bays and giant sculpted rock pillars standing high out of the water. We ride into Kipili on the glassy water.

Thursday 29 July

We bid farewell to Sosoliso and Simon, the villagers and our hosts who have come to wave goodbye. We don't have enough fuel to take both boats, so Mashozi, Ross, Jon and I are heading north in *Bathtub*. Nkonkoni Rob and Ian are going to tow *QE2* around to historic Ujiji where we will meet in three days' time, *I presume*. If we don't pitch they will launch *QE2* and come looking for us along the eastern shore of the lake.

Kirambo, our first stop from Kipili, has a welcoming buzz as the Bujumbura–Mpulungu ferry is about to arrive. But the shoreline 50 kilometres north of the town becomes inhospitable – sheets of rock fall steeply into the dark water and the *Kusi* brings waves crashing onto the dangerous shore. There is no place to tie up a boat or make camp. The sun is dropping quickly over the distant hills of Zaïre and we will need to find a camp soon or spend an uncomfortable night rolling around in *Bathtub*, anchored off some point in high winds.

And then we spot it – a tiny sandy cove with a handful of huts clinging to the rocky slopes of a small amphitheatre open-ending onto Lake Tanganyika. Judging from the energetic waves from the fishermen and their gestures for us to come ashore, it looks as if we will be welcome, and, anyway, we don't have an alternative.

As we land, the fishermen and their families all gather around us excitedly. I show their headman, Leonard, a letter of introduction from the chairman of Kipili village (you can never have enough stamps and letters). Never before have we been shown such hospitality. Firewood and charcoal are immediately offered to us as we prepare our camp in the middle of the village. Even the fishing camp dogs are friendly.

The grass huts of Kaswende are built on plinths of slate-type rock, each with their own little thatched kitchen. Higher up on the hillside is a thatched long drop toilet, and everything is spotlessly clean. One of the fellows has on a Union Jack shirt and speaks a few words of English. By now we all have a few words of Swahili, and for the rest we make do with sign language. We have an early night under the stars.

Friday 30 July - Kaswende fishing camp

It is around 4 am and still dark when a paddle is beaten against the side of a large wooden canoe. This is followed closely by the crowing of a rooster, the camp alarm clock. In no time at all the fishermen are up and about, some pulling in the night net, others going out onto the lake, paddling furiously against the *Kusi*, their canoe loaded with an enormous net.

The large catch from the night net is divided into baskets for the occupants of Kaswende. There is no squabbling or shouting as people take their share. We are told that none of these

On Lake Tanganyika as in other parts of Africa, certain organs of the crocodile are valued as magic. Some parts dried and powdered are used to induce fertility in women – Crocodile gall bladders are said to contain a virulent poison. 'Witchdoctors' have disposed of their enemies with this poison for thousands of years!

fish are for sale, just for the pot. I am humbled when we are given the biggest fish, appropriately named English fish, for breakfast. Mashozi gives Maria, the headman's wife, a string of Zulu beads and in return we are given a papaw.

Here the people are reaping a rich harvest from the lake, everyone in the camp is healthy and well fed. Their main source of income is from netting *daaga*, which are sun-dried and sold in bags up and down the lake.

I take Headman Leonard and some of the villagers on a boat cruise to the next village, letting Leonard steer. It makes his day as he circles in the bay, waving for all to see. We're all boys at heart, I guess.

From Kaswende, we make our way to Ikola where Johann Boytler, our missionary friend from Kipili, has left 100 litres of fuel for us. We have a letter to a Mr John Zongwe

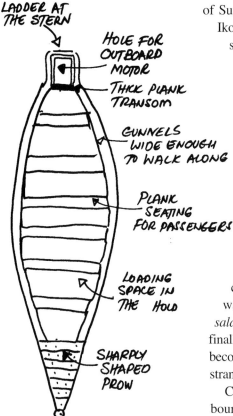

LADDER AT THE STERN

HOLE FOR OUTBOARD MOTOR

THICK PLANK TRANSOM

GUNNELS WIDE ENOUGH TO WALK ALONG

PLANK SEATING FOR PASSENGERS

LOADING SPACE IN THE HOLD

SHARPLY SHAPED PROW

LAKE TANGANYIKA BOATS - HAND - CRAFTED BY FUNDIS

of Sumbwe Ikola, in whose care the fuel has been left. Ikola is a fairly large village by Lake Tanganyika standards. It has a Catholic church, an old grey Land Rover, two or three tiny shops, an immigration office and a boat-building yard under a tree – but no John Zongwe. Eventually, after a frustrating time in the hot sun, walking from place to place, brandishing the letter and practising my 10 words of Swahili, it is suggested that we take off to the next village where there is a Mr Kamba. He is a member of the Moravian Church, and should therefore know Johann Boytler of Kipili's Moravian mission.

Nothing happens quickly in Africa, and Tanzania is no exception. Here our European ways to hurry and demand have to be kept in check or we will seem extremely rude. Another hot walk through another dusty village. Countless *salaams*, *jumbos* and *habaris*, and much handshaking finally bring us to the house of Mr Kamba. I am now becoming concerned, for without the fuel we will be stranded in this somewhat inaccessible place.

Chairs must first be found – one from the neighbours and one from the hut next door – before we are ushered into the coolth of the mud-brick home. Still there are not enough chairs to go round and Mr Kamba of the Moravian Church has to sit on a bag of rice. After more handshaking all is quiet as I ceremoniously draw the letter to John Zongwe from the pocket of my rugby shorts and hand it politely to Mr Kamba.

But it is not that simple. Our host cannot read, and so a suitably educated fellow is called for. All smiles and, feeling quite important, he reads the letter out to his hushed and expectant audience. It is in Swahili and urges Mr Zongwe to give Mr Kingsley (who wears shorts and a big beard, and who has pump-up boats with two engines on each) 100 litres of fuel that has been left in the care of John Zongwe. Everybody smiles and nods wisely. Through the letter reader, who also speaks a little English, they explain that there is a Mr Zongwe, whose first name is John, and that he lives at a fishing camp at Sumbwe. It is there, among a long line of wooden kapenta boats, that we find John Zongwe's home – but no John. Fortunately, his wife agrees to part with the fuel against the letter. We gratefully siphon off the 100 litres into *Bathtub*'s containers and head north to the Mohale Mountains.

We soon leave the sandy beaches of Ikola behind as we travel along a steep, craggy shoreline, the high slopes heavily wooded with trees coloured in a profusion of muted winter shades. We are thinking of turning back when we find a small, uninhabited sheltered cove, a storybook smugglers' den with a tiny pebble beach. We unpack our charcoal cooker, paraffin lamp, food trunk, camp chairs and sleeping bags. The cove provides ideal snorkelling and spearfishing; Ross spears a nice-sized perch and Jon adds two more.

We gut the fish, opening them up to grill over the fire. A few deep incisions are made along their flanks and some salt is rubbed into them, a simple method with tasty results that we have learnt from the local fishermen. We still dream of steak, egg and chips, however, and 'menus of the mind' is a frequent word game around the campfire. The fish are great eating with our ever-ready pasta, all washed down with a Primus beer.

A fishing party of eight young bloods in a plank canoe, heavily laden with nets, visits us at sunset. They are all from Zaïre, but make a living from fishing in Tanzania where things are more settled. Each one of these young fishermen has a body that the members of health clubs work out for hours each day to achieve. Their exercise comes from rowing their canoes against wind, rain and choppy seas with large handcrafted wooden paddles. They have to bring the fish harvest ashore or go hungry. These guys take great delight in giving us a rowing display that would impress even the crews from Cambridge and Oxford. It is dark by the time they return to our camp to present us excitedly with yet another fish. In return we give them a packet of macaroni, explaining that one cooks it like rice. I imagine that the cooking and eating of the macaroni will be accompanied by much mirth as they wonder in amazement at the *wazungu*'s eating habits.

The moon is almost full and bathes our pebble beach in soft light throughout the night.

Saturday 31 July – Mohale Mountains

The *Kusi* has started early, but we decide to push on as we are already packed. So out into the swell we head – and what a swell. Heavily loaded, we have to run at full taps to avoid constantly losing power by stalling up the swells. This is punishing stuff for boats and engines, but the Mariners keep going as we race down and over the wave tops of Lake Tanganyika, heading for the lee of Kibwesa Point and Edith Bay.

Seconds after rounding the point we are in dead calm water, the swells still crazily careering round the point in search of another vessel bound for Ujiji. But there are none; all the dugouts, wooden canoes and the large lake taxis are safely anchored in Edith Bay waiting for the *Kusi* to blow itself out, which at this time of the year normally happens by three or four in the afternoon. The sandy beaches just north of Kibwesa and in Edith Bay are superb. We spend most of the afternoon snorkelling, the cichlid nests visible in the crystal clear water. Woodlands and tall yellow grass come down from high hills to border sandy beach after sandy beach – paradise found.

Finally the wind abates and we point *Bathtub* north. Nothing could have prepared us for the splendour of the next stretch of coast to Luagala Point. Steep mountains tower above the lake, waterfalls tumbling hundreds of feet through thick tropical forests. Secret coves, beaches and thickly wooded river mouths invite us to explore this region, a part of the Mohale Mountains Game Reserve, an area with an abundance of chimpanzees. As the sun sets over Zaïre, the water turns to gold. Not to be outdone, the full moon rises over the mountains, providing sufficient light for us to find a pebble beach guarded by high hills and towering trees.

Sunday 1 August

It seems that our old friend the *Kusi* is determined to accompany us all the way to Ujiji, and the swell quickly picks up, waves coming in from everywhere. We cannot afford to run along the shoreline and need to head straight across the bays to conserve our rapidly diminishing fuel supply. Mashozi is jittery at times like this, feeling that we are taking unnecessary risks. But we arrive four hours later, having crossed two massive bays and passed the mouth of the Malagarasi River.

The waves are pounding onto the beach at Ujiji. The large wooden boats all lie at anchor, their noses pointing into the south wind. Our timing is perfect, for as we arrive offshore *Thirsty*'s lights flash in recognition. We create much excitement with our classic North Coast ski-boat landing through the waves, and arrive with only a cupful of fuel to spare.

We drive directly to the historic site where Stanley met Livingstone under the mango trees. This is an important moment for me. A year ago I had glibly written it into our itinerary, and now we have finally made it. We all pose for photos under the simple memorial that now stands there and reads: *Under the mango tree which then stood here – Henry Mortimer Stanley met David Livingstone – 10th Nov. 1871.*

We decide to camp here for the night and Mashozi and I lay out our bedroll under the mango trees between Livingstone's memorial and a smaller stone that reads: *On February 14th 1858 Burton and Speke reached Ujiji whence they explored Lake Tanganyika.*

The little museum at the site is totally empty, other than for some local artists' impressions of the historic meeting and two life-size papier-mâché models – one of Livingstone, cap raised above his head, the other of Stanley. The staff gives a delightful account of the historic event, having learnt their script parrot fashion, carefully including Stanley's famous phrase: 'Dr Livingstone, I presume?' The area is surrounded by enormous palm trees, its dusty streets and mud huts little changed since the time of the slave trade, except that in Livingstone's time the lake came up to the foot of the steps of the museum below the mango trees. Now it is nearly a kilometre away.

Monday 2 August

The beach at Ujiji is fascinating, littered with wooden boats in various stages of construction. There is a strong Islamic influence in the town and most of the boat builders wear embroidered fezzes. The market and main street are also interesting, providing you don't get knocked over by a *mutato*. These taxis delight in racing down the main street, a dusty, potholed road flanked by restaurants, tailors, fruit vendors, music dens, and *dukas* that sell everything imaginable. The hand-written signs on the shops are extremely bright, enticing all to enter in their sometimes comical English. The girls are beautifully dressed in colourful wraps and the palm trees add to the enchantment of the place.

Mashozi and I buy a great big piece of beef at the market. Brushing off the flies, we carry it back to our Livingstone camp, together with pineapples, bananas, oranges, papaws and an assortment of vegetables. A great feast follows.

The afternoon sees us in Kigoma, a vibrant harbour and railway town of stalls, *dukas*, restaurants and quaint little hotels. A visit to Kigoma is incomplete without seeing the impressive, but now unkempt, railway station, its colonial architecture a reminder of the former days of German East Africa. This is the end of the old German railway line that starts in distant Dar es Salaam, 1,200 kilometres away. The building of the railway line was interrupted by the Maji Maji Rebellion and was only completed by the Germans just before the outbreak of World War I. The route from the lake to the Indian Ocean was also the route along which tens of thousands of slaves were marched to the coast in a trade so despicable that Dr Livingstone called it 'the open sore of the world'.

Patient local travellers sit or sleep on the station platform, their woven baskets of sun-dried fish piled high. Food is cooked on little charcoal stoves, babies suck greedily from their mothers' breasts, and bare-chested boys pull huge loads on rubber-wheeled wooden carts. There is an air of expectation as people glance down to metal tracks that disappear into the distance. The train was due yesterday.

Kigoma's wooden boat harbour lies north of the main harbour where ships from Bujumbura and the ferry call. It's a delightful place and I'm sure a customs official's nightmare, as the large hand-hewn craft ply their trade between Tanzania, Zaïre and Burundi. Boats with names such as *The African Mariner*, *Butterfly* and the *Safari Queen* are loaded with bicycles, drums of fuel, charcoal and, salt, and even the odd backpacker. Sacks and drums are piled everywhere, battered trucks and Land Rovers moving in and out to drop off or pick up loads. Deals are being done in tiny reeded restaurants offering Safari lager, Primus beer and tasty kebabs. The area is shaded by large palm trees. No cranes, no jetties, no offices; just the good old African informal trading sector at its best.

At the docks we chat to the Danish shipbuilders who are repairing the *Liembe*. Like the *Chauncy Maples* of Lake Malawi, the *Liembe* is the lovely old lady of Lake Tanganyika. Built in Germany and shipped in pieces to Dar es Salaam in German East Africa, she arrived at Kigoma by train in 1913, along with 20 German shipbuilders who toiled through the heat and malaria. In 1915 she was launched as the *Götzen*, after explorer Count Götzen. During World War I, the Germans scuttled her outside Kigoma, but when the British took over it was Winston Churchill (then in the admiralty) who had salvage experts refloat her. In 1927 she was ready to sail under her new name, *Liembe*.

In the evening we discuss the next leg over drinks and samoosas on the veranda of the old Lake View Hotel. Tomorrow we will need to weld up *QE2*'s trailer springs, which took a severe beating between Kipili and Ujiji, and then move north to Lake Victoria.

Tuesday 3 August

To have slept at the site where Stanley met Livingstone has been a fitting end to this lake adventure. We pack up and pull into SA Garage, one of those places that fix, repair and weld, and somehow keep a fleet of brightly coloured lorries and buses operating over horrific roads. The trailer springs literally fall apart in our hands! With true bushveld mechanic ingenuity and $200 later, new Land Rover springs are fitted onto *QE2*'s trailer. This means spending the night at the Kigoma Railway Hotel. Mashozi and I take a simple room that has a cold shower and a flush toilet. Bloody luxury!

We watch the sun set over the lake – a hazy ball of orange. Across the bay we can see heavily laden boats leaving for Bujumbura, and in the distance I hear a long and mournful whistle as the Dar es Salaam train finally announces its late departure for the coast.

The Queen of Africa's Great Lakes

Homemade wooden scooter

Lake Victoria, a giant saucer of a lake, is the largest in Africa. This vast inland sea was given its present-day name by Speke after he reached its shores in 1858. What a change from the Rift Valley lakes of Malawi, Rukwa and Tanganyika.

Wednesday 4 August

We pull out of town for Lake Victoria, *QE2* bouncing along proudly on her new springs. The national road to Mwanza is tarred for only a few kilometres, whereafter it becomes a dusty, stone-ridden track. The area is thick with borassa palms, their nuts used for producing palmnut oil. Hundreds of bicycles loaded with 20-litre plastic containers of oil are making their way to the Ujiji and Kigoma markets. We also see dozens of palmnut vultures.

Leaving the lake behind, we climb up onto open grassland. Villages abound, their inhabitants working in the rich red soil of the surrounding fields. All along the road people are walking and riding bicycles. Rough-hewn wooden scooters are also popular. Made from the fork of a tree, they have wooden wheels, handlebars and decorative plastic mud flaps. Not only are these large scooters great toys for the children, but they are also put to good use by adults and children, who use them to carry firewood, water containers and other goods. The drivers push them uphill and then jump on for the downhill bits, which results in a number of comical accidents.

We are only able to average 15 kilometres an hour on this stretch – and even then we shear the bolts on *QE2*'s trailer's hitch and have to make running repairs. At one point I go on ahead of the vehicles and walk for at least six kilometres before they catch up with me. The passing locals are intrigued when I tell them I'm walking to Dar es Salaam. There is red, red dust everywhere – in the air, in your nose, in your hair and between the toes. And the road is crawling with bicycles. It will take some time to reach our destination, but there is no other way between Lake Tanganyika and Lake Victoria. We camp on the side of this dusty road as our clock, the orange-red sun, sets in the west. It has taken us a full day to do 130 kilometres.

Thursday 5 August

The horde of early-morning gawkers become dancing gawkers as they join the Afrika Odyssey members, who all take up the beat of Boney M's 'Hark the Herald Angels Sing', everyone dancing away to a premature Christmas carol playing on the radio. Then, in an effort to get them to move away while we have breakfast, we go through a mock religious ritual, wailing and singing 'Cocky Robin' and gathering around the fire. This, however, only adds to the interest. Gawkers are a fact of life in Africa – especially Tanzania – where all gather to the rallying cry of '*Wazungu! Wazungu!*'

There is evidence that the early German colonial road from Kigoma to Mwanza was laid with stones and packed over with gravel. Saloon cars I'm sure once travelled easily along it, but now the stones have been ripped up and there has been no maintenance for years. The only vehicles we encounter are trucks and 4x4s whose drivers, on seeing us, accelerate and head straight for us, only veering off at the last moment, some with hooters blaring and lights blazing to increase the effect of their Rambo-style driving.

I don't know if many of the people have been told horror stories about *wazungu*, or if few have ever seen white people in this remote area of Tanzania. Whatever the reason, it is difficult to get used to the sight of women grabbing their babies and running off to hide, sometimes tripping over themselves to get away from us. Kids often run off scream-ing at the top of their voices to crouch out of sight in the long elephant grass until we have passed. In some of the bigger towns the kids are braver and have obviously seen martial art movies. The cheekier ones burst out from their group to give a few karate chops and kick-boxing steps at our passing vehicles, often falling over in the dust as they do so.

The odd pedestrian, however, is totally oblivious to us. One fellow, touched by the trop-ical sun no doubt, is walking along a deserted stretch of track in his birthday suit, smiling benignly to himself, in a world of his own. Another chap, dressed only in a tattered T-shirt but no trousers, lurches out at the vehicles and then proceeds to gyrate and wobble his hips. This bushveld stripper would be a great success on ladies' night at a down-town pub!

Maize stacks, full granaries, dust. We cross the
Malagarasie River as it makes its way down
to distant Lake Tanganyika, through a
game-rich wilderness. Dust, dust, a fuel stop
at Kibompo, dust, and finally, after nearly 10 hours of
travelling and having covered only 200 kilometres, we make
camp under some trees just off the Mwanza road.

Friday 6 August

A stretch of tar in unbelievably perfect condition leads up towards the Rwandan
border and Kigali. We immediately have a kiss-the-tar ceremony. Passing lorry drivers
inform us that a peace agreement was signed just a few days ago in Arusha and that all is
quiet in Rwanda. It's tempting to push on to Rwanda's Lake Kivu, but we decide to carry
on to Lake Victoria as planned. Our stretch of tar is short-lived, for as we turn north to
Biharamulo it soon deteriorates into the red, dusty, potholed track we have got used to over
the last three days. But we are making good time and hope to be on the lake by nightfall.

Ross and I are singing on the back of *Thirsty* when we hear the left back wheel on
the boat trailer wobble and screech. The wheel bearing has collapsed. Our spare was
stolen in Zambia, so this could mean we are stuck here for several days while Ian makes
the 600-kilometre, two-day round trip to Mwanza, providing of course he is lucky
enough to find a replacement that's the right size. On the up side, we've broken down
opposite a banana plantation, so at least we'll have some shade while we wait. Nkonkoni
Rob noticed a mission station a few kilometres back, and we decide to go there for help
and advice before Ian rushes off to Mwanza.

We cannot believe our luck when we get there. Some Swedish people at the mission
station have only just received some bearings for a trailer that they are repairing. By
divine providence they are exactly the correct size, and within a few hours Ian has fitted
them, making a new oil seal from a piece of mattress.

More dust and finally we reach Biharamulo. We want to launch our boats into Lake
Victoria at Nyamirembe, and take the narrow track down to the flat land leading towards
the lake. With only about 50 kilometres to our destination, the setting sun dictates that we
camp at the foot of a giant anthill on a wide plain dotted with trees. No sooner have we
got a fire going than two game scouts arrive – one armed with a rifle and both thoroughly
drunk. It appears that we are camping illegally in the Biharamulo Game Reserve, which
runs along the western side of the road to Nyamirembe and includes Rubondo Island, for
which we are heading. But we are allowed to stay for the night once we persuade them
that we are not poachers and are not carrying firearms. After much handshaking and many
*karibu*s they lurch off across the plain and back to their beer pots.

Saturday 7 August

Nyamirembe pier was originally built by the Germans, and from here coffee and other
supplies were transported across the lake. Now there is just a village of about 4,000
people, a small market, a derelict Fisheries station, a school and a couple of hammer mills.

The wooden fishing boats have just come in with the night's catch of Nile perch which are being gutted and scaled near the pier. Their entrails are fed to a massive flock of marabou storks that share the catch with the locals, the giant birds striding and wading like long-legged undertakers among the people. It's an amazing sight.

We camp on the lakeshore, on a patch of grass without dust but with hundreds of gawkers. We use our normal solution, ringing the camp with an old rope, and put up our sign that reads *Afrika Odyssey Members Only*. To enforce this perimeter we appoint two local *askaris* (guards). It's a pity to have to do this, but in some situations it's the only way; otherwise you have gawkers all over the camp. Thanks to old-world discipline, few, if any, ever duck under the rope. But the little kids still opt for ringside seats, sitting next to the rope, commenting on every move we make. This invariably calls for an impromptu English lesson, generally directed by Mashozi. And, of course, everybody wants to be a pen pal – I just wish Nkonkoni Rob would stop giving his address as c/o The Queen, PO Box 1, London.

9 August - Interview with a Lake Victoria fisherman

I spoke to Joseph, a local fisherman this morning. At 5 am, while it was still dark, he rowed his hired wooden canoe out into the narrows between Butwa and Rugea islands on his own. He put out a 200-metre handline, with 10-centimetre-long hooks baited with one *daaga* (small kapenta) every two metres. The hooks are made from old bicycle spokes. Joseph moved slowly forward until he felt a bite. Today he caught just one mighty fish of 25 kilograms, coming back in at 7 am. The early morning is the best time for fishing, for it is when the massive *sangara* (Nile perch) are feeding. His best day was in May when he caught 25 large *sangara*, the biggest of which weighed about 80 kilograms. He took these fish, opened them up and smoked them unsalted over a fire. He sold them to the fish merchants, sharing the money with his family.

'I'm a good fisherman and I will stay a fisherman all my life. I used to go fishing with my father when I was only five years old. The biggest *sangara* caught here must have been 300 kilograms. Such a fish needs 15 people to carry it and the owner sells it off in pieces like a beast at a butcher's shop. Once when I was fishing with my father, a massive storm came up and capsized our canoe. We only just managed to swim for the shore. Three people drowned last year in a storm. We have no life-jackets. Some cannot even swim. Yes, fishing has many risks but, if it's your time, it's your time.'

FISHING METHODS LAKE VICTORIA

WOODEN CANOE

WOODEN FLOATS

3m DEEP

BAIT IS SMALL DAAGA

LINE WITH HUNDREDS OF HOOKS MADE FROM OLD BICYCLE SPOKES!

10 August 1993
Nyamirembe, shores of Lake Victoria

Hi Debbie

We've made it to our next great lake - Africa's biggest in fact. You would not have believed the road to get here though - hell! The last couple of days we've spent exploring the little islands in the south-western corner of Lake Victoria. This is such a beautiful section of the lake. Rubondo Island was incredible, and luckily it is a nature reserve so there is plenty of game. We saw sitatungas, vervet monkeys, bushbuck, crocs and hippos, and were overawed by the fantastic birdlife. We saw no elephants, but plenty of tracks.

It was Jon's birthday while we were there. Mashozi and Nkonkoni Rob decorated the breakfast table with palm leaves and flowers and we all signed a homemade card, celebrating with freshly squeezed lemon juice. Obviously a colonial game warden enjoyed a slice of lemon in his G&T. High trees, massive creepers and tropical rain forest make the island a wonderland, its shores softened by wild date palms and sandy beaches.

The inhabited islands are almost totally deforested and heavily populated. Thank God for some far-sighted planning on Rubondo. We also visited Izumacheli Island, which isn't a reserve, and then Magaf and Kenyatta islands, before heading back to Nyamirembe where we'd left the vehicles with the Fisheries officer.

Our guide and friend for this part of the Expedition has been Mr Ernest Camion Joseph, the divisional secretary for the Nyamirembe division, Biharamulo district, Kagera region. It has definitely paid to have the divisional secretary with us at times!

The people here supplement fishing by growing cotton as a cash crop, and cultivating food crops such as rice, maize, bananas, sweet potatoes and cassava. Some have large herds of zebu cattle, which they graze on the floodplains. We're now going to head across to the south-eastern side of the lake to do some exploring there before we go to Nairobi. We'll definitely give you a ring from there.

Keep well

Kingsley

Wednesday 11 August – A ferry ride

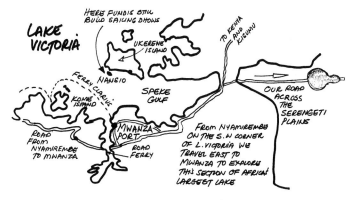

The *MV Clarius* was built in the early sixties by the British in the dockyards of Kisumu, Kenya. It must have been a fine ship in its day, but now its plank decks, woodwork and general condition are suffering from the decay of African socialism, and it has a huge ding just off the stern where it was rammed by another ship. The *Clarius* leaves from Nyamirembe every Wednesday at 8 am for the Lake Victoria port of Mwanza, Tanzania's second biggest town. This is an opportunity for Mashozi and me to experience local boat transport on Africa's largest lake. The rest of the pilgrims are taking the boats and vehicles round to meet us at Mwanza.

There is great excitement as she pulls away with three loud blasts of the ship's horn. We are the only passengers in the small second-class cabin, but the third class is packed. Everybody is colourfully dressed for the trip to Mwanza, travelling with loads of dried, fried and smoked fish, banana *pombe*, live chickens in woven crates, sweet potatoes, pineapples and sacks of Nile perch gizzard. This, dried like parchment, commands a high price from Asian and Korean buyers in Mwanza, who, we are told, export it to be used as surgical thread. We have hardly left the pier when scores of live chickens are unceremoniously slaughtered on deck, the feathers tossed into the lake as we steam past Rubondo Island. These are to be our lunch.

Our first official port of call is Kahunda (at the unofficial ones banana boats roar out to bring passengers to the ship as it stops for a few minutes). The ship's master simply runs the *Clarius* up onto the white beach, nearly ramming some excited traders in a canoe who only just manage to paddle furiously out of the way. This all delights the vibrant crowd that has gathered to trade, embark or simply gawk at the fully laden ferry. Giant woven baskets of fish, covered in grass and bound with sisal string, are dragged on board off plank canoes that bring them to the side of the ferry. These bundles, some weighing up to 250 kilograms, are pulled aboard and thrown onto a platform scale. Piles of paper money change hands in all this chaos, and I shudder to think of the returns, if any, for the Tanzanian Railways who run these ferries. Amid the loading chaos, fruit sellers jump on board, the ship's passengers eagerly grabbing at the bananas and pineapples for sale, and little cigarette sellers dart about, getting the odd slap from the bursar. The master waits the allocated time, then gives a few short blasts on the horn and moves off without any thought for those getting on and off the ship. Some passengers throw their trade goods or baggage overboard and jump into the warm lake waters.

Our other ports of call are Maisome Island, Lushamba and Kome Island. A friendly fellow in a spotless white outfit serves us a lunch of chicken, rice and boiled bananas washed down with mugs of sweet tea. We have the privilege of knives and forks while those on deck eat with their hands. Now the beer begins to flow from the canteen and the second-class cabin soon fills up with people, noise, and brightly dressed girls who flirt outrageously with crew and passengers, intent on plying their age-old trade.

Ross and Nkonkoni Rob are there to meet us at the Mwanza docks, cold beers in hand. They have had a trouble-free drive, arriving only minutes before us. The Mwanza Yacht Club allows us to camp there and use the facilities. We again launch the boats into Lake Victoria, our plan being to explore this part of the lake, using the yacht club as our base.

Thursday 12 & Friday 13 August

I like Mwanza with its decayed old colonial feel and the comings and goings of the ancient sailing dhows and ferries from across the lake. I like the bustling market and the Indian shops that sell bicycles, pots, pans, radios and colourful cloth to traders from the islands and lakeshore who've come here to trade their fish, cassava and bananas. I enjoy eating on the streets, the taste of the goat kebabs and the cold beer at sundown while seated on the veranda of the yacht club, our boats tied up at the jetty. Most of all I enjoy being part of a great adventure that around every corner holds new and exciting surprises. Like Burton and Speke, I too have been smitten by the 'madness' of African exploration and adventure.

We head north-east up the lakeshore to camp on a beach where the vast Serengeti Plains stretch down to touch the water. To the west the sun sets over Africa's largest lake and to the east lie the open plains of one of Africa's most fascinating wildlife sanctuaries.

Saturday 14 August

I am woken by a gawker from the previous evening who heralds the dawn, disturbing the tranquillity of the Serengeti plains with a loud 'Hello my friends'. As I emerge from my tent he bids me a cheerful 'Good morning, grandfather'. Deciding to pull his leg, I angrily reply: 'How dare you call me grandfather. I'm only a young man.' He stammers an apology, but, by now thoroughly sick of early morning gawkers, I tell him that I am going to report him to the District Chairman (as a joke, of course). This has the desired effect, and he and his friends disappear from sight, leaving us to have our breakfast in peace.

After the delights of mealie meal porridge, a mug of camp coffee laced with condensed milk, and bread toasted on the braai grid and topped with peanut butter and jam, we go through the routine of loading vehicles and checking oil and water. This done, we set off through Ndakaba Gate and into the Serengeti.

Our plan is to head north-east through Tanzania's great Serengeti, and then to cross Kenya's Maasai Mara and travel on to Nairobi where we will gather our thoughts, seek a few Western comforts, and meet up with old friends. We also need to research Ethiopia and plan the second half of this adventure.

I can tell that the pilgrims are in need of a break. We've been on the go for months now and everybody is starting to feel the pace. We are all tired, not only from the constant hassle of making and breaking camp, loading and off-loading, packing and unpacking, and the ongoing worry about the safety of our equipment – always a threat in lands of haves and have-nots – but also from the endless bombardment of the senses by

LAKE VICTORIA

RUBONDO ISLAND

FISHING CAMPS

KOME ISLAND

NYAMIREMBE EXPEDITION BASE

FROM LAKE TANGANYIKA

ROAD TO MWANZA

? ALL O.K!

an ever-changing kaleidoscope of scenes, sights and sounds. Sticking wherever possible to the waterways, camping on sandy white beaches and islands, and having the boats and vehicles to do as we please, make it very special, but physically exhausting. Also tiring for me is the never-ending decision-making, which I consult Ross on a lot of the time.

I write in the journal, sitting alone under a shady acacia. The Serengeti Plains stretch out around me – hot, dry and dusty, the yellow grass desperate for rain. The vehicles are in the distance. One trailer wheel bearing has gone and everybody is gathered around repairing it (thank God we have a spare for this one). Around me, topi, wildebeest, zebra and Thompson's gazelles graze. I hope no lions are lurking in the grass. This is unspoilt Africa – it's all that I've ever dreamt of and more.

The wheel bearing replaced, we are soon on our way to the Serengeti's Seronera Camp, through the haze of a sandstorm caused by the excessive dryness and a strong wind that started this morning. The Maasai word for this region is *serengef*, which means 'an extended place', and that it certainly is. Animal populations are on a grand scale: we drive past at least 10,000 wildebeest and thousands of zebra and Thompson's gazelles.

We reach the luxury lodge, which is a touch 'buggered', but far better than expected for a government lodge. After our long, hot, dusty ride across the Serengeti Plains we make straight for the pub, which has a wonderful view and is built into the massive boulders of a koppie. The Tusker lagers slide down the hatch, and soon we're all jolly.

Everybody's got Nairobi fever and our land journey through the Serengeti ecosystem is part of the wind-down after the long but exciting months of travelling rough. Our budget doesn't allow us to stay in the lodge, but in any event we prefer the bush – although Mashozi does make a wistful remark about a bathroom, and I notice a couple of the pilgrims glancing longingly at the menu.

Lions roar throughout the night. Pots bang and a hyaena cackles in the darkness. Here there are no fences, just the endless plains and the rocky outcrops so favoured by cheetah.

Rift valley jewels &

Cheetahs in the Serengeti

The Great African Rift Valley has truly captured our imagination and is one of the main factors that are making this waterway expedition possible, for along the floor of the Great Rift is strung a fascinating, shimmering necklace of lakes. Ahead of us lies the challenge of Kenya's Rift Valley lakes, lakes with names like Navaisha, Elementaita, Nakuru, Bogoria and Baringo, not to mention Lake Rudolf - the Jade Sea – now known as Lake Turkana. It's the world's largest desert lake and one of the most desolate and dangerous places in Africa.

the Jade Sea

Sunday 15 August

We wake up to find that a hungry hyaena has stolen a cooking pot which we find a distance away, somewhat dented but thankfully still serviceable.

What an exciting way to pass between two countries: across the Sand River from Tanzania's Serengeti to Kenya's Maasai Mara. Driving north through the Serengeti, we round one bend and see literally thousands of head of game in a small valley – elephants, buffaloes, eland, Thompson's and Grant's gazelles, hartebeest, zebra and wildebeest. We stop the convoy of two red pontoon boats and expedition vehicles covered in stickers that look so out of place in this paradise. This small area, teeming with animals, is a microcosm of Africa as it must have been seen by the early hunters and explorers.

At the entrance to the Maasai Mara we again fall foul of officialdom. It appears that one is not permitted to enter Kenya this way. But, two $20 bills and a promise to clear customs in Nairobi later, and all is fine. We spend the night on the banks of the Sand River, surrounded by the sounds of zebra, hyaena and lion. *Lala salaam*.

Monday 16 August - The Mara and the Maasai

Our arrival at Keekorok Lodge is quite a shock and we all have difficulty adjusting to the sight of scores of tourist-filled minibuses, their khaki-clad passengers armed with long lenses, Out-of-Africa hats and loud voices. A Maasai warrior in full regalia and sporting an American accent is too much for us, and we quickly move on from this commercialized place, unable to make the adjustment after several months in the bush. I guess we will find Nairobi difficult at first. We are the gawkers now, the pilgrims unable to take their eyes off anything female. We look a sight – burnt black by the sun, very dusty and travel worn.

The Mara is a paradise at this time of the year, and we head east through tens of thousands of wildebeest, all part of the annual migration from the dry plains of Tanzania's Serengeti. This must be one of the most dramatic wildlife scenes in Africa, the massive herds moving among lions, hyaenas, buffaloes, elephants, zebra and giraffe. Grant's and Thompson's gazelles also dot the plains.

Unlike some parts of Africa, the cattle-loving Maasai co-exist with the wildlife, grazing their herds among the wild animals of the Mara. The exception to this are the *Morane*, the age-set warriors, who still need to spear a lion to prove their manhood. I am entranced by the red-ochred Nilotic Maasai, and the long-haired *Moran*e who traditionally only eat meat and drink blood and milk. They are the epitome of the 'noble savage' with their long lion spears, ostrich plumes and decorated war shields. I sit down with a group of elders dressed in red tartan *shukas* as they watch their cattle being herded into the pallisaded cattle kraal, around which stand their small mud and cow-dung huts shaped like loaves of bread.

The Thompson's gazelle is named after the great explorer Joseph Thompson, the youngest man ever to receive a gold medal award from the Royal Geographic Society. This he was given for being the first European to walk through Maasailand in 1883, so opening a path through to Lake Victoria. To survive he passed himself off to the fierce Maasai as a laibon, a Maasai spiritual leader. This he pulled off by chanting Scottish incantations, tearing up bits of white paper and throwing them in the air, dancing jigs, foaming up water with Eno's fruit salts, spitting, blessing, and even removing his false teeth and displaying them! His journal makes fascinating reading.

The Maasai women admire Mashozi's Zulu bangles and she their beadwork and jewellery. I make the decision that if I survive the Expedition I will come back to East Africa to spend time in these wild places with the Maasai. My soul demands it.

It's cattle market day in Narok, the capital of Maasailand. We drive slowly into town, the streets full of traditionally dressed Maasai, cattle and beaten-up old Land Rovers. This 'cowboy town' has great atmosphere.

At the little stone Usoboko Farmers' Hotel we have a meal of *nyama choma* and *ugali* with *sukuma wiki*. The place is full of people socializing, the traditional Maasai walking tall on sandalled feet, carrying their sticks, their *shukas* over their shoulders. These great pastoral people seem somewhat out of place among the plastic chairs and loud music of the Usoboko Hotel, and I can see some delightful old fellows are battling with the modern surroundings, their sticks getting caught up in the plastic chair legs, their earrings and traditional jewellery shining brightly in the electric light. Rich from cattle sales, they are ordering glass after glass of milk and plates of *nyama choma*. Wads of rumpled Kenyan shillings are stuffed into their leather pouches.

Tuesday 17 August

We grind out of Narok, edging our way forward through a huge herd of cattle being driven by three lop-eared Maasai elders with long sticks. They tenderly move the cattle out of the way – no whipping or stone-throwing. The Maasai truly love their cattle, believing that all the cattle on earth are the property of the Maasai.

We cross the floor of the Great African Rift Valley. There are no game fences here, and giraffes, their necks bent forward, move across the vast plains of short whistling thorn. Ahead of us lies the distinct shape of Mount Longonot. Recently a young bush pilot, showing off to his girlfriend, attempted to circle his small plane within its extinct volcanic crater. The 2,776-metre-high Longonot is now their burial site.

We stop at the old Halia Church that serves as a memorial to all those Italian prisoners of war who died building the twisting road that takes us up and out of the Rift Valley. It winds past wooden curio shacks showing off Maasai shields and sheepskins, and past heaped piles of rich earth built up like tables to display the Kikuyu harvest of green mealies, cabbages, potatoes, peas, strawberries, carrots and broccoli, Yes, the British have been here! We put on jackets and roll *Thirsty*'s canvas roof closed. It's a grey, damp day in the highlands of Kenya.

We hit Nairobi at rush hour, get lost repeatedly and have to keep asking for directions. The streets are chaotic after the peace and quiet of wild Africa – colourful *mutatos* hoot loudly, their conductors leaning out of the doors and windows, vendors shout their wares, and street children mill around the boats and vehicles, pointing and laughing at my beard. An ancient lorry loaded with charcoal overtakes a donkey cart on a blind rise. The driver of a crammed bus seems to have a death wish as he roars down the crowded highway into the city centre, coloured lights flashing, chromium hooter trumpeting and the words *My Mother's Love* emblazoned on the back. Welcome to Nairobi, the safari capital of the world!

I've got mixed feelings about being here. I hope we don't break the magic of the Expedition by getting caught up in the city, but I see Nairobi as the halfway stop. Our vehicles, outboards and other equipment all need urgent attention. I'm sure it will work out.

Finally we reach our destination in the suburb of Karen, named after *Out of Africa* author Karen Blixen. Our base camp is in the grounds of a private home that serves as the Kenyan offices of Group Africa. Soon we are all ensconced in a well-known Karen watering hole and restaurant, The Horseman. This sociable place is to become our second home in Nairobi ... straining even further the already tight expedition budget!

Nairobi 18–23 August

On 30 May 1899 the so-called Lunatic Line, the railway being built to connect Mombasa on the coast to Lake Victoria, reached Nairobi – *Nyrobi* or *Nyarobe* in Maasai, meaning 'a place of cold water'. For Mashozi this time in the city is an opportunity to soak in a hot bath and wash off the months of hard travelling. Clothes are washed and ironed, vehicles and outboards serviced. The pilgrims gallivant, and our new recruit arrives from Botswana: Rob Caskie, whom we'd met at Shakawe, has been able to join us. For him it's a dream come true as he's always wanted to visit East Africa. Rob Caskie's job is that of expedition photographer; he's great fun.

Tuesday 24 August

How exciting to be hooking up the boats again, everything washed and clean, oiled and greased, punctures fixed, and the entire team a few kilograms heavier thanks to Nairobi's good living. We make our way back down into the Rift Valley and cross the Lunatic Line to reach *E-na-iposha*, the original Maasai name for Lake Navaisha. The lakeshore was once prize Maasai grazing ground, but now a lot of it is highly productive farmland used for growing flowers for export. A great deal of this Rift Valley lake is, however, still unspoilt, and we camp under the giant yellow acacias that fringe its shore.

As we launch into the sparkling waters of papyrus-fringed Navaisha, the air is crisp and clear. The birdlife is terrific, hippos plentiful, and we fish for tilapia and film the pelicans and waterbuck with Mount Longonot as a backdrop. Early settlers who found this place to be a tranquil paradise include the famous lion man George Adamson and his artist wife Joy, who are remembered for the film *Born Free*. Their home, Elsamere (after the lioness Elsa), is today a museum. We arrive there in time for tea and cake and the feeding of the black-and-white colobus monkeys that inhabit the grounds. So English!

Hi Debbie,

Trust you are well. Greetings from Nairobi, our halfway point, and for us a taste of 'civilization' after the months of exploring. Our journey is proving to be an exhilarating experience, one that has become a way of life.

We've met with some of the old settler families in an area that still has some of the romance of Karen Blixen's 'Out of Africa' days. Beautiful colonial homes, wide verandas, horses, dogs, Land Rovers, and 'The Club'. And everywhere the friendliness of East Africans. There is still something nostalgically romantic about visiting the old race course on Nyong Road, and having drinks at the Mutiaga Club, the Thorn Tree Bar and the New Stanley. We've been doing our own measure of gawking from the veranda of the historic Norfolk. Between resupplying the expedition and servicing vehicles and boats, there's still been time for a dusty drive to the edge of the Nyong Hills to watch the sun set over the dry African Rift Valley.

We were invited to the mayoral chambers, so got into our long trousers and clean expedition T-shirts for the occasion. The Mayor of Nairobi, a lovely, cheerful fellow, signed our expedition scroll and presented us with a City of Nairobi crest.

Pesos are a bit short with all our available cash going into fuel and provisions. Tomorrow we set off to add lakes Navaisha, Elementaita, Nakuru, Bogoria and Baringo to our waterways list. Then it's far north to the world's largest desert lake, still referred to by the 'old school' as Lake Rudolf, now called Lake Turkana or, more lyrically, the Jade Sea. For a taste of this we plan to take our boats across the lake to croc-infested Central Island and then on to the wild eastern shoreline.

Exciting? Yes! Dangerous? Probably!

All our love
Kingsley and the Team

At last light we tie up the boats and are soon comfortable around the campfire. It's good to see that the spirit of adventure is still strong after eight months: everyone is delighted to be back 'on safari' as they would say in East Africa.

Wednesday 25 August

Our first visitor of the morning is an uninvited hippo who walks purposefully towards Rob Caskie, our new recruit, who is lying in his sleeping bag. Rob looks up startled. With hardly a second's hesitation he runs for cover, sack-race style, his sleeping bag still around his feet. It is a comical sight indeed, which results in Rob instantly being named Kiboko – 'hippo' in Swahili – not only because of this funny incident but also because of his portly frame. But it doesn't end there. Next minute I come racing back from the long drop into camp with the angry *kiboko* just a few metres behind me.

Still laughing, we go to visit the old Lake Navaisha Hotel that served as the original flying boat station. Pictures on the walls of the hotel show a bygone era, the flying boat anchored off the hotel, old station wagons lined up to take the guests 'on safari'.

We leave Navaisha and head west along the Mombasa–Kisumu road. Our next jewel among Kenya's Rift Valley lakes is Elementaita, and we stop to ask directions from a roadside *duka*. The directions are good, but we decline lunch, a large, boiling pot of sheep heads. The road is really bad, but eventually we arrive at the tip of this tiny but exquisite lake. Once again our camp is on the lakeshore under giant yellow acacias with a view of the thousands of pelicans and flamingos. I unfold my green East African canvas-and-wood safari chair, and, as I write in the journal, the air is filled with birdcalls.

Thursday 26 August

It's difficult to leave Elementaita, but we're on expedition and it's forever forward! We head further west to Lake Nakuru, which is close to the bustling market town of Nakuru, a watch-your-kit-watch-your-back type of place, and extremely colourful and noisy.

Lake Nakuru is part of a national park, fenced because of its proximity to Nakuru town. It is, however, one of the most beautiful of Africa's small parks, which ornithologists describe as the greatest bird show on earth, with its more than 400 species. The lake, its white crusty edge leading out into open grasslands, reflects the blue sky and the pink and white hues of tens of thousands of lesser flamingos. These birds mass in the warm alkaline water to feed on the abundant algae that is cultivated by their own droppings, while the thousands of pelicans feed on tilapia, a type that can withstand the alkalinity.

There are buffaloes, giraffes, rhinos, waterbuck, a large male lion, a leopard too, and the largest euphorbia forest I have ever seen. We cannot launch the boats into the shallow water and wouldn't want to disturb the peace anyway. *Nakuru* in the Maasai language means 'place of swirling dust', and as we leave a windstorm blows the white soda ash across the shoreline of the lake, creating an amazing mood with the buffaloes and waterbuck appearing like ghosts through the haze. We cross the equator in the dark and finally reach our next expedition camp on the shores of Lake Bogoria. As we arrive at Fig Tree Camp, the massive yellow tree trunks are silhouetted in the moonlight and the light of a raging campfire, and the pilgrims who went ahead of us are already merry with Tusker.

119

Friday 27 August - Lake Bogoria

I wake up, unzip the tent and nudge Mashozi awake. In front of us is one of the most breathtaking sights I have ever seen in Africa. Lake Bogoria is set in a volcanic moonscape, the surface of its waters coloured pink and white by perhaps two million flamingos. Its hot geysers spurt steam and white smoke into the early morning sky. In the background the eastern face of Africa's Great Rift Valley plunges into the lake, a giant sheet of rock, its surface thick with vegetation, crevasses and waterfalls. While we are admiring this wonder, a kudu tiptoes though our camp of yellow and green sycamore figs, and drinks daintily from a freshwater stream that runs through the camp into the warm waters of the lake.

For breakfast we cook potatoes and eggs in the hissing, steaming cauldron of one of the geysers. Nkonkoni Rob perches on a rock, dangling a string bag of eggs from a paddle into the cheerfully boiling geyser. As the breeze changes he is engulfed in steam – an instant sauna. Just what he needs after all the Tusker he drank last night.

We spend the day filming and exploring this incredible lake with Duncan and Lourens. A bath in the stream at our campsite is a welcome relief from the midday heat of this Rift Valley cauldron. Because there are no fish in this alkaline water, the fish eagles here feed on flamingos. Later in the day I witness a most uncommon sight – tawny eagles sharing a treetop perch with a fish eagle. I see the fish eagle dive into a flock of flamingos, talons outstretched. As the flamingos catch sight of his shadow they lift into the sky in a great pink and white commotion of flapping wings and dragging feet. Nevertheless the fish eagle is successful. How could he go wrong?

Once again I sense that everyone is feeling the pace, myself included. Nairobi wasn't a break, and we will have to call a few rest days. Ian Adamson is struggling with a severe leg ulcer caused by a jab from the spine of a Nile perch on Lake Victoria. These leg ulcers, from which everybody has suffered (right now Ross has even got them on his hands), are extremely dangerous if not kept clean – a difficult task when we spend our time in and out of the water. So it's not an uncommon sight to see the Afrika Odyssey members limping along, their feet bandaged with surgical plaster, as course after course of antibiotics is consumed with pasta.

When we are all hot and tired as we are today I wonder if we shouldn't have broken the expedition into two halves – north and south of the equator. But enough of that. We are committed now and other travellers we meet are amazed at what we have achieved. I'm proud of the fact that we are still a highly spirited and cohesive team, motivated by the constant store of surprises that Africa springs on us.

Saturday 28 August - Lake Baringo

It's a perfect day and we launch our boats into Lake Baringo, a freshwater lake just north of Bogoria. Strangely, the crocodiles here, while plentiful, do not seem to eat humans. I am amazed to see the locals bathing and washing clothes right alongside these reptiles. However, there is one reported case of a man rushing into the water to try to pull his goat from a crocodile's clutches and being seized upon by the crocodile in all the confusion. Despite this, the local Njemps people sit astride balsawood canoes and row with their hands while fishing the glassy brown lake. They agree that here humans are safe from crocodile attack, and the hippos, they say, do not trouble them either.

On an island in the middle of Baringo is Island Camp, consisting of a tented camp and a pub serving excellent grub. The owners obviously think we've got a hungry look. They're fascinated by our journey and invite us to enjoy a delicious lunch. This is the sort of hospitality that we've found throughout our journey, from African villages, mission stations, remote outposts, and now here. We question our hosts about Lake Turkana, our next destination, and are warned to be careful of the extreme heat, high winds and huge crocs.

Sunday 29 August - The journey to Lake Turkana

The steep climb out of the Rift Valley soon has us changing from shorts and T-shirts to balaclavas and blankets. We stop to buy roasted green mealies, cooked on the coals of roadside fires. Finally our convoy drives into the farming and frontier town of Kitali, situated high up on the Rift Valley Escarpment.

As we pull into the filling station we are mobbed. A tall Rasta man kisses Mashozi on both cheeks. Others seize my hand and proceed to shake it up and down like a water pump handle, and the pilgrims are helped down from the vehicles. Confusion and excitement reign. Only then does the Rasta man point to the headline accompanying a double-page spread in today's edition of *The Nation* newspaper (the result of an interview that we gave as we left Nairobi). We are all there, in black and white – our expedition team, boats and vehicles instantly recognizable. With true journalistic zeal the bold headline

Having fun in the boiling hot geysers of Lake Bogoria with Duncan McNeillie (centre) and Lourens van Rensburg (right). Laid-back Ross relaxes on the extreme right.

Rob Caskie, a farmer, adventurer and wildlife man from the Natal Midlands, joins us in Nairobi. As a keen amateur photographer, Rob has landed the task of documenting the expedition. He is a great storyteller and communicator and doesn't drink (I hope he doesn't give his share to Nkonkoni Rob). After Rob's brush with a hippo, he's nicknamed Kiboko - 'hippo' in Swahili. KIBOKO CASKIE turns out to be great fun and gives the expedition a new energy.

reads: 'SOUTH AFRICAN FAMILY ON DANGEROUS MISSION TO SPREAD ANTI-APARTHEID MESSAGE.'

Mashozi seems to be getting special attention, not only from the Rastafarian, but from others in the crowd who eagerly, but with great respect, shake her hand. I realise this is because in the article I jokingly gave her age as 102!

The expedition convoy leaves the cheering crowd of well-wishers to wind down the steep escarpment to the very floor of the Great African Rift Valley and into the harsh, semi-desert moonscape of Turkanaland.

We stop to buy charcoal along the road, and two Turkana ladies come out from their rough beehive homes to conduct the sale. Our first encounter with these amazing people, with their beaded necklaces and earrings, and their Mohican hairstyles, gives us the impression that they are proud and haughty.

Further along the road, where we stop at a little *duka* to buy some Cokes, the people and their lifestyle are like something out of *National Geographic* magazine. Through an interpreter we arrange to call here on our way back. We give them a date and leave them money to pay for a few goats and to brew up some traditional beer. For this get-together we request that there be traditional singing and dancing. The Turkana love the idea, and after much nodding and handshaking we're off into the heat.

Our last town on the way to Lake Turkana is Lodwar, where Jomo Kenyatta was interned during the Mau Mau uprising. It is dusty, fly-ridden, hot as hell and unbelievably fascinating. Here a large number of the Turkana still dress traditionally. The men wear ornate headpieces of coloured clay and ostrich plumes, tall spears and old 303 rifles. The straight, long-limbed bodies of the girls are covered in ochre and adorned with ornate leather aprons, bangles, beads and necklaces.

From Lodwar we head east across dry camel country to the shores of Lake Turkana. Once again there's the exciting feeling of a new and unexplored waterway. This time it's the mystical Jade Sea, another name for the lake because of the green colour it goes when its alkaline water is stirred up by the wind. As expected, the heat and desolation of the landscape are indescribable. The wind howls, causing white-topped green waves to crash on the volcanic shore. A few Turkana are huddled in the shade of sighing palm trees, watching over their camels and goats. The sand and wind blow in our faces, and our voices are carried away in the wind. It will be impossible to launch the boats until the wind dies down.

At the village of Kalokol we meet David Ebenyo, a Turkana who speaks English. He agrees to be our guide and, as always, involvement with a local brings the adventure to life. The wind finally drops sufficiently to allow us to launch. We leave *Thirsty* and *Vulandlela* at Fisheries and, with life-jackets on and everything tied down, we're soon bouncing across the lake. Ross and I are now so familiar with our boats that we understand every angle, pitch and roll – feet firmly in the straps, one hand on the wheel, the other on the dual throttle controls. The pilgrims are hunched against the green spray, the familiar smell of suntan cream and outboard oil filling the air. Once again we experience the incredible feeling of freedom and joy of the unknown. We cross the entire lake, passing Central Island to the right and south of us. Our objective is to get to the wild eastern shoreline and explore the island on the way back.

Our campsite on the eastern shore of Lake Turkana has an eerie strangeness. We off-load our tents and equipment on a black sandy spit. We hope it will shelter the boats from the crazy winds that we know will come up during the course of the evening and tomorrow morning. Now, in the late afternoon, the water is completely calm, broken only by *Bathtub* trolling up and down in search of one more fish for the dinner table. Because of the heat of the Jade Sea, we quickly run out of fresh drinking water, and have to drink lake water, which tastes like a good dose of unflavoured fruit salts. I'm sure it will keep us regular.

The area is completely wild, and we are the only people in this rugged, wide-open country. There is not a beast, not a fisherman, not a dugout canoe in sight, just the odd croc lying in the shallows. The shore is covered in Nile perch bones, massive vertebrae indicating the size of some of the monsters that must have been dragged up from the depths of this brak green water. David explains that, until fairly recently, this spot was inhabited by fishermen, but that they were killed by bandits from Somalia. This sort of idle chatter does wonders for one's sense of well-being. I keep glancing up into the rocky moonscape for a glint of sunlight on a rifle barrel, hoping not to have to play host to a bunch of these trigger-happy *banditos* on camels.

This lake is not everybody's cup of tea. For most people it is just too hot and inhospitable. Its insane winds whip the waves into a frenzy and I am grateful for our sturdily built boats and motors that have been prepared for heavy sea work. David was terrified by some of the waves we went through this morning and we make sure that he never gets into the boat without a life-jacket on. We do not wish to add to the high number of fatalities caused by Turkana's wild winds and waves. Sir Vivians Fuchs' expedition to Lake Turkana in 1934 lost two men whose bodies were never recovered – no doubt this was the work of the fierce crocs.

Lake Turkana has the world's highest Nile crocodile population and as such is not the ideal place to go swimming. But, with the intense heat (it averages 54°C in certain parts), we just cannot resist the odd dip off the boats, in deep water, way out into the lake.

Countless rivers and waterfalls occasionally flow down into the lake, and as they tumble down from their rocky heights they bring with them massive boulders. But clearly this is something to be seen only a few times in a man's life, for now they are bone-dry. It has been known not to rain here for up to five years at a stretch.

Tonight the wind comes up early and soon the coals of our campfire are blowing around restlessly, providing a good heat on which to cook the day's catch.

It's difficult to imagine that this lakeshore was once verdant, with large trees growing in the black soil, and that situated further north up the lakeshore is Dr Leakey's Koobi Fora, where early man took some of his first faltering steps.

Monday 30 August - Central Island

From a distance Central Island does not look like much: just a desolate shape on the horizon. This unique triple-cratered island covers no more than five square kilometres. However, by the time we tie up our boat at the base of the island, we have more of a sense of the eeriness of the place. One of the craters is completely dry, a gaping hole that once belched smoke, lava and volcanic ash into the air, and the other two are now full of water.

The island is a nesting ground for big colonies of waterbirds, but, like some African Galapagos, it really belongs to the reptiles. Nile crocodiles breed here in their highest concentration in Africa. During breeding season (usually in April/May) the newly hatched crocodiles break out of their nests to race, squeaking loudly, down to the crater lake, where they will pass their first season.

We tread with extreme caution as we make our way up to the summit of the island along a difficult path that runs along a razor-backed ridge. A fall to the right would mean a drop of several hundred metres into the larger of the three crater lakes. The deep water would no doubt break your fall, but you wouldn't have the time to swim for the shore before you were snaffled by a croc relishing a welcome change from its normal diet of Nile perch. A fall to the left would be into the dry crater, and would end with the thud of certain death.

But we remain on the path and reach the summit safely, panting and blowing, more as a result of the intense dry heat than the climb itself. In the excruciating heat of the afternoon we find some shade in a shallow cave, and drink cup after cup of sweet tea. A large quantity of sugar is necessary to disguise the brak-tasting water of the Jade Sea. If you did not keep on drinking in this climate, you would very soon dehydrate and get into serious trouble.

Sunset on Central Island is taken straight out of picture-book Africa, and, as happens in so many hot, dusty, semi-desert areas, nature puts on a special sunset show that somehow makes the heat of the day a little more bearable. Nothing, however, prepares us for the demonic wind that comes up during the night. Enamel plates take off like flying saucers, camp chairs are blown about like autumn leaves, and a hurricane lamp is knocked over and smashed.

I lie with my sleeping bag over my head, fully awake and wondering what the Lake Turkana Special Effects Department will think up next. The screaming of the wind is relentless, and every now and then the red *High Velocity* button is pressed, along with the yellow button marked *Severe Sandstorm*, while the blue *Icy Spray* button is used with gay abandon to whip up spray off the surface of the lake and splash it willy-nilly onto the apparently sleeping, huddled forms on the island.

Tuesday 31 August

By sunrise everybody looks miserable, but we are still able to laugh. After exploring some of the less rocky western shoreline around Ferguson's Gulf and Kalokol the wind drives us off the lake. We trailer the boats and head south, away from this harsh desolate place.

Our interaction with the tough, warlike nomads of the area is not yet over. When we reach the village where we arranged two days ago to have a feast ready on our return, well over a hundred Turkana are waiting. The Turkana social worker who organized the gathering is nervous. The people, he says, have been here since early morning, the goats have been eaten, the beer is almost finished, and the young bloods are spoiling for some action. The men are armed with spears, bows and arrows, and wrist and finger knives. Small groups of dancers are leaping into the air amid a shrieking, singing, clapping crowd. I know I am seeing something that I might never see again. I'm 6 feet 4 inches (190 cm) and am dwarfed by some of the warriors who insist that we dance with them. A sort of honey beer is passed around and men dressed in leopard skins and ostrich plumes do a warlike dance, while the ochre-smeared unmarried girls eye the men.

Our guide nervously mentions that things are getting a bit unsafe and suggests we should move out immediately. I invite a delightful old man to come for a drink with me. He has a good strong face, is robed in a red tartan wrap and wears camel hide sandals and a wild plume of ostrich feathers. I am determined to have an interview with this proud nomad, knowing that opportunities like this are rare. We help him into *Thirsty* and take off down the road to a small eating house where I order some fried goat meat, *chapatis* and cold drinks. We go out into the back courtyard of the enterprise where a mat has been spread out for us, the mud wall of the hut serving as a backrest.

I sit down with our Turkana friend and an interpreter. The old man tells me that the most exciting thing in his life thus far was the death of his father. He was happy for his father who had lived such a full life, having taken part in many raids against the Pokot and hunted many wild animals. The old man also tells us about the significance of the charm tied to his right leg just below the knee. He explains that what looks like an ornamental piece of bone is actually the scale of an ant-eater, indicating that he too is a great hunter who has lived close to nature. The ant-eater or pangolin is rarely seen, and for this reason it has more value as a kill than an elephant or a leopard. Armed only with a traditional spear and shield, he killed his first lion when he was quite young.

The man has just married his fifth wife, a young girl valued at 200 camels and many goats. He has also, like his father, taken part in raids, and has killed two men in raids retaliating against the theft of cattle. Asked whether he has taken part in any recently, he responds that they are now illegal, but, after a brief pause and with a knowing look, he admits, yes, he has taken part in a recent raid.

I am interested to know what this successful and proud man could still wish for, and am more than a little surprised by his answer. He tells us that he once heard of a strange animal that lives across the sea in a desert land similar to his own. A tall animal that hops on its hind legs and has a pocket in front in its belly. 'I would wish to see such an animal before I die.' Through the interpreter I am able to confirm that the old man's wish is indeed to see a kangaroo. In Africa things are never as you expect them.

12 September
Malindi

Hi Debbie
Just to let you know we're still going strong and have reached the Kenyan
coast after a long haul down from Turkanaland. Mombasa opened its hot,
steamy, sleazy arms to us. The mayor added a letter to our scroll and a
welcome party was held in our honour. I even got to meet local resident
Lorenzo Riccardi, the great adventurer who crossed Africa from east to
west, travelling from the mouth of the Rufiji to the mouth of the Congo
River in inflatable boats. He presented us with an autographed copy of
his book. What a jolly character! As we launched our boats into the bay,
he slapped me on the back and shouted 'Cape to Cairo! Good luck! You
must all be bloody crazy!'
    After exploring the bays and creeks around Mombasa we travelled
north to Malindi in the wake of Vasco da Gama's fleet, which arrived
here in 1498. In Nairobi I heard about a Malindi local called Renaldo
Retief, a direct descendant of the Boer leader, Piet Retief. Yes, the
same one who was murdered, disembowelled and then impaled by the Zulu
king Dingane. But the settler blood flowed strong in the Retief family
and Renaldo's father trekked to Kenya.
    Renaldo immediately made us feel at home, offered us his bush camp
on the Tana River, and has helped us make arrangements with the
officials to launch QE2 and Bathtub from Malindi to travel north to the
old Tana mouth estuary and then on to Lamu.
    The empty boat trailers will be towed to Lamu with a police convoy as
the road has become unsafe. Recently a group of German adventurers was
hijacked and robbed of their vehicle and belongings, including the
clothes they were wearing. The four of them had to walk to the nearest
village stark naked. Can you imagine the reception?
    We are all well, and looking forward to tackling this magnificent coast.
Hope you are managing to hold the fort back home.
Siyabonga
Kingsley

In the wake of an Arab dhow

Launching an East African dhow

Creaking, lantern-rigged dhows have traded on Africa's East Coast for over 2,000 years, leaving Africa on the monsoon wind laden with slaves, ivory, coconuts, cowrie shells and mangrove poles and returning from India and Arabia with dates, carpets, glassware and cloth. Here the blood and cultures of Africa and Arabia have mingled to become a fascinating Swahili mixture that is unique to this coast. Even the name Swahili is derived from the Arabic word Sawahil which means 'the coast'.

Monday 13 September

Despite a strong south-easterly monsoon at Malindi, we steer out onto the open beach to launch through the surf. It is a rough ride and *Bathtub* gets tripped up by a freak wave, putting both props screaming into the air and giving Nkonkoni Rob and me quite a fright. One-and-a-half hours past Ras Ngomeni we begin to look out for the break in the high white sand dunes that we have been told will indicate the Tana River mouth.

It's always rather nerve-wracking to come through a rough shore break into an unknown river mouth or estuary. Renaldo warned us to take it wide and come in from the north to avoid a long sand spit running out from the southern bank. We have to run parallel to the coast, between the waves – not the best way in the rough – before we race, relieved, into the sanctuary of the estuary. There is a delightful camp here, where we take a welcome afternoon nap, before cruising upriver into the mangroves for a mud bath. We're watched by a lonely hippo who bellows its approval at each of the mud bathers' wild antics.

Tuesday 14 September - Maulidi in Lamu

We are up before sunrise preparing the boats in an attempt to beat the wind. The Tana River camp is totally protected behind the dunes, so we don't realize that the wind has been blowing hard throughout the night and that the sea is mountainous. But, undaunted, we shoot out through the mouth and over the sandbar, nosing into a terrible sea. The wave sets are only a few metres apart with very little room to run or turn, so we have to take it on the nose. We have a safe but bumpy exit into the Indian Ocean bound for Lamu, about 75 kilometres to the north. Out on the ocean, waves seem to be coming from every direction – not the sort of thing we were expecting off the tropical Kenyan coast. Here we are again, travelling with Murphy.

Between the Tana and Lamu the numerous reefs and rocky outcrops keep us constantly on guard. The waves are breaking over the bows and everybody is wild-eyed and soaking. I am skippering *Bathtub* with Ian and Nkonkoni Rob as crew. We have a lot of the luggage tied down under a blue tarpaulin, and they cling to the top of this like two trussed fowls going to market on a rainy day. Ross is skippering *QE2*, and with him he has Kiboko, Mashozi and Jon.

We have a very wet but trouble-free ride through to Lamu, but both Kiboko and Mashozi are quite adamant that they are not going back to Malindi by boat. Mashozi took considerable strain, hurting her back on one of the thousands of severe bumps and bounces. It has been bad enough running with the south-eastern monsoon; the thought of going against it is pretty daunting.

Lamu is something of a legend, one of the last viable remnants of the Swahili civilization, the dominant cultural force all along the coast until the arrival of the British.

We head straight for the old town and tie up among a number of Lamu dhows, their crews amazed that we have travelled up the coast in these small boats. We immediately put the word out for Abdullah Bob, a delightful old dhow captain whom we befriended some years ago. Within a few minutes the said Abdullah comes running down the waterfront shouting 'Mr King, Mr King'. From that moment on everything is taken out of our hands, and, in his charismatic way, Abdullah Bob rushes us through the port authority formalities and then customs. We meet the customs officials under a tree as the customs building has been burnt down in riots against the failure of the administration to provide adequate security. (Somali bandits recently attacked a bus en route from Malindi to Lamu and many were killed.)

We are soon settled into the Pool House, a revamped old coral house built in the traditional Swahili style with delightful little rooms, their hand-carved four-poster beds draped with mosquito nets.

As good fortune would have it, we are in time for Maulidi, a week-long celebration of the Prophet Mohammed's birth. With processions and dances, it involves the whole town and attracts pilgrims from all over East Africa and the Indian Ocean. There are to be dhow races, a swimming race and even a donkey race down the main street.

We fall asleep to the amplified sounds of a eulogy to the Prophet that is delivered from the rooftop of a nearby mosque and which lasts several hours. The mosque is only a few metres from our white-washed room above the 14th-century town, where donkeys still have the right of way on the narrow streets, and the only motorized vehicle is the District Commissioner's Land Rover.

WE TAKE TIME TO EXPLORE THE LAMU ARCHIPELAGO, FINE BEACHES, ANCIENT RUINS, THE DHOW RACE, MAULIDI CEREMONY, MANGROVE SWAMPS AND THE ISOLATION & BEAUTY OF KIWAIYU NEAR THE SOMALI BORDER

Wednesday 15 September

The festive mood of Maulidi is tangible, as dhows arrive from Pate, Dhow Island, Faza, Siyu, Kisingitini and Kiwaiyu. Some of the dhows that have come a long way are motorized, and all are festooned with flags and bunting for the celebrations. We've left our boats at the harbour in the care of one Mohammed who makes sure that they don't come to any harm.

Travelling by local dhow, Abdullah Bob accompanies us to Pate Town on the Island of Pate, about an hour's run from Lamu. We approach the island on the high tide with the *Kusi* (the south-eastern trade wind) blowing strong and gusty as it has every day since our arrival at the coast. This wind blows from May to November, and brings rains and rough water. At this time of the year the inshore channels of the Lamu Archipelago are used for most boat movements. The north-eastern trade (the *Kaskazi*) blows from December to April, bringing summer's calm clear water and heralding the start of the fishing season. Strong winds are occasional, but storms are rare.

The town of Pate does not have the fine houses or the tourist infrastructure of Lamu, but it was, in its time, a great place, its people ruling over a large area. There are only about a thousand souls living here now. The limestone coral buildings are mostly unpainted, but all the atmosphere of an ancient Swahili town survives in the narrow streets.

Pate's farmers make a living mainly by growing a cash crop of tobacco in the ancient plot ruins of Pate's walled town. The crumbled walls of what were once schools, mosques and homes now separate one farmer's tobacco from his neighbour's. We leave Pate a little more aware of how life must have been in the archipelago three or four centuries ago. Apart from the Arab dhows with cotton sails, and the natural beauty of mangrove channels, beaches, palm trees and baobabs, the area is rich in history – a living museum to Swahili culture.

Thursday 16 September - The Lamu Dhow Race

In no time at all we get into the rhythm of life on Lamu. The muezzins' cries soon blend one into the other, as do the tides. Everything seems timeless as we walk the narrow streets, or move slowly from one restaurant to another. It is no wonder that Lamu ranked with Katmandu as a 1960s hippie paradise.

Despite this reputation, Lamu has a strict Islamic code and only at Prestley's Inn can one legitimately obtain a cold beer or spirits, and it often runs out of stock. Guy's Restaurant has beer mugs of delicious iced tea on the menu, but, when this is ordered with a wink and knowing nod, a tankard of real beer arrives with the mango and orange juices that Lamu's restaurants serve so well. Please, sip your 'iced tea' with decorum and try not to roar cheers as you quaff litre after litre of Ceylon's best.

We start the day with a trip down the channel that separates Lamu Island from Manda Island and leads to the village of Matandoni. It lies in a state of calm, the occupants of its palm-thatched huts moving slowly along its sandy streets, the tides washing in and out through the mangroves.

The village is best known for the building of traditional dhows, and a 150-ton behemoth of mangrove ribs and mahogany planks is under construction at present. A thing of great beauty, it is being constructed completely along traditional lines by master dhow builder Fundi Shishi, who learnt this ancient craft from his grandfather. This is one of the largest dhows to be built here and, as Shishi explains, the largest he has ever tackled. He has been working on it for just over a year and it will take two years to complete.

Using a traditional bow drill and adze, and with no drawings or plans to guide him, Shishi performs wonders, cutting the long mahogany planks to shape with deft strokes of an adze. The sturdy branches for the giant mangrove ribs have already been selected individually for their natural bend or twist to fit the shape of the dhow. The finished product will be launched in a colourful ceremony as many hundreds of people roll her on coconut tree trunks down to the water's edge to await the high tide when the waters of the Indian Ocean will embrace her. What a monument to a man's life this will be, and I'm sure that if one listens carefully on the day, one will hear the voice of Shishi's grandfather whispering praise in his ear.

As we move in and out of harbours such as Lamu, we are constantly surrounded by dhows. The most common form of these fascinating craft seen in Lamu harbour is the *jahazi* with its wine-glass shaped transom, broad but gracefully curved belly, and bow rising perpendicular from the water. Lamu's *jahazis* are quite different from Zanzibar's ones, which have a railed or sloping bow and a much squarer transom. *Jahazis* can always be recognized by the strips of woven coconut-fibre matting affixed to their sides to reduce splash. They also invariably have a wooden eye, or *macho*, attached to each side of the bow beneath a curved, decorated tailboard which is connected to the timber of the hull just below the bowsprit. *Machos*, which are round, hand-carved discs, embellished with a star and crescent in the traditional Swahili colours of red, white and black, are attached to all dhows on the Swahili coast to keep the boats safe and allow them to avoid obstacles at sea. These fairly large dhows can carry more than 30 occupants and are used to ferry mangrove poles, building sand and limestone coral blocks throughout the archipelago.

We cut our visit to Matandoni short and rush back to Lamu to catch the Maulidi celebration dhow race. The excitement has been growing for some days now, with the competing dhows all parading up and down the waterfront, their crews beating drums, blowing whistles and conch shells, and generally attracting attention to their prowess as sailors. The race is taken extremely seriously – there is a floating trophy and great prestige for the winning dhow and crew.

Abdullah Bob presents us with machos *('boat eyes') to attach to our boats to ward off danger.*

There are three divisions to the race. The first is the *mtori* class, the small sailing canoes. The second and most popular class is the *mashua*, the medium-sized, very fast, shallow craft. The third class, with only a few entrants, is the *jahazi*.

The waterfront is massed with thousands of spectators, some, like ourselves, with their own boats with which to follow the race. Many others have clambered aboard local dhows that are not racing, all in an effort to get closer to the action.

The two hot favourites in this class are *Peace Villa*, her brand-new sail shining white in the sunlight, and *Mandela*, a smart-looking dhow, her crew all dressed in green and white. Abdullah Bob is with us on the rubberduck. He, in his day, won seven times, but he no longer races and will not race again for fear of losing the great reputation that still causes many people to greet him as 'captain' as he roams the streets of Lamu. Abdullah Bob becomes very animated as *Peace* takes the lead, shouting encouragement at the top of his voice. Every sailing trick in the book is used, as the crews juggle current, tide and wind in the age-old craft of dhow sailing. By this time the spectators are at a fever pitch with Abdullah Bob so worked up that he almost falls overboard as the crowd chants 'Peace, Peace *Kiboko ya*!' to much handclapping from other waterborne spectators. All this

THE MASHUA CLASS IS MADE ALL THE MORE EXCITING BY THE CREWS' AMAZING ABILITY TO HANG OUT ON THE TRAPEZE, OR SHOULD I SAY 'WALK THE PLANK' FOR IN THIS CASE THE TRAPEZE IS SIMPLY A STOUT PLANK THAT CAN AT ANY TIME BE STUCK UNDER THE GUNNELS ON ONE SIDE AND OVER ON THE OTHER — AT RIGHT ANGLES TO THE DHOW

MASHUA TYPE OF SAILING DHOW.

WALKING THE PLANK

PEACE VILLA

THIS ALLOWS THE MASHUAS TO SAIL AT GREAT SPEED AND A GOOD DEAL OF EXCITEMENT — BALLAST IS BY WAY OF SANDBAGS WHICH CAN BE EMPTIED TO LIGHTEN THE LOAD! WATER IS CONSTANTLY SPLASHED ONTO THE SAIL TO KEEP IT STIFF.!. SUCH IS THE MAULIDI DHOW RACE IN LAMU !!

excitement obviously has a good effect on the crew of *Peace*, who, with a clever tack, manage to gain 50 metres on *Mandela*. Rounding the buoy outside Peponi's Hotel, they run with the wind for the home stretch through to Lamu, jettisoning their sandbag ballast as they do so. They cross the finish line just ahead of *Mandela*.

As is the custom, hundreds of spectators swim out to the winning dhow and clamber aboard, all chanting and dancing. So many in fact that she begins to sink, dripping bodies everywhere. She floats to the surface as the hordes are borne off by the water. The crew then leads a chant down the waterfront, and, as part of the general celebrations, everyone, myself included, is seized upon bodily by the crowd and thrown off the waterfront into the sea. Fully clothed and sopping wet, we walk up to the market square, where, in front of the old fort, the winners are presented with trophies. Even the donkeys seem excited and the speeches are interrupted by raucous braying.

By late afternoon people have gathered in their thousands outside the Riyadha Mosque, founded by Habib Saleh, a Sharif (descendant of the Prophet) from the Hadhramaut (Yemen) who settled in Lamu in the mid-19th century. He and his group introduced a new freedom to the daily prayers, including the use of musical instruments, singing and spontaneous readings from the Koran.

Today an area outside the mosque is cordoned off with mangrove poles into sections, a different dance routine being performed in each. In one, a tall elegant fellow dressed in white Arab costume, complete with headdress, dances with sabres, tossing them into the air and clanking them together to the beat of drums, cymbals and tambourines. Several hundred others beat stout mangrove sticks against the horizontal poles of the pallisading, creating a throbbing beat that can be heard throughout the town.

In another section, hundreds of Muslim gentlemen clad in white *kanzas* and embroidered skullcaps go through a simple but dignified dance routine, with each performer holding an identical walking stick in front of him. Many have paper notes of local currency protruding from under their caps, and all gaze steadfastly in front of them, concentrating on the leader and the somnolent chant.

The male spectators stand on one side of the square, and on the other stand the women, many of whom are clad in the traditional black *buibui*. Some are partially veiled revealing only their beautiful eyes, which they are adept at using to their full advantage. Outsiders tend to get the wrong impression about Swahili culture, for, while women are indeed restricted in their public lives, in private they have considerable freedom. The notion of romantic love runs deep in Swahili culture, with love affairs, divorces and re-marriages being the norm.

The entire celebration has a light-hearted charm to it. Even the little children have been smartly dressed for the occasion, and the green and white mosque is lit up with twinkling lights. As the sun sets over the coconut palms behind Lamu, the women and children quickly disperse and the men go into the mosque to pray. The festivities are over for another day.

Friday 17 September - Takwa ruins

Abdullah Bob arrives early to escort us to the Takwa ruins. He explains that we should be careful today as the festivities have taken on a political note, with Islamic Party of Kenya (IPK) demonstrators determined to advance their cause. The IPK has been refused recognition by the Kenyan government as a political party and this has recently caused serious riots in Mombasa. Today, riot police have moved into Lamu from the mainland and feelings are running a bit high. We decide to let Lamu town simmer while we travel by dhow to the nearby Takwa ruins.

To get to the ruins we travel up a narrow mangrove channel. The only village along here is, surprisingly enough, a Luo village. The Luo people here, who hail from distant Lake Victoria, make a living mining limestone coral alongside the village. For the Luo, considered the best stonemasons in Kenya, it's a far cry from home as they toil in the coastal heat, cutting stone from the dry coral beds of Manda Island. These are then loaded onto dhows and transported to Lamu and Shela to be turned into fine traditional Swahili homes.

Takwa must have been a flourishing town in the 16th and 17th centuries. But today the well-kept ruins lie in peace under giant acacia and baobab trees, disturbed only by occasional tourists who arrive from Lamu by dhow, or by the elephants which, I'm told, often swim across from the mainland to Manda Island. Locals tell us that it was here that a young elephant was attacked and killed by sharks while making the crossing.

By the time we get back to Lamu the procession from Habib Saleh's tomb to the Riyadha Mosque is in full swing. The narrow streets of the town are swamped with people, the procession jamming the route between the waterfront and the mosque. Drums are competing with tambourines, and women dressed in black *buibuis* clutch their children, and stare out from doorways and windows onto the highly excited procession of men and boys. The IPK demonstrators have cordoned themselves off with rope, political banners raised above their heads as they loudly chant their slogans. The riot police have sensibly stayed out of sight and the procession remains noisy but peaceful.

The crowd disperses as it becomes dark, and our expedition goes off to Ali Hippies. Ali is a delightful little guy, portly with a cherubic round face, who wanders the streets of Lamu inviting people to his humble home. Taking off our sandals at the door we are ushered into a small, extremely hot room, the bright paraffin pressure lantern adding to the heat. Once we are all seated on mats on the floor, Ali brings us a bowl of water, explaining that we are to wash our right hands, as there will be no utensils with which to eat. The Swahili custom is to eat with the right hand, leaving the left to clean the more unsavoury parts of the anatomy. The food is excellent, the menu consisting of prawns and *chapatis*, an Ali's yummy (a savoury doughnut filled with crab meat and onions), and curried red snapper on a bed of rice, all washed down with cups of tamarind juice.

After dinner Ali invites his entire family into the already crowded room for Swahili music, with Ali on keyboard and the kids on drums, which consist of a number of plastic containers. A tiny fellow who can't be more than six or seven years old beats the smallest drum. He has great rhythm, but keeps on falling asleep.

Late into the night, while the children are memorizing the Koran for a contest, the sound of their young voices drifts in and out of our Swahili bedroom, borne on the ebb and flow of the *Kusi* wind.

18 -22 September - Up into the Lamu Archipelago

We planned to leave with Abdullah Bob this afternoon for a safari north towards Somalia to explore the Swahili towns and islands up to Kiwaiyu Island, a long thin stretch of land to the north of this fascinating archipelago. But Abdullah Bob, being a senior man in the nearby village of Shela, has to stay behind to assist with the recovery of the body of a young man who drowned there this morning. In his place we are given Ali Roy, a nice enough youngster who chews constantly on *miraa* taken with chewing gum. So, with Ali Roy chewing at the bow of *Bathtub* and Mashozi on my left, we set sail for our expedition north. The rest follow in *QE2*, loaded with rations, tents, bedrolls, spearfishing equipment, a few changes of clothing, some flour for making *chapatis* and paraffin for the lantern.

The Lamu Archipelago is a cluster of hot, low-lying islands tucked into the coast near the Somali border. Very few tourists venture here. Lamu and its neighbours have a special appeal – life here moves at the pace of a donkey or a dhow. On the way we pass many a dhow full of passengers returning from Maulidi – the boats still flying colourful bunting and the passengers all still in a festive mood, waving cheerfully at the able fleet bound for Kiwaiyu and the north.

From Lamu we travel through the narrow Mkanda Channel, lined with mangroves. This is sometimes a difficult dhow passage as there is very little room to tack. We leave Manda Island behind, pass little Manda Toto with its lovely white beach, and head on across a bit of open sea to Mtangawanda on the southern tip of Pate Island. It is possible to keep to the leeward side of the island, which is a great help as the south-eastern monsoon is still making life difficult. This is the joy of the Lamu Archipelago – one can travel in the lee of the islands, provided of course that the tide is right. At low tide this becomes a world of exposed, tide-washed sandbanks stretching for kilometre on kilometre. The scores of mangrove islands then stand proudly above the water's edge, revealing their shining black network of roots.

About halfway up Pate Island, we pass the ancient town of Siyu set well back from the main shoreline at the end of an inlet that cuts into the mangrove swamps. The town was a flourishing centre of Islamic scholarship from the 17th to the 19th century, and apparently something of a sanctuary for Muslim intellectuals and craftsmen. It is still famous for its woodcarving and leatherwork. Siyu-carved doors are among the most beautiful of all Swahili doors, with distinctive guilloche patterns and inlays of ground shell.

We pass Faza and Kisingitini, the two northernmost towns on Pate Island, and travel across open water to the little island of Ndau, before making our way to the fascinating island of Kiwaiyu that will be our base for the next few days. Because of the layout of the Lamu Archipelago, we are able to look west, back towards the mainland and across a vast expanse of water. It is a unique experience to watch the sun go down over the Indian Ocean.

The area around Kiwaiyu is idyllic and we spend the next couple of days exploring. We stroll the beaches at low tide and one day, when the tide is high, Ross and I take *Bathtub* all the way to the Somali border.

I get the opportunity to sail back to Lamu with the crew of a local dhow. It is timeless travel – the creak of the mainsail, the whispered commands between the skipper and crew with their intimate knowledge of their surroundings, the large hand-woven straw hats, a gnarled weathered hand on the hand-carved tiller bar, the massive hand-stitched sail pregnant with wind. We break the journey to braai fresh fish over fibrous coconut husk coals. Soon the minarets and swaying coconut palms of Lamu come into view and we tie up outside the burnt-down customs post in Lamu's old stone town.

Do we really have to push onwards to Cairo and the Med? We've been lulled into the slow rhythm of Lamu's deliciously lazy atmosphere, and it's a tempting thought to call it a day and spend the remaining fuel money on living it up in Lamu. But we must be strong. Time and money are running out and we need to keep moving.

Thursday 23 September

We bid farewell to Mohammed and Abdullah Bob, who presents us with some *machos* or boat eyes. Both our boats now have 'eyes' attached to either side of their consoles, a Swahili touch that I hope will bring us good fortune.

Finally we get away, having missed the morning bus convoy in which the three daily buses ride with armed *askaris* in case of Somali bandits. I just hope that, with the colourful boats and 4x4s with people perched on top of them, we might look like some sort of convoy. Down a long straight stretch of road we see a group of people gathered. My heart leaps into my mouth, but not for long. We soon realize that the laugh is on us – the 'people' are actually baboons! I have to confess that before leaving Lamu I suggested to Ian that we keep both vehicle hubs in, just in case we needed to engage 4x4 hastily for a quick getaway through the bush and ilala palms. Mashozi also bandaged her finger over her wedding ring – no Somali bandit is having that.

We take the road down to Kipini at the mouth of the Tana River, our plan to spend a few days further exploring Kenya's greatest river. It is a spectacular and wild place, unspoilt and full of crocs and hippos. The narrow sandy track down to Kipini winds through coconut palms and indigenous trees. We soon arrive at the sleepy, palm-fronded village where we meet with the chief of the area, Muhammed Jima. He accompanies us down to the river mouth and soon we have a delightful camp on the river bank: white sand and palm trees with a view up the river and south down a huge sweeping bay of never-ending white beaches. Life sure is hell on the great Afrika Odyssey Expedition!

Friday 24 September - Up the Tana River

The Tana is magnificent as it breaks out from a tunnel of extremely high mangrove trees into the bay. This morning the sun has lit up the high wooded banks and we all clamber aboard *Bathtub* and, with a local guide to show us the way, commence our expedition up the Tana River.

After only a few kilometres we have already seen our first hippos and crocodiles, the crocs heading off the muddy mangrove banks and into the brown water at the sound of the outboards. The mangrove belt soon breaks into rainforest type vegetation – you could be forgiven for thinking you are on the Zaïre or Amazon rivers. The area is virtually unspoilt and, while the locals do cut mangrove poles, this practice seems limited, probably on account of the hippos and crocs, of which they are terrified.

We stop at the Pokomo village of Ozi, noticeable from the river only by a few dugouts on the bank and some palm-thatched, mud-walled huts nestling among the giant trees. The hospitable inhabitants welcome us warmly. A number of them are perched in one of the trees, picking seed pods, the insides of which are filled with a soft cotton-like fibre which they use as mattress packing.

A colourful character, thickset and bowlegged, beckons us to follow him. He is the village blacksmith and invites us to sit down and observe him practising his craft. His bellows are made from two old cement bags; strong and pliable they do a great job of supplying air through two pipes into a little open forge fire burning with locally made charcoal. He is busy with pieces of old aluminium pots, melting them over a very hot fire. It takes quite a while to melt, and while we wait some people skim up a tree to gather green coconuts. We are each presented with one, a neat hole cut in the top from which to drink. Once the blacksmith has melted the aluminium, he pours it into a small mould pressed into mud. A piece of iron, the back-end of a spear blade, sticks into this mould. Once the silver liquid has set, he removes the spear blade, now complete with a shiny new handle. We all clap in appreciation as he raises the newly forged weapon for us to see. Proud of his achievement and delighted at our response, he breaks into a wide smile. For me these are the special moments of the expedition.

The vegetation remains dense and tropical for some distance beyond the village. The muddy banks indicate that it is tidal a good way from the sea. Higher up the river we begin to see breaks in the vegetation, beyond which stretch wide-open, grassy floodplains dotted with outcrops of doum palms. Huge herds of long-horned cattle graze in the distance.

Then, to our amazement, we come across several villages of very tall, egg-shaped huts standing like giant thatched Easter eggs, silhouetted against a massive plain. These structures are inhabited by the Orma, tall, thin nomadic people bearing a resemblance to the Maasai. Our guide, whose English is limited, seems ill at ease and explains that few of these people speak Swahili. As luck would have it, one of the Orma speaks a little English, but even he seems shy and reticent. He explains that the Orma are pastoralists who came originally from Ethiopia.

CLOCKWISE FROM TOP LEFT:
Local transport. There are smiling kids wherever we go. The beach at Ujiji – Thirsty pulling Bathtub out of the lake. Nkonkoni Rob trying out a wooden scooter.

Lake Victoria,
the Queen of the Great Lakes

CLOCKWISE FROM LEFT: *Our journey took us across the untamed Serengeti and Maasai Mara where, amid the predators (among them leopards and lions), we followed the annual buffalo migration.*

COLLECTION OF ALL SORTS OF THINGS FROM THE PARK IS NOT ALLOWED
BY ORDER WARDEN

ABOVE: In a traditional Maasai enkang (village). *BELOW*: Maasai men on the Olololo Escarpment. *RIGHT*: A young Phokot woman with her baby.

The menu in the inset reads:

"KARIBU"
BREAKFAST
RIFT VALLEY FRUITS
* "FLAMINGO" PANCAKE
* BACON "ALA BUSHPIG"
* FRY EGGY
* BEANS "ALA FARTO"
TEA, COFFEE & TUSKER.
ASANTE SANA.

TOP CENTRE: Beautiful Samburu maidens. ABOVE: Maasai enkadji – a mud and cow dung-roofed hut. INSET LEFT: Expedition menu. BELOW: Ross poses with two Phokot women near Lake Baringo.

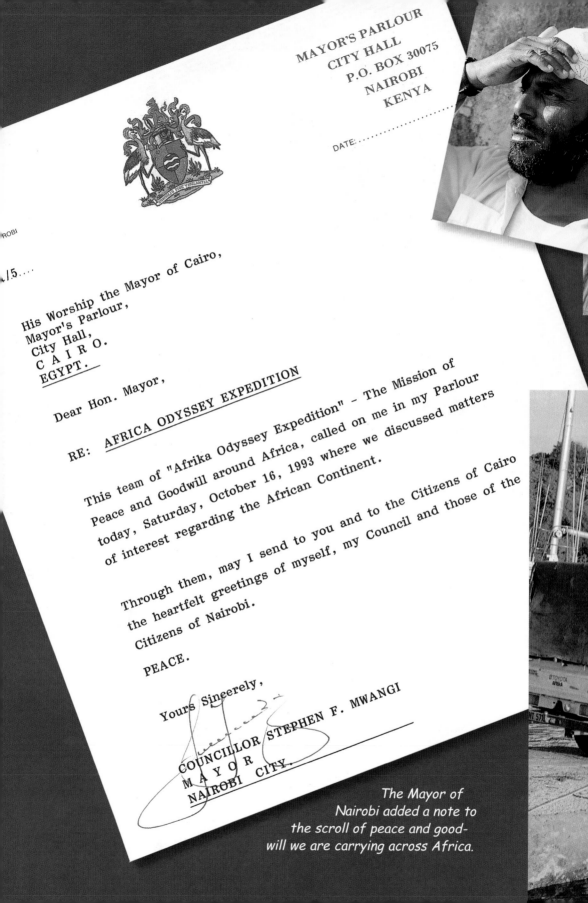

MAYOR'S PARLOUR
CITY HALL
P.O. BOX 30075
NAIROBI
KENYA

DATE:................

ROBI

.../5....

His Worship the Mayor of Cairo,
Mayor's Parlour,
City Hall,
C A I R O.
EGYPT.

Dear Hon. Mayor,

RE: AFRICA ODYSSEY EXPEDITION

This team of "Afrika Odyssey Expedition" – The Mission of
Peace and Goodwill around Africa, called on me in my Parlour
today, Saturday, October 16, 1993 where we discussed matters
of interest regarding the African Continent.

Through them, may I send to you and to the Citizens of Cairo
the heartfelt greetings of myself, my Council and those of the
Citizens of Nairobi.

PEACE.

Yours Sincerely,

COUNCILLOR STEPHEN F. MWANGI
M A Y O R
NAIROBI CITY.

*The Mayor of
Nairobi added a note to
the scroll of peace and goodwill we are carrying across Africa.*

TOP LEFT: *Abdullah Bob and Mohammed –
our Lamu men.* ABOVE: *Local Swahili markets
are our main source of food supplies.*
THIS PICTURE: *We launch into the bay in
Mombasa – the start of our coastal journey.*

East Africa's Swahili coast –
the ancient Land of Zinj

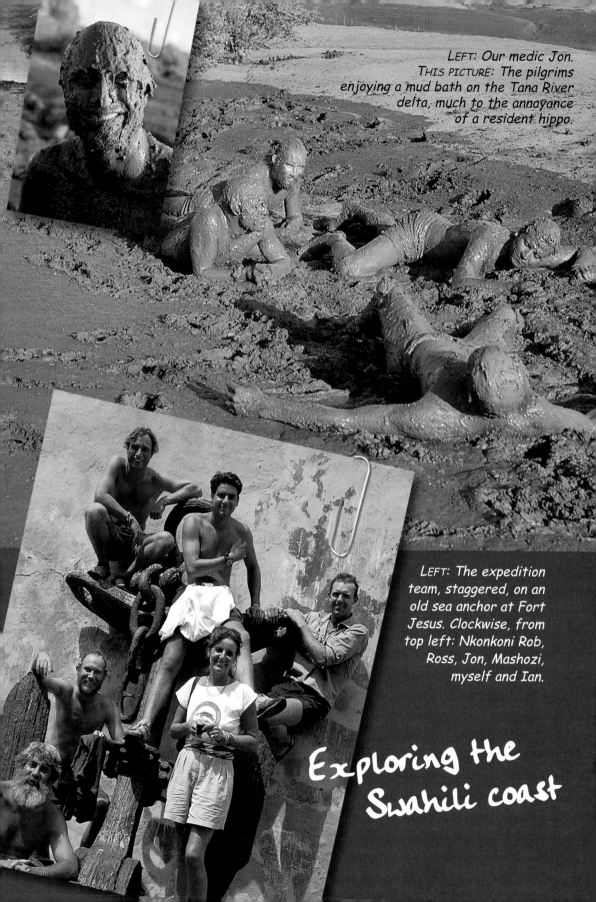

LEFT: Our medic Jon.
THIS PICTURE: The pilgrims enjoying a mud bath on the Tana River delta, much to the annoyance of a resident hippo.

LEFT: The expedition team, staggered, on an old sea anchor at Fort Jesus. Clockwise, from top left: Nkonkoni Rob, Ross, Jon, Mashozi, myself and Ian.

Exploring the Swahili coast

Being from Zululand I am intrigued by the similarity of their homes to beehive-shaped Zulu huts. Saplings are bound together in much the same way that the Zulu do, but these huts are a lot taller and more sharply pointed, with very narrow slits for doorways. With my stout frame, I find it impossible to squeeze through, but at least my endeavours bring chuckles of mirth from the women and children who have gathered shyly to observe the visitors. The men, dressed in blue shawls and long flowing *kui-kuis*, remain aloof, but once they become used to our presence they invite us to take some tea with them. While we are seated on cowhides beneath the shade of a solitary tree, one of the little boys, unable to contain his curiosity any longer, reaches forward timidly to feel the hairs on Ross's legs. Obviously few, if any, white people come this way and hairy legs are a novelty. The Orma people no doubt find us as strange as we feel them to be a people from a forgotten age.

We make our way back down to the mouth of the Tana. The sun is behind us and the snaking brown river is as smooth as glass. It's almost dark by the time we get to the beach, but there is time to take a swim in the sea and wash off the sweat and mangrove mud that clings to our legs. Soon the smoke rises from the campfire. What a comfortable feeling of fulfilment, sitting barefoot in the sand, the body burnt brown from the sun, the mind full from a day's exploring. A cool sea breeze keeps the mozzies away.

Saturday 25 September

We get up early to reach the town of Wito in time to catch the bus convoy to Malindi. In Wito there is quite a buzz with the last of the three buses having just come in from Lamu. The police officer in charge of the roadblock at Wito remembers Jon from the trip up to Lamu with the vehicles. Saturday, he says, is a good day for bandits – this with an outburst of laughter. Yes, we should ride with the convoy for safety. No, officially petrol is not available in Wito, but with a note from him to a local shopkeeper we can get some petrol – through the back door. This is Africa, and soon we are siphoning petrol from old cooking oil containers, using a tin jug as a unit of measure.

The last 90 kilometres through to Malindi is bloody hell towing boats. The lorries and buses have left a ruin of potholes and ruts on this, an apology for a road. But we eventually arrive, hot and tired, at Silversands campsite in Malindi, and at sunset we go down to the coral beach to visit the Vasco da Gama monument.

26-27 September

It rained during the night, but now it is hot and humid. The south-east monsoon provides the only relief as it blows cool air from across the Indian Ocean, rustling the palm trees and inviting us to spend a day of rest here at Malindi. But we've decided to move on to Tiwi Beach south of Mombasa to prepare for Pemba, one of Tanzania's Spice Islands.

We take a slow drive past Lorenzo Riccardi's place, but he is away in Nairobi. The Perrilli inflatables from the Rainbow Expedition are piled up in the yard, half inflated and lying under tarpaulins, like old explorers waiting for the next expedition to happen.

Having made our way south via Wasini and Shimoni, we camp just north of the Kenya–Tanzania border at the Pemba Fishing Club, established in 1962 by avid fisherman, Pat Hemphill, who still lives in the area. The club is well known for holding over 70% of all Kenyan and 40% of all African marlin records. It is also famous for its Ten to One (10:1) Club, the weight of the fish caught being 10 or more times the breaking strain of the line used.

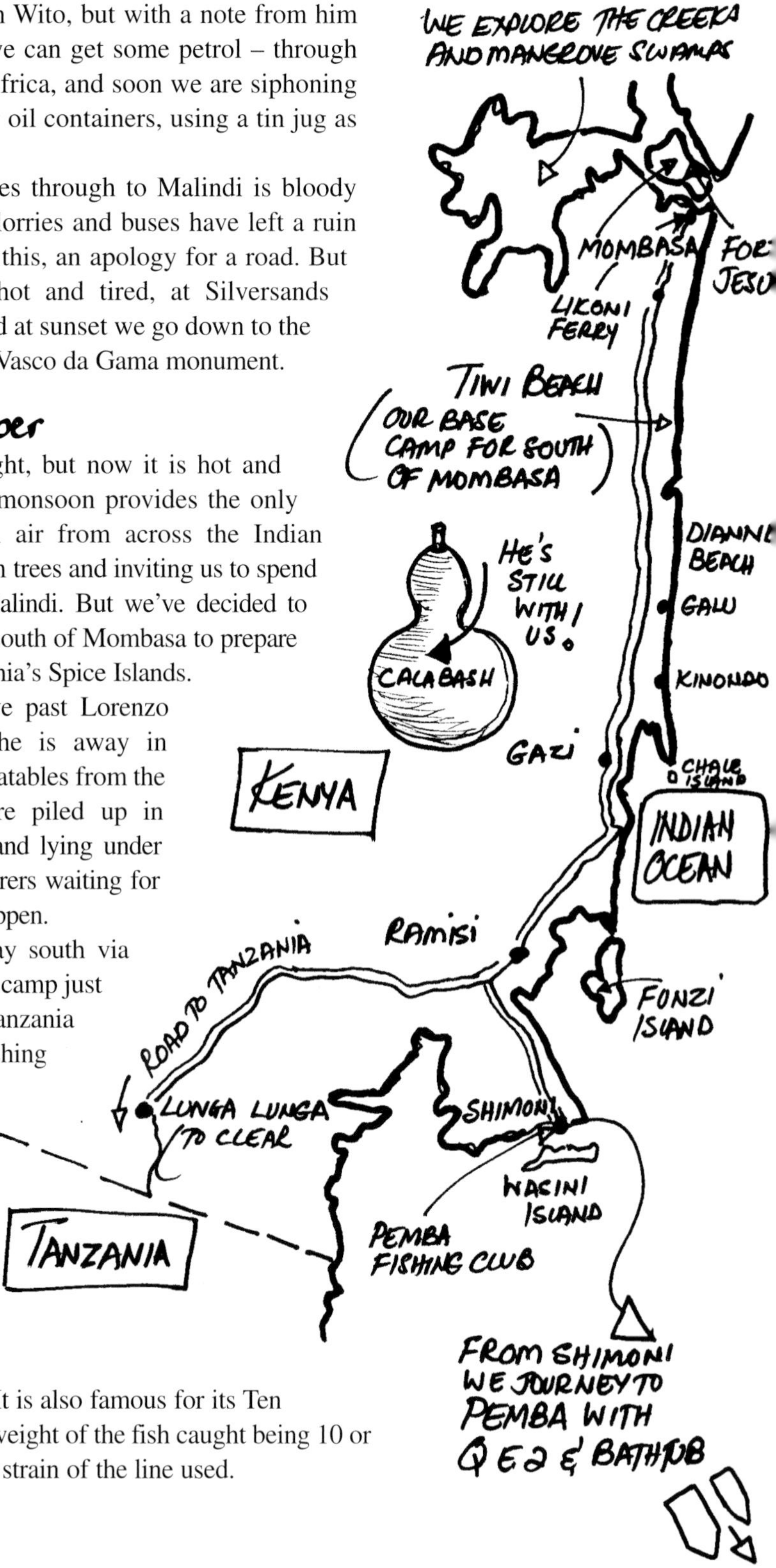

WE EXPLORE THE CREEKS AND MANGROVE SWAMPS

MOMBASA FOR: JESU

LIKONI FERRY

TIWI BEACH
(OUR BASE CAMP FOR SOUTH OF MOMBASA)

DIANNE BEACH

GALU

HE'S STILL WITH US.

KINONDO

CALABASH

GAZI

KENYA

CHALE ISLAND

INDIAN OCEAN

RAMISI

TANZANIA

FONZI ISLAND

ROAD TO TANZANIA

LUNGA LUNGA TO CLEAR

SHIMONI

WASINI ISLAND

TANZANIA

PEMBA FISHING CLUB

FROM SHIMONI WE JOURNEY TO PEMBA WITH QE2 & BATHTUB

In the 1930s Alex Hemphill and his son Pat would come down to Dianne Beach to fish. In those days there were no hotels, just virgin bush down to the water's edge. They went out to sea in an old plywood boat with a Seagull engine that started first time cold, but was a real bitch to start when warm. Pat eventually moved down to Shimoni as he had heard many a tale of great fish to be caught there. He was the first person to offer charter fishing at Shimoni, with a sleek fishing boat, the *White Otter*, 44 feet long and powered by two Foden diesels. She was launched in 1961 and to date she has travelled the equivalent of about five times around the world and landed over 1,000 marlin.

Tuesday 28 September

Pat advises us to clear Customs at Shimoni prior to leaving for Pemba Island. The customs office has to be especially opened for us and detailed forms need to be filled in. We have to pay port tax, navigational tax and crew tax. There is no immigration office at Shimoni so, unfortunately, I have to take off to Lunga Lunga on the Tanzanian border to get us all stamped out of Kenya. I don't think too many tourists try to leave Kenya this way. All this takes time, but, as always, if one remains patient, smiling and friendly, it invariably comes together. Remembering of course that Africa owns the time!

Wednesday 29 September - Bound for Pemba

We launch both boats into the Wasini Channel bound for Pemba Island, which we are told is roughly two and a half hours to the south-east. The wind blew throughout the night and even now it is rustling the tops of the coconut palms. But the sea is calm, and for most of the way we travel in the lee of the island.

The *White Otter* set off some time before us, and we catch up with her just off Pemba. Keeping her in sight, we too put out a few feathers into the deep blue of the Pemba Channel, rated as one of the finest fishing grounds in the world.

So here we are, Jon and I in *Bathtub*, the rest in *QE2*, the two boats loaded with tents, pots and pans, drinking water and the general mish-mash of expeditionary kit. In the distance is *White Otter*, the sun glistening off her white hull and blue trim as she rides proudly through the small swell. Won't it be a laugh, I think, if we are the ones to land a marlin. I hope that the *White Otter* passengers, paying $500 per day for the boat, would see the humour of the situation. The thought no sooner leaves my mind than I hook into what seems a sizeable fish. Within 45 minutes I've landed a big yellow-finned tuna. Foul hooked, but, when a fish is in the boat, it's in the boat. This one will make an ideal gift for the customs officer in Wete – something to smooth the way and ensure a happy stay on Pemba and its surrounding islands.

We ride into Wete, a small, sleepy port on the north-eastern tip of the island. I have an idea of what to expect from Customs and Immigration as we tie up next to a dhow, and, with the gift of the tuna as a sweetener, a few small 'remembrances', our scroll, our never-failing letters and lots of smiles, we are through. They can't believe that we haven't come off a yacht and that the two Gemini rubberducks aren't the 'tenders'. Few outsiders arrive at Wete, so it is quite an occasion.

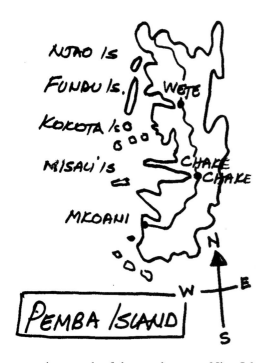

NJAO IS
FUNDU IS.
KOKOTA IS
MISALI IS
MKOANI
N
W—E
S
PEMBA ISLAND

Wete is suffering from general decay, but the people are most friendly as we shop in the market for rice, tea, sugar, bread, beans and fruit. Old barges lie rotting in the mangrove mud, graceful steel ladies who once carried spices and fish to the mainland. A decorated cast-iron electric light pole, forged in Bombay, stands on the corner of the pier next to the immigration office – an old corrugated iron shed bearing colonial lettering indicates this was once the property of the Pemba Wharfage Company. This must have been a bustling little port in colonial times, and I feel, as I have so many times before in Tanzania and Mozambique, that ours is a journey of re-discovery.

Our camp for the night is on Fundu Island just south of the gap between Njau Island and Fundu. The small, deserted beach faces towards the setting sun, its fine white sand surrounded by a horseshoe-shaped bank of coral. It is spring high and there is just sufficient beach above the high-water mark to pitch our intimate camp. During the night the boats drag anchor and Ross and I race around in the surf in our birthday suits. We really do need sand anchors!

Thursday 30 September

I walk a distance down the shoreline of Fundu Island, which, at low tide, is a beautiful maze of white beaches and exposed coral banks carved into a thousand different shapes by wind and tide. It is spring low and the exposed reef is alive with people from the nearby village, all hunting in every nook and cranny for anything they can sell or eat: shells, sea cucumbers and octopus – even stone fish, their deadly spines cut off before they go into the pot. How much longer can nature continue to provide as the population multiplies?

A local woman indicates that I should crawl through a hole in the cliff face, saying that it is *mzuri sana*. Not knowing what to expect, I creep through into a huge cave, much of it open to the sunlight from above, that leads off into smaller caves and passages. It obviously fills with water at high tide, but now at low tide it is completely dry, the floor fine white castor sugar sand. The colouring is out of this world, with giant stalactites hanging from the ceiling. Standing alone in this breathtaking setting I am suddenly struck by the eeriness of the place. What ceremonies have taken place here? I realize that the Swahili ladies who were hunting for octopus under the low-tide rocks have moved on, showing no desire to step into the caves with me. Pemba is known for its voodoo and witchcraft. Have the walls of the place ever been lit by firelight and have they ever echoed to strange cries and the beat of the African drum? I hurry back to share my exciting find with the others, and I must say, once full of people, the place takes on a happier and friendlier tone.

Later, when we are out on the water, two strongly built men in a canoe greet us. One is a happy elfin character who, in pidgin, introduces himself as Masoudi and offers to show us a big hole with water and fish. Without further ado he jumps into *Bathtub*, leaving his mate in the canoe. The hole is a beautiful rock pool sunk deep into the coral and overhung by the roof of a shallow cave. It is full of tiny tropical fish, and Jon notices a few crayfish when he and Ross dive in with fins and masks. On the same day we've discovered an Aladdin's cave and a mermaid's pool.

We also have a small paradise beach on which to camp. A few metres out to sea a coral ledge drops off into deep crystal-clear water, providing excellent diving and fishing – some of the best in the world. To the north of our camp, just around a corner, a deep-water channel runs into a protected lagoon. We can even get fresh water from Masoudi's village well. It is also full moon, our camp bathed in moonlight at night, and we decide to stay on. No one is in a rush to move from our newfound paradise. Pemba and her islands are proving to be all that we've dreamt about, and, for me, the ideal chance to have a much-needed rest – I've been feeling the pace a bit lately.

In the afternoon, after a brief rainstorm that has us diving for cover, Nkonkoni Rob, Jon and I take off in *Bathtub* for a bit of sport fishing. Each trolling a feather, we travel north in deep blue water. Ahead of us birds swoop and dive into the water, a sure sign of fish ahead. Soon we are among a shoal of tuna, silhouetted by the setting sun as they leap out of the water. All three rods take simultaneously, ratchets screaming as metre after metre of line peels off the reels. Alas, these monsters are too powerful for our light-weight tackle and within seconds we have all lost our feathers, and our dignity. The tuna still frolic around the boat, winners of round one. Little do they know that we have one rapala left on the boat, which Jon soon has in the water. Within seconds the game is on and Jon's rod is bent almost double. But time waits for no man and as Jon prepares himself for the fight, the sun settles on the horizon and then disappears.

Under normal circumstances this would have been a problem for three men in a small boat, miles from camp and fighting a great fish. But luck is with us tonight, and soon the ocean is lit by a soft glow from the full moon, providing enough light for Jon's epic battle to continue. It takes well over an hour to bring the giant yellow-finned tuna to the gaff (the gaff in this case being a sharpened tent peg, curved into a hook and bound with baling wire onto a stout piece of mangrove). A good clout from the anchor prevents our fish from leaping around the boat and we are soon heading for home 'by the light of the silvery moon', with enough protein to keep the AOE alive and well for a few days. We don't have a scale but the tuna certainly weighs more than a full 25-litre fuel container – a measure of weight we are now all accustomed to.

Saturday 2 October

The day starts with a ride just out beyond the reef accompanied by dolphins. As they frolic around the boat, Ross and I put on masks and snorkels and hang off the side of the boat for a better look.

Our friend Masoudi Omari Juma invites us to pay a visit to Kimeleyani Village, where he lives. Masoudi, his two wives and 15 children make a living from fishing and collecting shells, which he sells from a small *duka* and in Mombasa. He also has a coconut plantation of 200 trees. Masoudi owns three boats, one small *mashua* and two larger ones, but what he really needs is a 40-horsepower outboard engine so that he can fish in the deep Pemba Channel. His dream is to make enough money to buy an outboard engine and get some nets for fishing.

Kimeleyani's thatched mud huts are dwarfed by tall palm trees. The people are amazingly friendly and not after anything in return. Apart from coconuts, there are bananas and cassava, and the few zebu cattle we see are in a beautiful condition – treated almost as pets. Masoudi is the perfect host, inviting us to take lunch with him. The food is served in true Swahili fashion with us all seated on the floor. First a bowl of water is offered for us to wash our right hands. This is followed by a simple meal of cassava and boiled banana with a small piece of fish, which we gave to him this morning, concerned that it would go off before we could eat it. Masoudi then takes us to his little shop, which I doubt has more than $20 worth of stock. He proudly presents each of us with a container of soap powder. This is great hospitality from a person who has very few material possessions. (Or has he noticed the state of our clothes?)

We are introduced to everyone in the village – brothers, aunties, uncles, fathers and grandfathers – and by the time we leave it is almost dark. The little kids all hop to push *Bathtub* off. We take off through the gap and round to our camp at Paradise Beach.

There a gourmet delight awaits us. Nkonkoni Rob has prepared an amazing meal, with starters of octopus and fish, a main course of bean stew, savoury rice and *chapatis* cooked Zanzibar style, and bananas as dessert. All this is set out on a low table made of empty fuel containers in an alcove of dry coral rock, lit by a number of candles placed in holes in the rock face. A little paraffin lamp burns on the table. We sit cross-legged on the fine white sand, savouring this moment to remember. By the time we walk to our bedrolls it feels as if we have been out to a fancy restaurant for dinner. We decide to stay on for yet another day – Paradise Beach on Fundu Island is proving difficult to leave.

Sunday 3 October

Nkonkoni Rob, Kiboko and I spend the morning fishing from a small *mashua* with a man named Sharif. Along with the two young boys who are the crew, we soon have the sail up and are heading towards the Tanzanian mainland. The skipper blows into a conch shell to bring up the wind. We trail a feather and a rapala, but no luck.

It's a great experience being pushed along by the *Kusi* wind in a hand-hewn vessel crafted in a way that has stood the test of time. As much as we admire the craft and the crew for their sailing ability, so they are over-awed by our outboard engines and rubberducks. The best place to fish, according to Sharif, is just to the north of Pemba Island. There you can catch monsters, but for such a trip you should have an outboard engine on the back of your dhow for the return trip against the wind.

I ask him if he has ever taken his dhow to Zanzibar or Tanga, and he replies simply: 'All this is possible if the wind is polite.' I wonder how many people have been lost at sea: no life-jackets, no navigational equipment, some of the fishermen unable to swim. But such has been the way of this coast for centuries of dhow travel.

Late in the afternoon I head back to Kimeleyani. We need a few supplies from the village shop and I am keen to find something unusual for Mashozi. Tomorrow is our 24th wedding anniversary, and I've picked up a few subtle hints from my better half warning me about forgetting the important occasion. I've normally got a terrible memory for such things, which invariably lands me in trouble.

At the village I buy an old wooden ornamental Swahili comb. It smells of coconut oil and is well worn with use, something I know Mashozi will enjoy. Back at camp I write a note and fold it into a small wad, pushing it between the long teeth of the wooden comb, taking great care to sprinkle a few grains of sand from Paradise Beach onto the paper before finally folding it. The romantic land of Zinj is obviously getting to me.

Monday 4 October – Our 24th wedding anniversary

We wake up early in our tent, kiss and exchange presents. Mashozi, who is good at these things, has had the foresight to buy a card in Kenya. I am pleased the note and comb are well received, and it appears I've made it through another anniversary – and what better place to spend it.

By 9 am the sun is already beating down as we pack up *Bathtub* and *QE2* for the little island of Misali, reputed to be very beautiful and excellent for diving. There are over 20 islands around Pemba, and we hope to visit as many as possible. First we call in at Wete to get supplies and charge the video camera batteries.

What an enchanting place Wete is. The 1950s Austin buses all have backs made from teak, and are known as *mbavu-za-mbwa* ('a dog's stomach') because of their corrugated wooden bodies that resemble a dog's ribs. These lovely relics thunder up and down the island on their bald tyres, and we decide that the Pemba experience would be incomplete without a trip in one at some stage.

Today Wete is abuzz as there are several large dhows in port and the motor dhow is about to leave for Tanga on the Tanzanian mainland. We hire one of the many bullock carts to transport our rations and water containers down to the boats, and finally leave for Misali Island with our new guide Salim, a bright young fellow who speaks reasonable English and is determined to get somewhere in life.

Lying about an hour south of Wete, with a deep channel running down the northern side, Misali Island is beautiful. But beauty is only skin deep, and Misali, with its deep blue water, its numerous drop-offs ideal for diving, and sandy white beach, has a few tricks up its sleeve. The first is sand fleas, which have everybody scratching and slapping. Lighting the campfire and setting up our chairs for the sunset over paradise, we discover the second with the arrival of some unwanted guests – rats!

As darkness descends over Misali, even more of the furry creatures come to visit. Some of them are the size of Jack Russells and soon Mashozi is sitting up in her chair, her feet up on a pot with all the lamps lit. She is terrified of rats. Damn! This hasn't turned out to be the ideal anniversary venue.

Next morning the area around our camp is covered in thousands of tiny footprints. We will not be spending another night here – not if Mashozi has anything to do with it.

Tuesday 5 October

On Misali I speak to Mr Muhammad Matoni, a fisherman from the port of Mkoani, who is in partnership with the owner of a small *galawa*, a large dugout with a single sail, a rudder and 'outriggers'. They go fishing for up to five days at a time, using Misali as a base, and bringing with them a few basic rations such as rice, salt and drinking water. During the time of the *Kusi*, they fish with small hooks and hand lines for reef fish about 20 metres offshore. On a good day they can catch over a hundred which they take to the market at Chake Chake to sell fresh. If the weather is rough they dry the fish on racks, but selling dried fish is not as profitable. During the time of the *Kaskazi* winds they go fishing way out into the Pemba Channel where the water is very deep. They use big hooks and heavy line because they are after the very big fish with long beaks (kingfish) or yellow-finned tuna.

The tide is up and we travel south past Chake Chake and Mkoani, Pemba's southern-most port. In the south there are islands dotted everywhere. We choose Makongwe, a small island just off Mkoani, once again arriving to find a tropical splendour of giant palm trees shading pristine white sand ringed by crystal-clear water.

Setting up camp is second nature by now, and Mashozi and I soon have our little love nest pitched right on the water's edge, the best place to be with the *Kusi* blowing off the water keeping the mosquitos at bay. There are sand fleas, but no rats.

Wednesday 6 October

I wake up at first light to find the high tide lapping just short of the tent door. Beyond the flap stretch miles of open sea, tropical islands dotting the horizon. The early morning sun makes the sails of the passing dhows and fishing *galawa*s glow white against the blue water.

We depart for Mkoani, which has the sleepy feel of tropical islands. The path to the village rises steeply from the port, which boasts a brand-new pier courtesy of a foreign aid programme. We use the old jetty, aged and broken, but easier for our small boat.

From Mkoani, Jon and Kiboko take the boats back north to Wete, the rest of us deciding to explore inland in a dog's stomach. The bus crashes through its gears, loaded to capacity. The people are laid back and very courteous, and you stop the bus with a faint *shish* of the lips. Swahili ladies in *buibuis* gaze at us with unabashed curiosity, their liquid eyes laughing at our unkempt appearance and poor Swahili. These old buses with their hard plank seats should be called bum-numbers. But we're used to bouncing along on rubberducks, and soon learn to tense our bums for every crater-sized pothole.

As we pass through the countryside we are accompanied by the constant smell of cloves, the mainstay of the economy. Three and a half million clove trees grow on terraces that corrugate the steep-sided valleys of the island. Our wooden bus swerves for bullock carts, bicycles, and ancient lorries, also with hand-made wooden backs, transporting the dried cloves to Wete. From here they are shipped east to be used in cigarettes and to produce the painkilling clove oil, not to mention the familiar cooking spice.

It's late afternoon by the time we get back to Wete and load up with enough fuel to reach the Kenyan mainland. By now we're friends with Customs and Immigration. They stamp our passports out of Tanzania and we explain that we'll spend the night at our

Paradise Beach and leave in the morning. *KwaHeri* and *Asanti sana*. We'll treasure our memory of your Spice Islands forever. Tomorrow we'll head north-east to the Kenyan coast and then on to Tiwi, south of Mombasa.

Sunday 10 October

We sadly say goodbye to the never-never land of Zinj. For me this coast will always beckon with the old wooden dhows of yesteryear, the clear blue water and tall coconut palms, their fronds whispering secrets to each other. I will never forget Sharif blowing on his conch shell to call up the *Kusi*; the cool *barazas* and narrow streets of Lamu; donkeys competing with the amplified muezzin call; Swahili women in *buibuis* sending messages with their seductive eyes; the paradise beaches and coral coves of the lost islands of Pemba; the grace with which the Swahili people accept the eccentric, uncouth *wazungu*; and the gentle *shish* of a request to stop the dog's stomach.

11-18 October - Nairobi bureaucracy

From Tiwi I telephone Nairobi, only to learn that we still don't have permission to cross Ethiopia and Sudan. While it is possible for foreigners to fly into both Addis Ababa and Khartoum, the borders are closed to land traffic, and as yet the new South Africa is not officially recognized by Ethiopia. I knew this when we left South Africa, but hoped that it would sort itself out. But it seems it hasn't, and my mood of doom and gloom deepens as we tow *QE2* and *Bathtub* across the wide-open plains of Tsavo to our base in Nairobi. Ahead of us lies one of the biggest challenges of the expedition.

It is moody and overcast by the time we reach Nairobi and I can taste the smog in the air. The clouds lift and, as we drive up Langata Road, the Ngong Hills reveal themselves, a reasonable welcome, I think, to a few days that I really am not looking forward to – days of embassies and negotiations. This will be the AOE's moment of truth. Will we be able to bypass bureaucracy, banditry and war to reach our goal – Khartoum, the Nile, Cairo and the Med? And so Mashozi and I

On Pemba we use bullock carts to transport fuel and drinking water to the boats. In the background is a wooden-bodied bus.

153

WE LEARN SOME BASIC SWAHILI'

CHAKULA – FOOD
MAJI – WATER
MKATE – BREAD
SUKARI – SUGAR
CHAPATI – UNLEAVENED BREAD
SAMOSA – THE FAVOURITE TRIANGLE
MANDAZI – DOUGHNUT & SWEET
MBUZI – MUTTON OR GOAT
KUKU – CHICKEN
SUKUMA WIKI' – GREEN SPINACH
VIAZI – POTATOES.
POMBE – BEER
NYAMA CHOMA – ROAST MEAT

OUR FAVOURITE BECOMES NYAMA
CHOMA AND CHAPATI – ROASTED
MEAT PIECES AND UNLEAVENED
WHEAT BREAD PANCAKES !!

get down to work, leaving the anxious pilgrims to sort out the equipment and hope for the best.

The Window: We start with Charles of Charleston Travel. If we can't get into Ethiopia through the front door, we'll have to do it through the window. We can buy return tickets from Nairobi via Addis Ababa and Khartoum to Cairo and back to Nairobi. Against these tickets we can get our visas, and then cancel our tickets, paying a small cancellation fee. Although we'll then have a visa, the fact remains that the land borders with Ethiopia are closed, and we need some sort of official letter to get us through the border. But, if push comes to shove, we'll go with the window method and try to talk our way through from there.

The Front Door: Our first step is to visit the SA Trade Commission in Nairobi. To sort out our *indabas* we are handed over to a Mr André Janse van Rensburg, and what a character he proves to be. We are accompanied by him on our visit to Mr Abdullah Alansreg at the Sudanese Embassy. If we can persuade the Sudanese to let us in, then we can approach the Ethiopians and, with luck, put pressure on them as the only stumbling block to the expedition reaching Cairo and the Med. We have already seen the Egyptians and they are extremely supportive.

I quote André: 'Well, Mr Alansreg, before Mr Holgate tells you his story about the incredible expedition, let me introduce the man. (Big puff of smoke from a cigarette that he has bummed from the Sudanese Councillor and a jerk at his baggy trousers, so bringing the crotch to a level just above his knees.) Well, do you know that Kingsley Holgate is a direct descendant of Burton, the famous explorer? Kingsley himself is an internationally famous explorer and not only does he have the personal support of our president, Mr de Klerk, but, more importantly in the new South Africa, Mr Mandela himself. And as you know, Abdullah (we have rapidly moved on to first name terms), my government and yours are forging ever-stronger links. So, please (another giant puff of cigarette smoke and a tug on his trousers – a dramatic pause for effect), I hand you over to Kingsley Holgate.'

I don't know what to say. Never before has a man become so famous so quickly, and I am dumbfounded. But a giant wink from André soon has me rattling through our scroll of peace and goodwill with all its mayoral wishes and letters, press cuttings and photographs. After such an introduction we simply cannot go wrong. Abdullah agrees to phone the Ethiopians and offers us a letter of introduction to ease our entry into Sudan. We are promised a guide from the border with Ethiopia through to Khartoum, an introduction to the mayor there, free visas and a guide to take us through to Wadi Halfa. Wow! It's all working.

By the time we get to the Ethiopians, they have heard from the Sudanese. Mr Levi at the Embassy of the Transitional Government of Ethiopia contacts his superiors in Addis Ababa, and after three nail-biting days we have our visas and a letter of introduction. That night I gleefully hand each pilgrim his passport with visas for Ethiopia, Sudan and Egypt.

Before we can head north we have to wrap up the Ugandan part of our expedition. This includes some of the most fascinating waterways in Africa. First we will cross the equator to Jinja and Speke's source of the Nile, at the top end of Lake Victoria, then head on to lakes George, Edward and Albert and the Murchison Falls. After that we will come back to Nairobi to prepare for the big push north. This will take us to Lake Tana – source of the Blue Nile – and on to Sudan's Omdurman and Khartoum, the confluence of the Blue and White Niles. Then we'll follow the united Nile through the Nubian Desert to Wadi Halfa, Lake Nassar, and on to Cairo and Alexandria in Egypt, where we'll finally pour our Zulu calabash of seawater into the Mediterranean. It's a huge challenge that lies ahead, but now, with our paperwork for the north sorted out, we've got a chance.

Tuesday 19 October

Funds are now extremely tight so we decide to do the Ugandan section with only *Bathtub* and *Vulandlela*. Ian is staying behind to service and repair *Thirsty*. We take the top off *Vulandlela*, throw a few things into the boat, and Mashozi, Ross, Kiboko, Nkonkoni Rob, Jon and I take off back down into the Rift Valley past Navaisha.

By the time we reach Nakuru we are into the first of what are known locally as the 'small' rains. These aren't small at all, and the pilgrims huddle in the back under a tarpaulin. We're soon drenched, and even the green carpet of tea plantations and misty views around the highlands of Kericho bring only small glances from the 'Cossacks' in the back (Ross and Nkonkoni Rob have bought sheepskin hats from a roadside vendor in an effort to keep out the cold).

It is dark by the time we reach the port of Kisumu on Lake Victoria. Our arrival at the yacht club is greeted with an almighty downpour, but, armed with a letter of introduction from the Mwanza Yacht Club, we soon have Tuskers in hand as we meet some of the members in the pub. Lovely old colonial furnishings speak of a bygone era, with wooden notice boards recording past sailing events. Great sailing fun must have been had here, but now the results of the races on the boards simply read *Not Sailed*. Most of the present members are from the local Asian and African community – Smiths, Gibsons and Jacksons have been replaced by Patels, Ramoches, Onyangos and Otienos. Very little sailing takes place these days and the sailing clubs have become social clubs, and very friendly ones at that. Yes, we can launch from the club. *Hakuna mutata* – no problem.

To the headwaters of the mighty Nile

Harvesting fish from Lake Victoria

Explorer John Hanning Speke reached the Nile on 21 July 1862 at a place called Urondogani, some 40 kilometres downstream from Lake Victoria. In his journal he wrote: 'Here at last I stood on the brink of the Nile ... most beautiful was the scene – nothing could surpass it!' Speke and his party then made their way further upstream and on 28 July reached the waterfall where the Nile tumbled out of Lake Victoria, so solving one of the greatest geographic mysteries of the time – the source of the Nile.

Wednesday 20 October

On the Kisumu–Jinja Road we cross the equator, hot and steamy, as one would expect it to be, and the vegetation becomes lusher as we get closer to the border at Busia. There is a bit of confusion with some hustlers at the Kenyan border, but through we go. The Ugandan border takes a bit of time, and from comments that are made it seems that not too many South Africans go through here. Finally with a big smile the official says, 'Welcome to Uganda – the Pearl of Africa.' He could well be correct.

There are crops growing everywhere you look – bananas, rice, maize, sugar cane, cassava, sweet potatoes, papaws, mangoes and oranges. The women wear colourful *gomesi,* flowing dresses with pointed shoulders, which are the traditional dress of the Baganda and Basoga people.

The tarred road through to Jinja is excellent, but the town looks like a film set from the 1940s. Though the corrugated iron-roofed shops with their wide verandas have an air of genteel decay, they are neat and clean, and there is a feeling of hope. There are thousands of bicycles, and the people are extremely friendly, the majority speaking good English. Jinja is Uganda's second largest town and its industrial centre. It is also at the source of the Victoria Nile. We all become very excited at the sight of the Napoleon Gulf on Lake Victoria: it's a new waterway and a new adventure.

Passing through Jinja, we head down to the water's edge to camp among the palm trees at the Jinja Sailing Club. We're next to the Nile Pier, a small market and charcoal trading station. Hundreds of tons of charcoal are brought across the bay from Bugungu and Bugolo. It is packed loosely into large wooden canoes with tatty patchwork sails.

We're soon relishing our first Nile beer. It looks as though Uganda will be great fun.

Thursday 21 October – The kill-me-quick fishermen

I write my journal sitting in the shade of an open bamboo-walled rondavel. In front of me is Lake Victoria's Napoleon Gulf, and just downstream is the source of the Victoria Nile. The spot was once marked by the Rippon Falls, although these now lie beneath the raised waters of the Owen Falls Dam. A handcrafted wooden canoe moves up and down, one man paddling, the other throwing a huge cast net. A Richard Clayderman tape produces background music from *Vulandlela*'s tape player. It is still fiercely humid and the heavy cumulonimbus clouds mushroom into amazing shapes over the source of the Victoria Nile.

In the afternoon we launch *Bathtub* out into Napoleon Gulf and back in the direction from which we have come, ending up at the fishing village of Namugungo in the Inganga District.

Namugungo's thatched huts have cast nets hanging from their eaves. Other nets for catching kapenta (*omena* in Uganda) are spread out like a fallen cloud on the beach, with fishermen sitting on them, stitching closed any tears. Over 30 large canoes are pulled up on the beach, beautifully made craft capable of carrying 20 to 30 people. The boats are somewhat longer and wider than those in the south, and resemble small versions of the Tanganyika lake taxis. Large pits have been dug in the earth over which metal grids are spread for the drying of fish. Woven mats cover the fish, fires glowing in the smoking pits. Unlike the giant Nile perch we saw in the south of the lake, these are tiny, averaging 15 to 20 centimetres. The unappetizing forms of smoke-blackened tilapia also lie on the racks; they command a good price at the Jinja market.

The equator crossing en route to Uganda

There are animals everywhere – turkeys, ducks, chickens, dogs, cattle and even pigs. This part of the lake is so different from the Tanzanian south. There is no socialist hangover here, no bureaucracy, just open friendliness. The visitors' book is brought out to us from the village shop, a little exercise book in which we are requested to sign our names under the headings *Day*, *Names* and *Omissions* (ours are the only names).

By this time heavy storm clouds have gathered, it is getting late and the wind is picking up. Time to go. The entire village comes out to see us off. Some of them are decidedly unsteady, tripping over the mounds of snails that have been dredged from the lakeshore to be dried and ground as poultry feed. We are told that the village drunks have been sipping on a brew called kill-me-quick. After loud farewells and much handshaking, we eventually get away from the kill-me-quick fishermen of Namugungo. We head into the chop before rounding the headland to run with the wind back to our camp at Jinja. It is almost dark by the time we reach our tents. The source of the Nile will have to wait till tomorrow.

THE VICTORIA NILE FLOWING NORTH TO LAKE KYOGA, THE MURCHISON FALLS AND LAKE ALBERT

VICTORIA NILE

UGANDA

KAMPALA

JINJA AND SPEKE'S SOURCE OF THE NILE

EQUATOR 0°

ENTEBBE

KISUMU

WINAM GULF

LAKE VICTORIA SPEKE'S SOURCE OF THE NILE

HOMA BAY

KENYA

N
W   E
S

Friday 22 October - Speke's source of the Nile

We launch our boats into the Napoleon Gulf. It is strange how the lake becomes the river and, as if to mark the spot, there is a small rocky hill on which stands a lone tree, iced white with droppings, its foliage stripped by the hundreds of birds.

Set above this rocky outcrop, in among giant palms and green lawns, stands a simple plinth which reads, *Speke discovered this source of the Nile on the 28th July 1862.* This is so symbolic for us, but what a shame that affairs in south Sudan are such that we are unable to continue from this point down the Nile to Cairo. Still, here we are, standing at Speke's source of the Nile.

On the opposite river bank stands a tall pillar overlooking the lake and the river. Somewhat neglected it is surrounded by cassava. How African, I think, that the place from which Speke first saw this source of the Nile now stands in the middle of a cassava field. After all, the locals lived and tilled the soil here long before the arrival of our friend Speke. The brass inlay for the lettering from the cracked marble slab below the pillar has long since been removed, and I imagine the small pieces serving as weights on a cast net.

Before the construction of the Owen Falls Dam, the lake must have tumbled over the Rippon Falls to form the Nile at this point. I can just picture the elegant ladies in their parasols, the men in their pith helmets, waiters running to and fro, small box cameras taking black-and-white pictures of tourists posing on the stone viewing platform that now stands deserted under a huge wild fig tree. Today all we have is a quickening of the river and some whirlpools as the lake crosses this imaginary line to become the Nile.

The water, clear and deep, is running swiftly, and in typical Expedition fashion we jump off *Bathtub* to celebrate the moment. The current is strong and we are carried down towards the railway bridge and the Owen Falls Dam and have to hop back aboard in a hurry to avoid becoming crocodile lunch.

From the source of the Nile we go back upstream to our camp. Packing up our kit, we set off over the Owen Falls Dam wall, across the Nile and on to Kampala. The road to the city is extremely good, passing through towering rain forests. The villages along the way are colourful, and never before have I seen so many bicycles and bananas. It is the rainy season and, as mid-afternoon approaches, the humidity and heat increase and the rain clouds gather.

It's Friday afternoon and Kampala is abuzz. We no sooner arrive than the rains come and the wet centre of Kampala is choked with traffic. But once the rain stops the air is clear and fresh, and the city is amazing. Thousands of people are gathered outside the football stadium, queuing up for a game, and there are brightly coloured markets and vendors everywhere. *Chips*-style policemen with khaki uniforms and white crash helmets stand next to their motorbikes. Poverty and squalor live alongside wealth and splendour, difficult bedfellows in a fast-expanding city where Fort Kampala once stood. Massive cumulonimbus clouds gather over the city skyline, lit by the setting sun, preparing for the next equatorial downpour. We make camp at the Salaam Yacht club on the shores of Lake Victoria. The area is choked with water hyacinth.

Saturday 23 October

We head out through Kampala, but can't resist visiting a Hindu temple next to the road. The priest informs us that this impressive temple, which is a carbon-copy of another in Kashmir, is not supported by a single piece of metal. After being told that this is indeed the second heaven, we are treated with great hospitality, departing for Lake Albert each with a little package of sweet cakes as is the Hindu custom.

From Kampala we take the road to Busunju, stopping to buy bread and bananas, plus beef from a roadside butcher who brushes off the flies with a banana leaf. Uganda is quite an expensive country for us; with just $500 to get to Cairo (though I know that Mashozi has an emergency stash) we are travelling and living as cheaply as possible: one meal a day and very few luxuries. Every cent has to go towards boat and vehicle fuel.

We slip and slide for 160 kilometres, wheels spinning and mud splattering, through thick equatorial forests of mud and potholes. We finally reach the town of Hoima which has its own wide, potholed, tar road and typical corrugated iron-roofed shops. There are bicycles everywhere: bicycles as taxis, complete with colourfully padded vinyl passenger saddles; banana-carrying bicycles with great bunches of green fruit hanging down each side of the carriers; firewood-carrying bicycles; and bicycles carrying enormous bags of charcoal as the forests of Africa are slowly destroyed. The people are ebony black here. The men's skin shines with the sweat of the equatorial climate, as wives and girlfriends are carried side-saddle on the ubiquitous bicycles. Hundreds of women tailors turn out colourful clothing on antique treadmill sewing machines, four or five machines to each store veranda. Everybody is extremely friendly, shouting out, 'Have a good journey.'

We leave this end-of-the-road town in north-west Uganda, taking a muddy track north to Butiaba on the shores of Lake Albert. Then the heavens open. I am one of the unfortunates in the open back of *Vulandlela*, together with Kiboko, Nkonkoni Rob, who looks like a wildebeest caught in a thunderstorm, and Jon, who, in his normal befuddled way, has a 'Why me?' look about him. By the time we have pulled a tarpaulin over the kit and ourselves, we are soaked. Fortunately, within an hour the sun burns down fiercely, and in no time we are all smiles and dry once more.

The view over the escarpment down to Lake Albert is breathtaking – hundreds of square kilometres of glistening lake bordered by the steep-sided Zaïrian escarpment to the west and a massive flat floodplain below us. It must, at one time, have been the floor of an even larger lake, walled by the eastern escarpment, on top of which we now stand in the company of a number of baboons who have also chosen this place for the view.

Butiaba turns out to be a has-been port. Old colonial buildings, some of them on stilts, stand in a haphazard line leading down to the edge of the water. An avenue of tall palm trees indicates the way to what was once the dockside. The sun is low over the hills of Zaïre and just to the north of us lies the blackened, wrecked hull of the *Robert Coryndon*. Its funnel, once a common sight on Lake Albert as it belched smoke up into the African sky, now sticks out at a despondent angle over a green papyrus reed bed, its final grave on the shore of Lake Albert. (The *Robert Coryndon* was named after the much-admired South African-born governor of Kenya, who died in 1925.)

With the large number of unruly gawkers present, many of whom have been into the kill-me-quick, we decide to push on towards the village of Ndandamire. We camp in fairly thick bush, which, apart from sheltering a few tired expeditionists, appears to be the favourite gathering place of our ever-present friends, the mosquitos. Having a little meat in the stew is a real luxury, which reminds me of home.

Sunday 24 October

We wake up to find that ants have eaten a hole not only through the tent floor but also through the backside of some shorts I'd put out to dry. But it's good to be back in the bush with the morning alarm of hundreds of birdcalls. It's hot and extremely humid by the time we get going. Passing through the village of Bulisa we finally cross an immense grassy plain to arrive on the shores of Lake Albert. There is a small fishing village with big wooden canoes bearing names such as *God's Love* and *To the Lord*. Marabou storks patrol the shoreline like Fisheries officers, their air sacs inflated to cope with the heat. Fish are stacked neatly on the drying racks.

By this time the humidity has reached an intolerable level, and the hundreds of villagers cannot believe the sight of these *wazungu*. It is midday, and, at a time when we should all be dozing under a tree, we are loading the boat, sweat pouring off us, as we prepare for our expedition up the Victoria Nile to the foot of the Murchison Falls.

Leaving the trailer and *Vulandlela* at the local police outpost, we finally get away from the huge crowd of excited onlookers. A barrage of directions is shouted at us, enough to confuse the most experienced of explorers. Within five minutes we are stuck on a sand-bank, but more directions from a nearby fishing canoe soon have us travelling up the main course of the Victoria Nile, flowing wide and strong from the north-east as it rushes down to Lake Albert. What an amazing delta this is, with the Victoria Nile flowing into the lake and the Albert Nile flowing out in the opposite direction a few kilometres away.

For the first 10 to 15 kilometres we stay in the delta, high papyrus reeds on either side. It becomes oppressively hot, and we decide to take a siesta in a thick evergreen forest on the eastern side of the river. After checking for crocodiles, we take a game track off into a clearing shaded by a canopy of trees, from which hang creepers of every shape and size. A pot of tea is soon on the boil: hot and sweet with fresh lemon, the perfect thirst quencher for these dangerously hot and humid conditions. Several cups of this witches' brew later, we all feel a lot better, but a siesta is out of the question because of the bloody tsetse flies.

Once it has cooled down we get back into *Bathtub*, but struggle with one of the outboards. The problem, as usual, seems to be dirty fuel, but, with just enough power to get on the plane, we move on up the Victoria Nile. By this time we have left the delta behind and are now in the main river. No wonder so much was written about this area by early explorers, missionaries, hunters and adventurers. Huge trees stand on the riverbank, giant crocodiles slide off the green papyrus banks and into the deep, wide river. Elephants graze on a nearby island. A small herd of buffaloes stands in the shade of an acacia tree. The birdlife is incredible. There are hippos everywhere: Mashozi sits in the front of the boat doing her hippo count, pod after pod, hippo after hippo. We count 837 hippos up to the Murchison Falls (named after the president of the Royal Geographic Society by the Nile explorer Sir Samuel Baker), a distance of only about 50 kilometres.

The mighty crocs of this Murchison Falls area are legendary – early game warden Pitman declared that he saw the oldest crocodile in Africa there, so massive with age it could hardly drag itself along the ground! The measurements of its footprints seemed to indicate that it was at least five feet across the body. Sir Samuel Baker, the great Nile explorer, reported a 30-footer below Murchison.

Rounding a bend in the river we come upon an awesome sight: thundering through a narrow gap in the rocks, the Murchison Falls roar down into a small, steep-sided bay, spray and foam everywhere. We drop Mashozi, Kiboko and Ross onto a small rocky outcrop, taking advantage of the calm water in the lee of the rock. It is their task to record this moment on slide and video. I skipper *Bathtub* up to the foot of the torrent, and at one stage the boat remains stationary, even though we are at full throttle, with foam and roaring water all around us. The current pushes us towards the rocks on the left bank, and I have to execute a tight turn and move back downstream to keep us out of trouble. Close to the foot of the falls, while we are still in turbulent water, a giant hippo looms, evidently quite at home in the rough water.

From our lone rock we make several 'white-water' excursions through waves and foam to the bottom of the falls. Mashozi is a little nervous at first, especially when a wave of white foam sweeps sideways onto the boat, covering the motors with a beard of shaving cream. We sight two giant crocodiles, their heads, snouts and eyes showing darkly above the white foam. They are swimming through! Who would ever have believed that crocodiles and hippos would live in such turbulent water?

After a few hours in yet another of nature's paradises, we set off back down the Victoria Nile in search of a campsite. An essential part of this waterway expedition is the sunsets. There's something so special about cruising on an African waterway at this time of the day. Everything goes quiet. Even the birds and animals seem to respect this magical hour. This is the time of day when one feels close to a greater being. The water has turned golden, the intense heat and humidity has passed. The hippos grunt lazily at passing *Bathtub*. Cranes strut in a long line down the western bank, looking like a formal changing of the guard, their golden fan-shaped crowns held high in true military style, as if they know they are Uganda's national bird.

We set up camp on a flat bank and soon the kettle is bubbling on a merry blaze. Camping has really become easy now – in a few minutes tents are up, battered chairs out and a paraffin lamp lit. Ross is a master at firewood collection and Kiboko is the 'coffee king'. Mashozi is soon comfortable in her East African camp chair, her favourite bottle of wine at her side – her special indulgence after a hot hard day. Nkonkoni knocks up a macaroni dish – my favourite.

The conversation round the campfire turns to the number of expedition days left to go, home and Christmas, family and friends, everyday life after the expedition ... that terrible feeling of reality. I'm sure we will all have a great deal of trouble re-adjusting after a year of high adventure.

During the night we are entertained by a cacophony of animal sounds. Hippos grunt only a few metres from our tents, not amused that we are camped on their nocturnal trail. I'm still not able to sleep through lions roaring, the unnerving sound close enough to rattle the fly-sheet on our small cottage tent. I nudge Mashozi and we sit bolt upright as the sound echoes across the delta. Hyaenas take up the challenge with their mournful whooping cry, and not to be outdone a leopard grunts in the darkness. Mother Nature lays on a spectacular show for these first-time visitors with lightning flashing and thunder rolling. Soon the equatorial rain drums down on the fly-sheet.

Monday 25 October

We wake to paradise and a giant pod of hippos that has come to stare. They must be the most inquisitive of animals, but great fun, never failing to amuse. But you need to keep reminding yourself that they are one of Africa's most dangerous creatures.

After sweet black coffee, we're off. As we run with the current, downstream to Lake Albert, the giant trees soon give way to papyrus reed. There is a slight chop as we bounce into the wind on the lake – lower back pain is a fact of life on a long rubberduck expedition! Turning west, we head for the Ugandan town of Panyimur and the Albert Nile. We do not have the fuel to go through to the Sudanese border at Nimules, but we feel it is important to do some of the great river – a symbolic start to what becomes the White Nile. How fantastic it would be if we could keep on going to Juba through southern Sudan, the great Sudd and Khartoum, but we were warned strongly against going into war-torn southern Sudan: you'll be shot like sitting ducks, we were told!

Only a few kilometres from the Victoria Nile we are travelling with the current, going north in an outpouring of water from Lake Albert. To think, if the river gods are with us, we will join these waters of the Nile again in a few weeks' time at Omdurman and Khartoum. We have to dodge the islands of water hyacinth, a big problem on this river.

We stop at the fishing village of Kalolo, where we are welcomed by Mr Jock. It is a tidy village, with fishing nets spread out on the sand. The finely crafted canoes are made locally. Fishermen's wives are gutting and scaling an assortment of catfish, herring, Nile perch, dogfish and others, all caught by net, one of which is being hauled in hand-over-hand at the moment. The pilgrims help pull in the heavy net, but it must be caught in a bed of hyacinth: with a great heave the rope breaks. So much for helping with village life! Mr Jock complains that the water hyacinth is indeed a problem and that the matter has been reported to Fisheries. Most of the catch, we are told, is sold fresh to buyers who come in by boat and on foot to make their purchases. They trade fish for nets from nearby Zaïre. The fish diet is supplemented by bananas, sweet potatoes, cassava and the occasional goat or beef dish. Such friendly people! Gone are the days of Idi Amin.

From Kalolo we turn back – fuel being in short supply – towards Lake Albert and Ndandamire. Once again the heat is intense and the gawkers somewhat drunk. But, hallelujah, the vehicle and trailer are safe. So, with some backslapping, smiles and handshaking, we give away expedition T-shirts – the international currency of Africa.

The view is quite beautiful and the air soon becomes cooler as we climb out of the Lake Albert system to Hoima. The road is narrow, muddy and rutted, just wide enough to take *Bathtub* and *Vulandlela*. Towering equatorial forest lines the road, and colourful markets appear in the middle of nowhere. How can a country devour so many bananas? They are everywhere. We camp outside a tiny mission church set high on a conical hill with a 360° view over Africa, and a magnificent sunset through the smoke of the cursed charcoal fires.

Tuesday 26 October
We push on in a cold and rainy equatorial Africa. The road is bad and it's tough going, but we are patient and soon arrive in wet and misty Fort Portal. We camp in the grounds of the aptly named Mountains of the Moon Hotel, a delightful colonial hotel built in 1928, with rolling lawns, palm trees, and really good food. Best of all is its pub – Old English with a warm log fire, comfortable chairs and pint after pint of Nile beer. Bloody luxury!

Wednesday 27 October - To the Mountains of the Moon
The rain and mist clear enough to give us our first sighting of the Mountains of the Moon. This is something I've dreamt of ever since reading Guy Yeoman's book, *To the Snowy Sources of the Nile, Ruwenzori Mountains of the Moon*. From Fort Portal (we nicknamed it Fort Pothole because of the road) we drop sharply to the Queen Elizabeth Park. One always has a vision of what a place will look like, and I envisaged the steep

slopes of the Mountains of the Moon to be covered in evergreen equatorial forest, dropping steeply into crystal-clear lakes. Instead, we cross a savanna-type plain of rich green grass and isolated trees. Golden brown Ugandan cob move across the plain, tame and contented, and everywhere buffaloes are chewing the cud. The area is totally surrounded by gigantic mountains. A lone lioness crosses in front of us and walks, shoulders hunched, towards a large herd of Ugandan cob. We wait for the kill, but she seems content just to stroll.

We drive through this paradise to spend a night camping alongside a deserted and dilapidated fish factory on the shores of Lake George. All the roofing has been nicked along with the doors and windows, but the well-built walls and floors of the enterprise stand strong, a reminder of a time when clipped British accents called the shots and Land Rovers, Standard Vanguards, Morrises and Anglias stood in a neat line outside the white-washed Fisheries office. But that was a long time ago and many things have changed.

In front of our eyes, the Mountains of the Moon throw off their heavy misty garments to reveal themselves naked in the setting sun, their glistening snow-

Nowhere in Africa do we see as many bicycles as in Uganda.

capped peaks shining white in the distance. To the east the sun sets over Lake Edward and Zaïre, and to the west the waters of Lake George change from brown to blue. Hippos grunt, an elephant trumpets in the distance, and pelicans fly home across the sun.

You would think that after 10 months in the saddle we would be getting bored with the wonders of nature, but, to the credit of the pilgrims, their enthusiasm for the expedition and the environment has only grown. There is something about the solitude and the wide-open spaces of Africa that is so close to peace. We are lucky people, but it is not always that easy; I think the most difficult thing in any expedition is proper leadership and good team spirit. If gossip and backbiting are allowed to take place, the expedition will be doomed to certain failure. Tolerance, not only for one another as pilgrims, but also for those people we meet daily, is a key ingredient.

In the deep rural areas the locals have most likely never seen such a circus – colourful boats and vehicles, tents, camp tables and outboard engines. Everyone comes to stop and stare, touch and feel, climb on and off, shove and squeeze. The humidity grows and tempers are short. We haven't slept well because of the hippos. We're sick and tired of putting up a little tent every night, sometimes sleeping on sticks and sometimes sleeping on stones. We'd murder for a cup of filter coffee, soft fried eggs, bacon, sausage, tomato, toast and marmalade. But here we are, trying to put a boat into the water. A few drunks lean against the vehicle for a closer look; one of them spits on me as he talks, excited to see and chat to the visiting *wazungu*. An officious official demands a permit; the man from Fisheries, who hasn't had a visitor in 10 years, wants us to sign a mouldy old visitors' book; the chief of police and a hundred of his friends would like a ride in the boat. The sticky heat is like syrup and the sweat runs into our eyes. Some fishermen on a wooden canoe want their picture taken, demanding a copy. Everybody wants to be a pen pal, and some in the crowd are amazed that white South Africans even talk to black people. With such a reputation to live down, there is even more need for us to remain patient in the ways of this continent. We carry the scroll of peace and goodwill with us wherever we go – proud to be part of the new South Africa and extremely excited and wide eyed at what we're seeing. It's not always easy, but the rewards are great. Take one day at a time and don't lose your cool. Tolerance. Smile a lot and, the more difficult the situation becomes, the more you wave and smile!

Thursday 28 October

The entire village turns out to see us launch *Bathtub* into Lake George, with Nkonkoni Rob, Mashozi, Ross and me on board. Kiboko and Jon kindly offer to take *Vulandlela* round to Katwe on Lake Edward. We agree to meet there at 2 pm. For them it's a beautiful drive through the crater lake area of the Queen Elizabeth Park. For those on the boat it's an opportunity to explore Lake George and the Kasinga Channel that joins lakes George and Edward.

Once into the channel we come across a herd of elephants taking their morning bath, the younger ones completely submerged at times. Thoroughly enjoying their swim, they break the water's green surface with a great splash, sometimes only a few metres from the boat. Others stand on the bank or in the shallows, drinking and eating from the lush vegetation. The steep bank of basaltic 'black cotton' soil shows a muddy black elephant path that climbs up from the river bank onto an open plain beyond. A lone tree signposts the top of the path, high mountains bordering the plain in the distance. With each passing *tembo* the path becomes muddier and muddier. These giant creatures are extremely comical as they engage four-wheel drive, sometimes dropping to their front knees as they finally engage low range, churning through the black mud in order to reach the top of the bank. One cow turns to look at us disdainfully and, with a wave of her trunk and ears, she trumpets a loud farewell before showing us her perfectly proportioned rear end.

As we move downstream from Lake George, now well and truly in the channel, it is as if we have been invited to a special party of the birds and the beasts. There are more elephants, this time with a full entourage of hippos swimming around the large herd, like lifeguards protecting a holiday crowd on a busy beach. But no flags or sirens here, just a loud pair of fish eagles specially hired for the occasion, each perched in a high tree. Their white necks arch backwards and forwards as they signal a warning cry to the excited bathers, two of whom have now swum out into deep water, their trunks sticking out of the green water like periscopes. Every now and then they emerge with a loud crash to lock trunks playfully. This brings angry grunts from the large, wide-mouthed lifeguards and further cries from the feathered sentinels, high up on their perch.

We cut the Mariners and drift. There is a sense of optimism in Uganda, a feeling of peace and harmony, long overdue in this troubled country. Local MPs have done a great job in getting this harmonious feeling through to the wildlife and people living within the Queen Elizabeth Park. Only this morning we saw buffaloes wallowing in a mudhole at the fishing village where we launched – people walked within a few metres of them and one old codger claimed that he even put food out for them. 'These buffaloes are our friends, we treat them with respect and they are polite.' Now on the channel we come across buffaloes lying in the shallows alongside a huge pod of hippos. Buffaloes move in and out of the water, the hippos lie grunting in a contented pod. Adding to all this beauty, the Mountains of the Moon have shaken off their shroud of mist and cloud, and are standing high and dark blue in the distance.

We accelerate and have to swerve sharply to avoid a large and somewhat belligerent hippo who obviously has not been attending the political meetings and is still behaving like one of Idi Amin's old guard. One of *Bathtub*'s pontoons would have provided him with an interesting bite. We are becoming complacent, which is a mistake with *kibokos*: more deaths are caused in Africa by hippos than any other wild animal.

Further downstream, on a small sandbank, are a large hippo cow and her newly born calf. Their hides shine black from water and mud, contrasting with a huge flock of pelicans; shining white in the midday sun they totally surround the mother and child. Unfortunately, the sound of our outboard engines soon has the hippos scampering for the safety of the water. The pelicans take off with a *swish* of their giant wings, their underbellies almost skimming the surface of the water as they escort us for several kilometres, before winging their way back to shore as if from a signal from their squadron leader.

There is so much to see that we have lost track of time. With only half an hour to reach the village of Katwe, we gun the motors, leaving behind us the wildlife paradise of the Kasinga Channel. Soon we're round the point, arriving in Lake Edward. Much larger than Lake George and somewhat clearer, it lies between Zaïre and Uganda.

We meet up with the rest of the party at the mad village of Katwe. It's into the kill-me-quick time of day, particularly scary when some of the imbibers are walking round with automatic weapons. What strikes us again is how the villagers are interacting with the wildlife. A pod of hippos lounges just offshore, quite content to be part of the fishing scene, as fishermen in their large high-prowed canoes, some with outboards, move between them and the land. Never before have I seen hippos so relaxed with humans.

Kiboko and Jon have not had any boating today, so, leaving Ross and Nkonkoni Rob behind to look after *Vulandlela*, Mashozi, Kiboko, Jon and I take off down the shore of Lake Edward. The water is like glass, and, as we get closer to the high mountains that border the lake on the Zaïrian sides, we are overcome by the desire to cross over to Zaïre for a swim in its waters. The water here is a great deal cleaner, but, with the rain clouds gathering, it appears dark and inky in the lull before the storm. Leaving Mashozi on *Bathtub* we leap overboard for a swim and a shampoo, having located a bar of soap. Kiboko balances his camera on an empty fuel container to take a picture of lonely *Bathtub* in the middle of Lake Edward, treading water furiously as he does so, for fear of wetting the most precious thing in his life – his camera.

Succumbing to the temptation to cross over into Zaïre was foolish and risky, not because of border guards, but because we are very short of fuel. I love a gamble and am taking a chance on creeping back on the still water, Mariners at half taps just on the plane. But halfway back the storm hits. The calm water is soon blown into restless waves. I have visions of us running out of fuel, the wind sweeping us back into Zaïre. The crew are skeptical and I bet them a bottle of Captain Morgan rum that we'll make it. Luck is on my side and we arrive back on the proverbial smell of an oil rag.

We bid farewell to lakes George and Edward and the Queen Elizabeth Park as we cross the Kasinga Channel and head south across the park and up the escarpment. I am not yet ready to leave this enchanting area, so we drive east along the top of a ridge that overlooks the park. As luck would have it, and at last light, we find a friendly game camp that allows us to pitch our tents. We eat a budget meal of sweet potatoes, first boiled and then fried in oil with a sprinkling of sugar. The locals tell us that chimpanzees inhabit the forested ravine below us.

Friday 29–Sunday 31 October – Back to Nairobi

We start off through high hills and tea plantations back to Kampala, travelling across broad plains – somewhat drier country with large-horned cattle and acacia trees, a bit like Zululand. The pilgrims constantly take refuge under a tarpaulin as the heavens open.

We overnight at Kisumu on the shores of Lake Victoria, a fitting end to the Uganda chapter of our expedition. My great dream throughout this expedition has been to travel down the entire Nile to reach the Mediterranean, but the war in southern Sudan has ruled that out. Now we need to go back to Nairobi to make our final preparations for the journey north.

Sunday sees us back in Nairobi after a long, cold, wet drive from Kisumu, through the beautiful tea plantations of Kericho and past our old friends, lakes Nakuru, Elementaita and Navaisha. It is freezing cold and the rain has lifted to reveal Mount Longonot, the rim of her volcanic crater clearly visible as we climb up and out of the Rift Valley.

It amazes me that things that would have been insurmountable a year ago we now take in our stride. If you really want to do something badly enough, you can do it. You must just break through the security barriers and liberate your mind. I've found that this very act of liberation is also a great opening of the mind: like a camera, it becomes open to receiving pictures. In the process, thousands of visuals flood in, clear and crisp, yours to enjoy. Roadside stalls, sunsets, people in traditional dress, well-kept cattle, lush forests, faces looking up at us as we pass in our boats and vehicles. The mind, uncluttered and clear, is fully able to receive the kaleidoscope of images that are Africa.

RIGHT: Ross's mobile Odyssey Pub. He gives the pilgrims too much credit and goes bust! FAR RIGHT: In Uganda you are aware of just how much a bicycle can carry. BELOW: Ross and Jon identifying fish species on the Albert Nile.

RIGHT: A celebratory plunge into Speke's source of the Nile.

Our Odyssey to the headwaters of the Nile

THIS PICTURE: We take Bathtub to the very foot of the Murchison Falls.

Faces along the North Road

What a fascinating mixture of cultures, including beautiful Borana women with braided hair; a Samburu woman with a wedding necklace of palm tree fibres and glass beads; Three Phokot girls in a row and Ross, just his eyes showing, dressed as a desert nomad.

professinal
Swimming Trainer

BELOW: A typical Ethiopian village scene - cooking njire over an open fire.

Ethiopia, a land so different from our home in the south. It's an ancient place that dates back to the legendary Queen of Sheba.

THIS PICTURE: Carrying butter to market

TOP: The hubbly bubbly - Africa's favourite. ABOVE: Outside a Borana hut at Torbi. INSET RIGHT: A carved headrest from the south of Ethiopia. RIGHT: St George and the dragon - Ethiopian art on a piece of goatskin. It serves as a bookmark for the expedition journal.

North to
Ethiopia

THIS PICTURE AND TOP: Thousands gather for the 'Timkat' festival, during which the moving of the Ark of the Covenant from Jerusalem is re-enacted throughout Coptic Ethiopia. RIGHT: An Ethiopian prayer stick.

CLOCKWISE FROM TOP LEFT: Greetings from the banks of the Nile in Sudan. Cameraman Tim Chevallier and our Sudanese translator 'Tuk-tuk' Husham. Camping in the Nubian Desert outside Wadi Halfa. An Egyptian policeman guides us through Alexandria. The bridge across the Blue Nile. On the bridge of the gunship Melik - our expedition base in Khartoum. Stopped by the war in southern Sudan, the old Nile steamers sit idle in Khartoum.

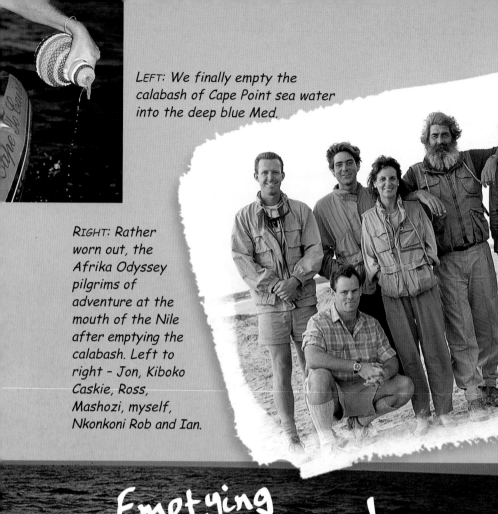

LEFT: We finally empty the calabash of Cape Point sea water into the deep blue Med.

RIGHT: Rather worn out, the Afrika Odyssey pilgrims of adventure at the mouth of the Nile after emptying the calabash. Left to right – Jon, Kiboko Caskie, Ross, Mashozi, myself, Nkonkoni Rob and Ian.

Emptying the calabash!

The long road through Ethiopia

Ethiopia is a unique country in Africa. It is an ancient Coptic land that is recovering from cruel socialist rule and war against neighbouring Eritrea. Although it was not part of our original route, passing through Ethiopia will allow us to experience two of Africa's most incredible waterways, the Blue Nile, and its mysterious source, Lake Tana.

Ethiopian gourd

Thursday 4 November

The bombshell hit with a phone call from South Africa yesterday. The media team will be meeting us in Cairo a week earlier than planned and we have to commit to an arrival date. We can't say no; we have a responsibility to the sponsors who've been so good to us, and if we are there in time we'll all have sponsored airfares back home. We've got used to travelling at Africa's pace, but now the race is on – 34 days to reach Cairo. On the positive side the tired pilgrims are delighted at the thought of finishing soon. Mashozi, whose difficult task it is to guard the purse strings, whispers to me that it is a blessing in disguise – the 'cat burglar' of Nsanje cost us dearly and we are low on cash. So our now impoverished expedition heading north is short of time and money.

Nevertheless spirits are high as we climb through the coffee plantations of Thika and onto the highlands of Kirinyaga, that 'place of brightness' also called Mount Kenya. Rising to 5,200 metres, this is Africa's second highest mountain, an extinct volcano of jagged peaks permanently iced with snow and glaciers. The local Kikuyu and Maasai have venerated the mountain for centuries as home of the great god Ngai, and Mount Kenya's twin peaks, Battian and Nellion, are named after 19th-century *laibon*, powerful spiritual leaders of the Maasai.

We cross the equator for the seventh time on our zigzagging journey across Africa. Leaving Mount Kenya behind us, we descend the steep escarpment in first gear, overloaded with fuel and supplies and towing boats. We are well rewarded with one of the greatest views in Africa.

The tarmac ends at Isiolo, where we feel as if we've crossed an invisible frontier into a region known in the old days as the NFD – the Northern Frontier District – the 'badlands' of northern Kenya. And badlands they certainly prove to be, with horrific road conditions. But what exquisite countryside: wide, flat plains as far as the eye can see. Sticking out of these plains, like sentinels guarding the northern reaches of the country, are massive green buttresses, high rock-faced castles, plum puddings and domes. Although this is still part of Kenya, the nomadic Gabra, Rendille and Samburu who inhabit these parts know no boundaries. Theirs is the life of wide-open spaces and livestock wars. They survive on the blood and milk of cattle or camels when out in the wilderness tending their animals.

It is in this piece of Samburuland, along the shaded Ewaso Nyiro River, that we see the most unusual of game species – the giraffe-necked gerunuk, which look like big impala with elongated necks; Grevey's zebras with their multitude of thin black stripes, named after a Mr Grevey who captured one and donated it to the king of France; and that loveliest of creatures, the exquisitely patterned reticulated giraffe.

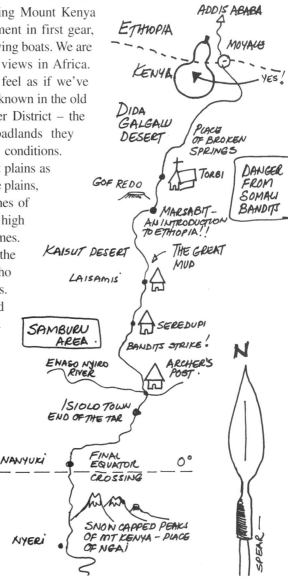

We camp against a rocky outcrop in thorn bush just outside Archer's Post, a dusty row of *dukas* that looks like the remains of a Wild West movie set. This is bandit country, but the military check at Archer's Post indicates that, while it is indeed safer to travel with an armed guard, things have been quiet since the rains. I don't stick around long enough to ask how exactly the rains affect local bandits – maybe the Somali's sit and chew *miraa* during this time. I reckon it must be safe to camp here as, back a short way, I saw a forward-control Land Rover camper parked just off the road. I presume that not everybody is as casual as we are and that he must have checked out the security situation.

Friday 5 November

We're up early – it will take us a full day to do the 180 kilometres through to the town of Marsabit. We bought a few broomsticks in Nairobi. The pilgrims carry these – riding shotgun style on the top of *Thirsty* – in the hope that from a distance we will look like an armed convoy. The beauty of this wilderness grows as we inch our way north, but we must be bloody crazy to be towing boats across this terrain. The road's a killer and we battle to average 30 kilometres an hour.

In the distance we see a Land Rover coming towards us. It's the guy we saw camping on the side of the road last night. He has two armed soldiers with him and has a sorry story to tell. During the night, just up the road, he was held up at gunpoint by three bandits who demanded money. They got some US dollars off the unfortunate fellow, but then a lorry appeared in the distance. Seeing the lights, the bandits told him not to move or they would kill him, and then hid in the bush nearby. But this was his chance, and, fortunately for him, his trusty Land Rover fired up at the first turn of the ignition key and he was off and out of there like a shot. I have a vision of this lone wild-eyed Englishman careening through the bush at full speed, heading for the lonely police station at Archer's Post. When we meet him he is still visibly upset and shaken. He is aborting his safari and returning to Nairobi. We will have to be more careful, and camp in towns or set up camp off the road at last light, out of sight of passers-by.

Next along the road is the Catholic Bishop of the area. Born in America, he lived in Italy and is now the Bishop of Marsabit and surrounds. He brings his Range Rover to a stop as if he were on the Le Mans racing circuit. 'Oh, you are great adventurers,' he roars with mirth and a twinkle in his eye. 'But the road,' he gestures with plenty of hand movements that lend his strong Italian accent even more authenticity, 'the road,' he repeats. 'They have come in the rain with their monsters, those terrible lorries, through the black mud. Oh, I hope you get to Marsabit. But your cars, they are four-wheel drive and you travel with boats, yes? God bless you, my friends.' And he is off with a roar that would make any Formula One test driver proud. His presence has lit up the desert plains. What a colourful character. I guess they have to be a bit crazy to live out here.

The beauty of the Kaisut Desert and the vast expanse of it all gives us an amazing lift. We come across a number of Samburu and Rendille nomads, strong young men with painted faces. They wear loose clothes and carry long sharp spears that are capable of killing a man with one thrust. Some of the blades are protected by leather sheaths, the points covered with a plume of ostrich feathers.

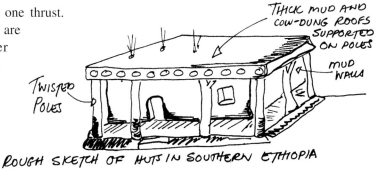

TWISTED POLES

THICK MUD AND COW-DUNG ROOFS SUPPORTED ON POLES

MUD WALLS

ROUGH SKETCH OF HUTS IN SOUTHERN ETHIOPIA

We then hit The Great Mud. This is not a country for pulling boats! Several overloaded lorries are blocking the road, the one closest to us being pushed by about 50 'cowboys', some of them from other lorries, which are also stuck. We can either wait several hours, or we can try to get around them. We decide to give it our best shot. The wheel track on *QE2*'s trailer doesn't run in *Thirsty*'s tracks, which makes this a lot more difficult. We slip and skid, and as we pass one truck *QE2* goes into a slide. With an almighty bang like a rifle shot she collides with the back corner of the lorry. Some of the fellows race for the scrub, others dive under the lorry, thinking that Somali bandits are attacking. Fortunately, being an inflatable, *QE2* has only burst a pontoon valve (hence the bang) and bounces off the side of the lorry. A lot more pushing and shoving, and we're finally past the lorries.

We stop to pick up two American girls perched despondently on a stuck lorry. We saw one of the macho Somali types give a rude sign indicating quite graphically what he would like to do to the two foreign girls, and we feel they will be safer with us.

Marsabit is situated on a hilly island in the desert. It rises 1,000 metres above the plains, the surrounding trees a tangle of foliage and lianas. Thousands of euphorbia cacti are in bloom and the sky is overcast and heavy with rain. It is almost dark by the time we slip and slither into town, boat trailers covered in mud and *Thirsty*'s exhaust starting to roar, a dead giveaway that the whole thing is about to fall apart.

We put up at some Third World digs, grandly known as the Kenya Lodge. The Amharic writing over the door is the first indication that we are nearing Ethiopia. The second is the friendly Ethiopian family who run the place. We are given a safe place to park our convoy, with two ancient security guards thrown into the deal.

For supper we have our first experience of an Ethiopian dish called *njire*, a large flat pancake made from a grain known as tef. To the uninitiated it resembles and tastes like a thin sheet of green sponge rubber, similar to a sponge dishwashing rag. Its only saving grace is the great variety of chopped up spicy food or sauce, called *wat*, with which it is served. You twirl a piece of sponge rubber through the *wat* with your right hand and then pop it into your mouth. '*Wat*' with going into Ethiopia, we are just going to have to get used to it, aren't we!

Saturday 6 November

We're up early heading in the direction of Moyale on the Kenyan–Ethiopian border and soon reach the first police checkpoint. Every roadblock's different, and at this one we sign a tatty notebook and the metal spikes across the road are pulled out of the way with a smile. We pass Gof Redo, a massive volcanic crater just north of the town, and soon we're into wide-open country, cold and wet, a cratered highland perched way above the Dida Galgalu Desert.

According to one source, Dida Galgalu means 'Plains of Darkness', although another account says it's named after Galgalu, a woman buried here after she died of thirst trying to cross it. Plains of Darkness strikes us as very apt, with the black volcanic rock stretching to the horizon, unbroken by a tree or even a blade of grass. This must be one of the most inhospitable places on earth, and certainly not a place to break down in.

The right-hand spring on *QE2*'s trailer is first to go. I am furious with Ian. He had 10 days in Nairobi to attend to this sort of thing, and now we are sitting in the middle of the Plains of Darkness with a broken trailer spring and no spares. The AOE has been a great learning curve. Such an expedition needs a jacked-up mechanic who can really solve problems and is motivated. But this negative thinking isn't constructive. We always make a plan and that is why the expedition is successful. Soon the spring is shored up with two planks bound together with 'Always tape' and tied into the gap between the leaf spring and trailer chassis with fence wire and old motorcar tubing. All this takes several hours, with many stops and starts before we come up with a foolproof solution that we hope will last all the way to Addis Ababa.

Earlier this morning we relieved a broken-down lorry of their armed guard, a taciturn fellow by the name of Dinow. This makes us all feel a lot more secure, but Dinow really is having a bad day. No sooner does he abandon the lorry for a supposedly quicker ride than he finds himself on the side of a particularly desolate piece of road in the company of some crazy adventurers who are binding up a broken spring with a roll of plastic tape branded Always Sanitary Pads in bold blue-and-white lettering (we'd been given a box of the multipurpose stuff in Nairobi). After an hour or three in the blazing hot sun, he hitches a ride with a passing lorry, leaving us in the middle of nowhere to the mercy of Somali bandits. May the fleas of a thousand camels be his constant companions!

Well, needless to say, we don't make Moyale, and it is late afternoon when we limp into the village of Torbi. We are informed that we will not be allowed to continue from here to Moyale without an armed escort or unless we are part of the organized convoy that departs from here every day at about noon. We chat to the administration police in the village, and they agree to let us have two armed guards, but there is no way we can leave now as it is far too dangerous. And no one, but no one, has Land Rover springs, new or second-hand, to sell or give away. To make things worse, one of the leaves on *Bathtub*'s trailer has now also broken.

Reverend Alex Guyo, a delightful chap, lets us sleep in Torbi's little Catholic Church. The veranda of this quaint church soon becomes a social centre and two Ethiopian hitch-hikers, Muhammad and Yared, join us. They are excellent company, and Yared agrees to go with us all the way through to his home in Addis Ababa. So now, in addition to the seven of us, we have a guide who speaks Amharic, his friend, two armed guards, and the two American girls we picked up. What the hell! We're all on the Great North Road to Ethiopia.

Sunday 7 November

Our two friendly escorts look sprightly and efficient in their khaki uniforms and berets, proud members of the Kenyan Administration Police. But before we can leave I have to meet with their commanding officer, who I feel is far more interested in his *chai* (conveniently the word for either a cup of tea or a bribe) than our safety. It takes a couple of Continental jackets and the promise of 100 Kenyan shillings to be paid in Moyale before we have a deal. So, hoping fervently that our springs will last and that the bandits are taking the Sunday off, we head into the desert. The fact that our guards exchanged fire with three bandits who ambushed the convoy just a few days ago does little for our confidence.

In Torbi we move ahead of the line of lorries waiting for the official convoy to leave at noon. If we break down, at least we will have the convoy behind us. The two guards sit in the back of *Thirsty*. James Ndungu, round-faced and shiny black, looks tough and confident, a bright white smile lighting up his ebony face, his whole manner exuding youthful energy. I just hope he can shoot straight. Shana Mohammed Diba is more mature. Born a Gabra, he shows the fierce fighting spirit of those nomadic people, and has seen a great deal of action fighting bandits from Somalia.

The bush becomes thicker and thicker after Torbi, and the escorts became more and more tense, especially when we reach the area where they had the recent shoot-out. They are great fellows, and they really seem to enjoy being our unofficial tour guides – I'm sure they are the first ever to escort rubberducks to Ethiopia. James Ndungu transposes his L's and his R's and blames the poor condition of the 'load on the rollies'.

By afternoon we are safely in Moyale, the frontier town astride the Kenyan–Ethiopian border. We use the last of our Kenyan shillings to stock up on fuel and then set off to the Ethiopian border officials (Kenyan side) for the moment of truth. This is the make or break of our expedition.

OUR ROAD TO THE SUDAN – BAD

GONDAR

LAKE TANA

BAHIR DAR

THE BEAUTIFUL BLUE NILE FALLS

MOTA

ABAY (BLUE NILE)

DEJEN

SUDAN

BLUE NILE GORGE

DEBRE LIBANOS MONASTERY

ADDIS ABABA

FROM LAKE TANA OUR NEXT OBJECTIVE IS TO GET OUR BOATS DOWN TO THE CONFLUENCE OF THE BLUE AND WHITE NILES IN SUDAN

We ask the two American girls to go in first without us, as we don't want them to queer our pitch. Shame, I really feel for them as they are refused entry and told to go back. Trying to look confident, I respectfully remove my hat, smile a lot and shake hands with everyone. We ask to speak to 'Mr Big', and with a flourish Mashozi brings out the paperwork from her tattered bag: the now bulging Afrika Odyssey scroll of peace and goodwill; the sealed letters from Nairobi written in Amharic (which we can't read and which probably say 'shoot the visitors'); the boat and vehicle carnets; and the passports. I hold my breath as 'Mr Big' tears open the envelope embossed with the Ethiopian government seal. With a furrowed brow he slowly mouths the words of the letter before saying, 'Please, you wait. I contact Addis.' And so, in the heat, we wait patiently. Africa, remember, owns the time!

Our mood of despair is finally relieved late in the afternoon with a handshake from 'Mr Big' who, with a broad smile, says 'Please you Mister, welcome to Ethiopia'. Phew!

But now the officialdom begins in earnest, starting with a two-hour search of all our equipment. The officers scrutinize Mashozi's make-up box (an old metal ammunition box that always gives us problems), Ross's Odyssey bar (they love the contents) and the medical kit. Even the little calabash, still full of sea water, is removed from its safe haven and passed from one customs officer to the other. They smell the contents, now really starting to *nuka*. Thank goodness for Yared, our hitch-hiker guide, whose translations save the day.

It's late by the time Customs and Immigration finish with us, and we camp in no-man's land between Kenya and Ethiopia. A bitch on heat seeks refuge in our camp and is followed by her noisy suitors. Hyaenas cackle in the distance.

Monday 8 November – 29 days to get to Cairo

Up early we strike camp. The boom is lifted with a salute by a veteran in a sun-bleached khaki uniform and old pith helmet. We're in Ethiopia at last.

After our experience with Customs I am expecting the worst from Ethiopia, but the Ethiopian side of Moyale has quite a vibe, different from any we've encountered in Africa. There is different writing, a different language, old Fiat lorries everywhere, Borana walking the streets with their camels, and pastry shops – a throwback to Italian occupation – that serve an assortment of doughnuts, cakes, biscuits and iced buns. In the little restaurants the steam jets of old-fashioned Italian espresso machines spurt hot cinnamon tea into little glasses loaded with sugar. Prostitutes smile from doorways.

Accompanied by the roar of *Thirsty*'s colander of an exhaust, and driving on the right-hand side of the road for the first time on our expedition, we hobble north towards Ethiopia's Rift Valley lakes. Then the roadblocks start, some of them rude and officious.

The scenery is incredible – savanna-type grasslands with scattered acacia trees, and the striking Borana with their cattle. Mountains of second-hand Western clothes (known locally as 'dead man's clothes') give colour to the dusty markets; in every village young men are playing table tennis in the shade of verandas and under trees, the old Italian signs telling of a bygone era. The road throngs with trucks, camels, goats, sheep, cattle, donkeys and horse-drawn carts. It is another world.

The roadblock at Yabelo is quite an experience. Everybody is high from chewing *miraa*, green slime oozing from the corners of over-relaxed mouths, automatic weapons pointed haphazardly. Luckily for us, this time the man in charge, complete with old cowboy hat, is friendly – our documents and Yared's translations are our saving grace.

The countryside is dotted with massive white and red-ochred anthills. We limp on across this unusual landscape until evening when we set up camp on the edge of an escarpment with endless valleys and hills beyond.

At about 2 am a vehicle stops close to our camp. Car doors open and there are voices. Fearing bandits, I leopard crawl to the pilgrims' tents and alert them. We grab our sophisticated weaponry – wheel spanners, a spade and a pick handle. After a short while the vehicle with its floating voices takes off into the dark. Ross laughs at his over-zealous old man, but one never knows.

Tuesday 9 November

We wake up to a group of Oromo gawkers – young boys and girls and an old fellow who promptly takes a camp chair and makes himself at home. He accepts a toasted bun, but has difficulty with the plum jam and peanut butter – a very different taste I'm sure from his usual *njire*. A beautiful girl from a nearby Oromo village arrives to sell us fresh cows' milk and butter carried in handsomely decorated gourds.

We have now left the badlands behind us and are in a world of greenery. Meadows stretch like lakes between towering evergreen forests and mountains. I had visions of dry barren conditions, but this is perfect farmland. It seems amazing that on a continent that is plagued by drought, one particular famine has created the misconception that Ethiopia is a food-starved, barren desert. Nothing could be further from the truth.

Ninety per cent of Ethiopia's population are farmers, and farming practices here have not changed in generations. The rains have stopped, and the wheat is being reaped by thousands of peasant farmers bending from the waist in fields of yellow that stretch to the horizon. Donkeys pull the crops from the fields on little carts with ancient iron-rimmed wheels. The wheat is threshed by oxen walking over it in circles. This is how Europe must have been before the Industrial Revolution.

We are travelling at a high altitude now, and there are no camels here, just tough little packhorses heading to market carrying *kocho*, a dairy product mixed with oats, the pack bundles wrapped up in banana leaves. As always the roads are crawling with Fiat lorries and pedestrians, the women bent over with firewood and other bundles, all carried on their backs. Local women grind their coffee on the tarmac, a good hard surface, and the process encourages roadside sales.

We need to stick to first gear low ratio down the steep hills, as *Thirsty* has developed severe brake problems, and we've put big *QE2* behind *Vulandlela*. One of the springs on the other side of the trailer breaks a leaf. We move on slowly.

Back in the African Rift Valley, we explore a chain of small lakes, Ethiopia's share of the Rift Valley lakes. The first is Lake Awasi next to the town of Awasi. Here horse traps with colourful canopies and rubber wheels, complete with springs (we're envious), serve as local transport. After the solitude of Lake Tanganyika and the other Rift Valley lakes that we've explored, we find Lake Awasi a bit too crowded. Nevertheless it is extremely beautiful and the thick fringing vegetation of wild fig trees is teeming with birdlife: fish eagles, silvery-cheeked hornbills, the endemic black-winged lovebird and a variety of terns, plovers, herons and other waders. Feeling that it's too populated to camp here, we move into the somewhat delapidated Wabe Shebele Hotel No. 2 where we are the only foreign guests.

Wednesday 10 November

After watching the black-and-white colobus monkeys performing acrobatic stunts in the trees of the hotel, we get an early start from Awasi. We have been pushing hard for days now and are all tired. One of *QE2*'s trailer springs is still tied up with Always, the other is running on a lick and a promise. The temporary repair to the spring on *Bathtub*'s trailer is holding well.

The busy countryside becomes drier and drier as we make our way along the floor of the Great Rift Valley. At the junction town of Shashemene we take a morning break at a spotlessly clean Ethiopian pastry shop, sitting down to fresh cakes and well-sugared cinnamon tea. In Ethiopia we feel we have left the Africa we know behind, especially now that we are well into the country. Here you have a sense of an ancient civilization that is frozen in time, owing to the feudal system under Haile Selassie, followed by the terrible ravages of war and Soviet influence.

The only hassle is the 'you-you' and the 'hey-you' brigade. The Cubans and Russians had no way of communicating with the locals except in limited English, which consisted largely of 'Hey you, come here!' Ethiopia has not had foreign visitors for years, and we're at the receiving end of *Faranji* Fever (*faranji* means 'foreigner'). On seeing us, crowds of people, mostly kids, go mad, screaming, 'Hey-you! You-you! Give money! *Faranji* you!' They tug and pull at our clothes, and we have to post a lookout on top of each vehicle to watch for itchy fingers around the boats and trailers.

At one stage, while I'm sitting in the open back of *Thirsty* with one leg out of the vehicle, someone tries to pull the boot off one of my feet! The thief, a teenager, spins

into the crowd like a top when I catch him behind the ear with a slap aided by the forward motion of the vehicle. The crowd fortunately see the funny side, pointing at him and howling with mirth. He obviously knows a one-legged man with a size 13 foot!

It is hot and dry as we leave the main highway and turn west along a dusty track that soon drops steeply down to what must be one of the loveliest Rift Valley lakes, Lake Shala. We get our first glimpse of blue water, shining brightly in the noonday sun and ringed by steep cliffs. The lake, the deepest north of the equator, is a 266-metre-deep crater, its surface broken by small volcanically formed islands.

We have been warned about bandits, but the only people we encounter along the lake-shore are a few herdsmen, who are extremely friendly. Armed with long sticks with a hook on the end, they shake the high branches of the flat-topped acacia trees, bringing down a rain of pods that are snapped up by the livestock waiting expectantly below. Volcanic rock pebbles dot the lakeshore, so light they float in the water. The hot springs in the north-east of Lake Shala are used by the locals to boil maize cobs and to bathe.

Flamingos wade in the shallows, showing off their pink wings in flight every time we get too close. An island in the centre of the lake is a breeding ground for pelicans that fish in nearby Lake Abiata. A few months ago we would have dallied here for at least a week, but now there's a sense of urgency. Forever forward!

At Shala the second spring breaks on *QE2*'s trailer. Kiboko, Ross and Ian tie it all together and put in a block. We now have a solid suspension, and let the tyres down to under one bar, our flat Continentals acting as our suspension. It must be hell on the tyres.

There are horses, carts, donkeys, Fiat trucks, pedestrians and you-yous in every village. Trying to avoid potholes, we finally hobble into Addis Ababa.

Ethiopia's capital lies in the central highlands at an altitude of 2,400 metres, making it the third highest capital in the world. We ease our convoy through the traffic, old blue-and-white Fiat taxis everywhere, street kids shouting 'Give me Birr! Stomach empty!' (Birr is the local currency). Fortunately we still have Yared to translate and guide us. He agrees to takes us to a hotel before he leaves us, but first we must visit his family and meet his girlfriend – for whom he has braved the Nairobi–Addis road. She's beautiful!

It's dark by the time we find a suitable hotel, which means cheap with safe parking. The pilgrims camp in the grounds and Mashozi and I take one room so as to have a lock-up and shower/toilet area. We are offered a lower rate if we vacate the room during the day. It appears there is a good daytime trade in girls and rooms.

Thursday 11 November

In the morning Ian and the team jack up each trailer wheel. The broken springs come apart in their hands. The hotel manager tells us that the only place to get replacements is at the springs section of Addis market. First agreeing on the fare, we throw the pieces of spring into the back of a 'blue-and-white' and are off to the market. The Markato, the commercial hub of Addis, is a vast grid of passageways with kiosks, shops and stalls. You can buy anything here – mountains of green *miraa*; camel saddles; ornate horse bridles; richly woven carpets; shawls, scarves and turbans; fly whisks; wooden headrests; intricate jewellery, and spices, fruit, vegetables and coffee beans.

We find the springs section next to the tinsmith and the pot-soldering sections. The springsmith's fire is roaring, and every shape and size of spring is being welded and beaten into shape. Yared, back with us as a guide, urges the smith to hurry our job, but he is more interested in beating the hell out of a massive Fiat lorry spring. 'Come back tomorrow' is the best that we can get. So, leaving our pile to be welded and tensioned, we wander back into the streets and burrows of the Markato, followed by a group of you-yous.

The language of AMHARIC is strange and difficult to our ears! But we soon learn a few magic words! TENESTALEGN – Hullo; SALEM – peace; CHIGGER YELLEM – no problem; and ISHEE! which means O.K.!

We decide to enjoy ourselves in Addis. Despite the poverty, the hundreds of soldiers, landmine victims and cripples, the shadow of socialism and the Russian vehicles, and the austere Revolution Square, the city is now, after the war, full of bustling hope and activity, lively pubs and eating places. In the hotel in the evening a troupe of white-robed musicians, beating a hand-held drum, tambourines and playing a simple violin-type instrument, approaches our table. With a shriek a young girl leaps forward. She's beautiful, her eyes shine and to the beat she twitches her neck and jerks her shoulders, building up to a fast jerky rhythm, her diminutive breasts wobbling furiously under her white cotton robe. She is joined by a male dancer who, facing her, also begins to twitch and jerk to the Tigrean Shoulder Shudder. The tempo quickens and their shoulders take on a dislocated frenzy – partygoers swig glass after glass of *taj*, a mead-like drink made from honey beer. It's cheap and has a kick on it like a mule. There's the aroma of roasting coffee beans wafting from the coffee ceremony taking place in the corner. We order *kai wat*, a delicious, fiery, orange-coloured stew with Hmmm! *njire*. Nkonkoni Rob overdoes the *tej* and is soon talking loudly. Ian mumbles something about springs and retires early to bed.

Friday 12 November – 25 days to Cairo
While Ian, Ross and Jon take off to the market to check on the springs, Kiboko Caskie writes letters, and Mashozi and I go into town to be tourists. It's late afternoon when we get back, to find that the boat trailers are jacked up, and the rebuilt springs are being bolted into place. Tomorrow we leave. But first there's some urgent and creative paperwork to be attended to. Using an old borrowed typewriter and a razor blade we make our vehicle papers valid for Sudan.

Saturday 13 November
There is a new feeling of optimism among the expedition members as we grind our way out of Addis Ababa, a strange city where Coptic Christians and Muslims live side by side, and where the rubbish dumps are shared by people, dogs and hungry hyaenas, all scrabbling to survive.

As in so many places in Ethiopia, the scenery heading north from Addis is quite breathtaking, with a slightly medieval feel to it. The 13th-century Coptic monastery of Debre Libanos is built on the side of a steep 700-metre-high sandstone canyon north of Addis. Our Ethiopian letters and scroll are shown to the high priest who allows us to camp in the ancient compound. We have a view of Haile Selassie's favourite church, built in the 1950s, its huge dome towering above the trees.

There is a Coptic festival taking place inside the church and we are invited to attend. The light streams through the stained glass window, assisting the yellow glow of the candles. White-robed monks and priests sway to the rhythmic beat of the ancient rawhide drums, and old men lean on their prayer sticks. The congregation lines up to be blessed by the high priest, who touches their Coptic cross necklaces to his lips. Smoking censers swing slowly from side to side, and the priests gather in a circle, moving forward in a shuffling, swaying dance that dates back to the time of King Solomon and the Queen of Sheba. We stand, hats off, in our old expedition clothes, mesmerized by the timelessness of it all.

In the grounds of the monastery we find monks living like wild animals in caves in the cliffs. Piles of old bleached bones and skulls lie in a huge open grave – Coptic Christians who were murdered by Muslims.

It's a cold and misty night. We put up our tents and huddle round a small fire. A tall man in an ancient overcoat, a rifle over his shoulder, paces up and down outside our camp.

Sunday 14 November

Outside the monastery we halt to gaze over the sandstone canyon across to the terraced hills and valleys that stretch forever. Long-haired gelada baboons scramble along the cliff face and a giant lammergeier circles overhead. Even a year wouldn't be enough to explore Ethiopia thoroughly, and I vow to return.

It is a thrill to be winding our way down the tortuous road through the kilometre-deep Blue Nile Gorge. The road, with its hairpin bends and stone viaducts, is a masterpiece of Italian engineering. Running against compression in first gear with the weight of the boats behind us, we slowly wind down to the bridge that crosses the Blue Nile. There are armed soldiers and I decide it would be crazy to stop and film the bridge. Here the river arcs south out of Lake Tana to rush down through the fearsome Blue Nile Gorge (unfortunately totally unnavigable in our boats), before gushing out of Ethiopia into Sudan. Our next waterway objective is perfectly clear – to reach and explore Lake Tana, source of the Blue Nile. This is Ethiopia's largest body of water and is dotted with islands that have long attracted monks and religious mystics to the lake's shores. We will base ourselves at Bahir Dar on the edge of the lake and explore the islands from there. What a great adventure!

Friday 19 November – 18 days to get to Cairo

From Bahir Dar on Lake Tana we snake up the dusty road to Gondar, capital of Ethiopia for 250 years and founded in 1635 by Emperor Fasilidas. We are amazed by its royal enclosure, the streets thronged with horse traps and serious-looking horsemen in

Bahir Dar, Lake Tana, Ethiopia
18 November 1993

Hi Debbie

Yesterday we launched our boats into Lake Tana, source of the Blue Nile - being more than 1,800 metres above sea level we had difficulty in getting them to plane. Here the attraction is not the lost tribes, big fish, crocodiles or hippos, but rather ancient Coptic monasteries, dating back to the Middle Ages, that stand like sentinels on the thickly wooded islands of the lake, guardians of the 2,000-year-old Coptic faith. These are holy places that have survived the recent war with Eritrea and the wasted years of Russian domination.

On one island in the lake a priest dressed in a long robe walked slowly, a cross in one hand, a smoking censer in the other. Over his shoulder was slung a rifle - a warning to bandits to keep away from the Coptic treasures. Huge wooden doors creaked open to reveal exquisite wall paintings. Our eyes took time to adjust to the low light. There was the smell of damp and bats.

On the wall in front of us Father Johannes was depicted with angel wings, delivering from Jerusalem the large iron keys that only a moment before had been used by the priest to allow us to enter into this inner sanctuary. Christ and his Ethiopian disciples were painted as white men; the prophet Mohammed was on a camel being led by the Devil. Leather thongs taken from the hides of 90 oxen tied thousands of saplings to the ancient roof trusses that supported the circular thatch roof. Outside the church a long piece of hand-chiselled iron stone hung as a gong to summon the monks to church. Such a place is the source of the Blue Nile, known here as the Great Abbai.

The next time we see this river will, I hope, be at Omdurman, Sudan. From here it's north to the Sudanese border. We just hope they're going to let us across. Hold thumbs.

Lots of Love

Kingsley, Mashozi and the team

traditional dress, as well as the great stone castle. While Ian is supervising another trailer suspension welding job, we visit the old Royal Baths and the elaborately decorated Debre Birhan Church, where the eyes of the painted angels seem to follow you around.

We ask the local lorry drivers their advice. 'Is it possible to travel from here down through the mountains to Sudan?' They gawk at our boats with amazement. 'You want to tow these? Such a thing has not been done before!' But they are able to reach the Sudanese border with their tough old Fiat lorries, so we figure, if they can, why can't we? We are only 180 kilometres from the border with Sudan.

Saturday 20 November - The road to Sudan

Along the rough road from Gondar everybody seems to be dressed in blue with tall hats. Peasant women with the finest features walk barefoot over the stony track that curves down to Sudan. There are pack-donkeys and packhorses, people and livestock unused to vehicles, and armed men everywhere. We pass a funeral procession, the corpse, wrapped in cotton, carried shoulder-high by bearers. Many members of the procession are armed with an assortment of weapons, from AKs to old muzzle-loading rifles. This is a land of bandits and old feuds. After a day of crawling along the rugged route, we camp in the dark, making sure to move off the road into the thick bush for our last night in Ethiopia. Sudan, here we come – or so we hope. Bean stew and rice!

Sunday 21 November

Today I'm driving *Vulandlela* with Mashozi alongside me. The road is narrow with a steep drop-off on either side. I ask Mashozi to check on *Bathtub*, which we are towing. She leans far out of the window to make sure that the trailer is still in the tracks behind us. Her Zulu bangles catch the door latch, the door swings open and she falls out of the truck with a thud and a scream. I instantly jam on the brakes. She's fallen onto a rock and slipped backwards, her head just centimetres from the back wheel. A split second more and her head would have been crushed. She is ashen with fright and her lower back is in agony. Medic Jon injects her with muscle relaxant and we feed her painkillers. She's so tough and she never complains, but I can see that she's in great pain.

We are about 100 kilometres from the Sudanese border, which can mean a full day or more depending on road conditions. First we travel through the normal patchwork fields with views that go on forever. It becomes a lot drier as we make our way through spectacular countryside with swift-flowing rivers, clear with highland water, and huge rocky outcrops. We are dropping out of the highlands now and the road to Sudan gets progressively worse.

The wet season has just finished, and the tough Fiat lorries on which Ethiopia's transport system relies have left tracks in the mud so deep that in some cases the *middel-mannetjie* is nearly half a metre high. This means considerable delays as we have to make detours through the bush.

Metal bridges along the way have been supplied by Britain, and the strong metal has remained in good order, lasting through countless floodwaters. Not so the planks that form the roadway over the bridges. In most cases we have to put each wheel on a steel girder, and with someone guiding, inch our way across, a bit like tight-rope walking. On this road we can only average about 10 kilometres an hour. It is really slow going, and the drivers are paranoid about breaking more springs. We must be crazy, but the alternative bridges have washed away and this is the only way to reach Gedaref and the Blue Nile.

We have left the stone walls and wattle-and-daub homes of the highlands behind. Now the countryside is dotted with conical grass hut villages, their top-notches etched against the dust-filled sky. There are healthy cattle everywhere and the fields stand high with ripe millet. Right now this is not a waterway expedition but rather a 'roof of Africa' rally towing boats, and the race against time is making everybody edgy. It really is a shame to have to rush the last leg of this fantastic adventure.

Eventually we make it through to Matema at the border. It has taken 10 hours to cover about 80 kilometres. Armed soldiers wave us to a halt. A young and rather nervous customs official tells us that we will have to go back to the village of Shedi, as at Matema they don't have a customs stamp. So tomorrow we'll have to go back to Shedi to find a man with a stamp.

We spend the night at a Matema hotel, a row of little rooms with cow-dung floors and a courtyard where some Ethiopian guests slaughter a sheep and roast it over a fire. Here also some Sudanese Muslims pray to Allah. A pretty waitress offers services other than food and honey beer, and I point to Mashozi and decline – everybody laughs. Loud music plays long into the night. This is our last night in Coptic Ethiopia. Tomorrow we cross into the land of Islam – that's if I can find the man with the stamp.

Monday 22 November

Taking *Vulandlela*, and travelling without the boat, the friendly Ethiopian immigration fellow and I race back down the dusty track to Shedi. Dodging camels and goats, we finally arrive in a cloud of dust. But no immigration official. We bang on the office door – nothing! My friend from Matema sees the look on my face and goes to the back of the house – more banging. The sun is starting to burn and I wait on the veranda with my little pile of passports. Rude shouts from inside the building indicate that at least there is life, and finally a dishevelled and red-eyed customs man appears, holding in his hand that great African treasure, so respected from colonial times – The Official Rubber Stamp and Ink Pad. And so finally we are stamped out of Ethiopia and I impatiently head back to Matema and the rest of the team.

Ethiopian tomb – the painting shows that the deceased was a rich cattle owner.

Tracks through the Nubian Desert

Following the old British railway line through the Nubian Desert

The guide book reads: 'Due to escalating civil war, present travel in Sudan cannot be recommended and is at your own risk. Travel in Sudan is only for the most adventurous and hardiest of travellers.' It is no wonder that the Sudanese are uncertain if, as an age-old proverb reads, Allah laughed or cried when he created Sudan.

Monday 22 November (continued)

Our doctored vehicle carnets get us through the Sudanese border at Galabat. On the other side it is intensely hot, and we have to travel in an armed convoy in case we encounter bandits. The Sudanese ride old blue Bedford trucks like camels, with their white robes flowing out behind them. The landscape is flat for miles, and the deep Bedford ruts and tracks are a killer.

Once out of the Sudanese badlands we travel alone. Four punctures later we are offered thirst-quenching sweet black tea in the village of Alum. Last night we drank the last of our booze, not wanting the Muslim Sudanese authorities to find any in the vehicles. The punishment is 40 lashes in public if you're caught with alcohol. It's going to be a long, hot, dry expedition across Sudan, but I'd rather keep my already sore back as the property of corrugated roads and bouncing boats.

Kiboko's skills with a high-lift jack are invaluable as we constantly jack *Thirsty* off the high *middelmannetjie*. Needing to replenish our water, we stop at a well surrounded by people and livestock. The heat is killing and the pilgrims gulp down water straight from the well. I have a tiff with mild-mannered medic Jon, telling him off for not using purification tablets, or boiling the water first. As medic he is responsible for the drinking supply. He gets annoyed with me, I feel bad, and we're all a bit tense as we push on. Later, while we are fixing yet another puncture by the light of the vehicle I apologize. I shouldn't have barked at him in front of the others. We shake hands. He really is such a good man. Ross is my right-hand man, and Nkonkoni Rob gets better as things get tougher. And poor Mashozi, who has held on through thick and thin, is doped up on painkillers, sitting in the front of *Thirsty* propped up and padded with pillows and sleeping bags. I suggest that we airlift her out of Khartoum, but there's no way she'll agree. She's come this far and for her there's no turning back now. We sleep in an open field of dry maize stalks. Pasta soup and bread; no grog!

Tuesday 23 November – Two weeks left

We are awake at first light. We realize with horror that the oil seal on *Thirsty* is damaged, but decide to push on in the unbelievable heat. We are all tired, and Mashozi is exhausted and in great pain from her back. We stop at a small roadside shop and Kiboko breaks the Odyssey record, chugging down 18 Cokes. Heat, heat, heat, and the race against time. At the agricultural town of Gedaref we put our watches back. Here it is the same time as in South Africa.

Suddenly smoke bellows from *Thirsty*'s left hub, and there's the smell of hot oil. We grind to a shuddering halt in the main street of Gedaref. The oil seal is gone, and the wheel bearings have collapsed and ground a furrow into the half-shaft. Ian, black with grease, sits in the road next to *Thirsty*, the wheel off, the damaged part lying in front of him. Tears run down his tired cheeks. He admits he knew about this problem in Nairobi, but instead of getting a new or second-hand half-shaft he'd had the old one built-up and machined. We're buggered! Our race against the clock is over.

I feel desperately sorry for Ian. I give him a few words of encouragement and suggest we get something to eat and drink in the shade of a nearby restaurant. The locals, some of whom speak English, are most hospitable, supplying us with tea, cold drinks, biscuits, cakes, and a guide to take us to every garage and spares shop in town. But no half-shaft. We find rooms in town as Mashozi is white as a ghost, and lying flat on her back helps the pain. Is it really all worthwhile? Shouldn't we just postpone the race, phone ahead and call it quits?

Wednesday 24 November

Wide-awake and refreshed, Nkonkoni Rob and Ross decide to extend their half-shaft search to the mud huts and semi-desert plots that make up the outskirts of Gedaref. I start thinking of Plan B: Go in one vehicle to Khartoum and fly a part in from South Africa. But then we'll miss the rendezvous in Cairo, and will have to come up with another plan to get home. We're certainly not going to give up. We *will* empty the calabash into the Mediterranean, come what may!

Next minute there's hooting and cheering. Ross appears, holding up an old weathered half-shaft! They found it lying in the sand among some junk in someone's garden. I can hardly believe it. It fits perfectly – a miracle when you think that our South African model does not match the current models that are imported into Sudan from Japan. By late afternoon we've resumed the race across Sudan, Africa's largest country.

The road to Khartoum is the best we've been on for weeks. Like wild men we race into the night. We can't wait to launch our boats into the Nile. Mashozi is weaker and feverish, and I wonder if apart from her back she could also have malaria. It's close to midnight by the time we find a rough but friendly hotel in downtown Khartoum. Mashozi's fever has broken and we take her to a doctor who says she does not have malaria, but should spend as much time on her back as possible. He gives her an injection, muscle relaxant and painkillers. Her X-ray shows nothing is broken; she's just badly bruised.

Saturday 27 November - Khartoum

Duncan McNeillie flies in again to record our adventure for MNet. With him comes cameraman Tim Chevallier, a delightful adventurer who brings an instant sparkle to the expedition. While I am indeed happy that the sponsors are getting the coverage, we now have the difficult logistics of getting more people and luggage to Cairo. But they're great guys, so what the hell ... Cairo, here we come!

We have to take our papers to the government offices in Khartoum to get permission to travel north through Nubia and to launch our boats into the Nile. There is also fuel rationing because of the civil war in the south of the country, and everything requires a piece of paper. It could drive you to lose your temper, but the people are just so friendly. Friendliness is almost a cult: 'Sudan, we are the friendliest people in Africa. Have some tea! Relax, come back tomorrow.' Bureaucracy and delays, delays, delays. It would not normally worry us but we are chasing for Cairo, and so for the first time we are at odds with Africa. Everything is *Insha Allah* – it will only happen with Allah's will. So be patient, don't get tense, it will happen in Allah and Sudan's own time.

Then I meet Husham Ahmed Abdel Halim. He owns a bright yellow tuk-tuk scooter and ferries me around Khartoum from one government building to another. A modern-day warrior, he takes us under his wing. Nothing is too much trouble. But after 24 hours and two visits to the government fuel depot we still have neither fuel nor papers.

Back at the hotel trouble is brewing. The pilgrims walked South African-style – in rugby shorts, towel over the shoulder, toothbrush in the mouth, no shirt on – from the hotel room across the courtyard to the communal shower. On the way they passed and greeted a Muslim woman covered in black. There is an uproar as a man in robes pulls out a 9-mm pistol and threatens to do in the expedition members. 'How dare you parade naked in front of my wife?' he screams in an American accent. Out runs the manager; seeing the pistol, he ducks back into his office. The pilgrims, keeping calm, try to sweet-talk the gunman, who is now almost foaming at the mouth. He waves his pistol in the air and then rushes off, intimating that he will soon be back with friends to sort out the team once and for all. The MNet crew looks on in amazement. Welcome to Khartoum.

Husham the tuk-tuk man warns us to leave immediately. He tells us that this is an isolated fundamentalist happening and not typically Sudanese. I believe him. He takes us to the Blue Nile Sailing Club, a grand name for Lord Kitchener's original old British gunship *Melik* that re-captured Khartoum from the Mahdi in 1888. The old gunship, now high and dry, is the clubhouse and becomes our expedition base camp in Khartoum. While we wait for our papers we launch *QE2* into the Nile. It's a great moment for us all and we use every drop of available fuel to explore the confluence of the Blue and White Niles and the surrounding islands. It's a privilege and a dream come true to be at the confluence of the two great rivers, the Blue and the White Niles. We cruise past the minarets of Omdurman and Khartoum. It's dark by the time we return to sleep on the deck of the gunship. Decks that once echoed with British commands and cannon fire, but that arrived too late to rescue Gordon of Khartoum, whose head was cut off by the Mahdi – a victory for Islam and a great embarrassment for the British.

Sunday 28 November - 9 days to D-day
Great news! Husham agrees to come along and guide us all the way down the Nile and through the Nubian Desert to Wadi Halfa. There's to be no mention of money. We're itching to get going, but we still don't have fuel or papers.

We visit Omdurman, where Gordon's head was cut off by the Mahdi. What a change all this is from southern, eastern and Central Africa. Here life is regulated by the muezzins' calls to prayer, white robes, palm trees and the ancient life-giving Nile. And so we wait.

Husham comes roaring into the grounds of the Blue Nile Sailing Club, holding in his hands our permission papers and fuel permits. There won't be enough fuel to get us to Egypt, but we'll make a plan as we go. What a relief! We fill up the fuel containers and prepare *QE2* and *Bathtub*.

Monday 29 November - Trek to Wadi Halfa
We are ready at 4 am and leave from the gunship *Melik* at the Blue Nile Sailing Club, hoping to catch the sun and the moon over the confluence of the two Niles, but our fearless leader Husham arrives late on his tuk-tuk. It is misty and cold as we cruise past Khartoum, North Khartoum and then Omdurman on our left. Finally we're heading down the united Nile, the waters of Ethiopia now mixed with those of Uganda. Ian and Kiboko are driving the vehicles down river to the town of Shendi where they will meet us. The wind is blowing straight up the river, and the chop is not good for Mashozi's back. This isn't going to be much fun. With a dark grey river and the sun a misty ball struggling through the tail end of a dust storm, this is altogether an unattractive morning. Is this to be the Nile?

But the hot sun soon burns away the mist revealing green cultivated lands shining brightly in contrast to their duned desert surroundings. Single-cylinder Lister engines with heavy flywheels driving antique water pumps suck the desert's lifeblood from the Nile. The water is poured into the hand-dug centuries-old irrigation canals that criss-cross this floodplain. Friendly farmers are at work, all in their *telebiar* and *emulas*, and hand-made wooden boats ferry people and donkeys across the river. This is the Nile.

We get to a rocky section, the banks high and steep, the rocks sand-blasted by the desert winds. The river is narrow and deep, flowing swiftly. Here we take one of our historic plunges, the third in this mighty river (the first was at Jinja, Speke's source of the White Nile in Uganda, the second in Lake Tana, source of the Blue Nile). I climb up high onto the rocks to sun myself, elated to be following the Nile again as part of its 6,400-kilometre journey from Lake Victoria to the Mediterranean. Late in the afternoon we take the boats out of the Nile at Shendi. We've covered a good distance and have got an excellent feel for the river. With such limited time, our plan is now to cross the desert to the Atbara.

As we are filming the two boats against the sunset, the security police move in. They look at our documents and assure us all is okay. But, as we are eating mutton stew and bread at the market, the heavies move in again. Our papers and passports are taken off us and we are told to wait in a dusty street where a crowd begins to gather. I've just been presented with an *emma* which Husham has wound around my head Sudanese-style, so we're looking like a bunch of half-disguised wild men. An old man who speaks some English is pushed forward by the crowd to utter his, 'You like Sudan? Sudan people very friendly. We friendliest people in all Africa.' But the heavies don't seem to typify this, and we are taken to a tiny white-washed room.

We sit like naughty schoolchildren waiting on a hard wooden bench outside the head-master's office. We wait and wonder. Even Husham goes quiet. These are the dreaded security police. This is a country known to harbour Islamic fundamentalist terrorist movements who don't like the West, and we wonder how safe we really are. Finally we are escorted up to an office. A senior officer walks in. He's been contacted on the radio. He goes though our papers and Husham explains. Mr Security smiles, the ice has been broken. We are most welcome. A terrible mistake has been made; a junior has misread the situation. What can they do to help us? Three hours later we are escorted out into the vast Nubian Desert. I feel weak from the tension.

In most cases the desert roads are faint, sometimes hardly discernible, tracks in the sand. We sit, Arab-style, on top of the vehicles. We've taken to wearing cotton scarves tied around our neck and faces as protection against the sun, wind and heat. With our headlights on bright and tyres let down to a soft bulge, we ride into the night. Husham asks directions at little mud villages where dogs bark and Nubians come out to give directions, drawing lines in the sand in the light cast by *Thirsty*. Other than *Insha Allah* ('If God wills') and *Salaam Alekum* ('Peace upon you'), we speak no Arabic, and have to rely totally on Husham. He no longer looks like the suave tuk-tuk man we met in Khartoum: dressed in a head scarf with only his eyes showing, he looks like a Nubian. We are constantly getting lost as strong winds blow the sand over the tracks and hours are spent digging the vehicles out of the sand, winching and pulling before finally we stumble across the desert railway line to Atbara. Dog-tired, we sleep in the desert under a tarpaulin on the sand. It makes a change from life in the office!

Tuesday 30 November

Once we're up, some nomadic Zebedias invite us into their tent, where they brew us breakfast coffee so thick that the spoon stands up on end. All they have is a tent in the middle of the desert and a small herd of camels and goats. Through Husham I ask the head of the family what his one dream is, and the answer is, 'My health and peace.' He asks if we can stay a week. Will we visit again? Will I roam the desert with him? Ross and Mashozi point to the vehicles. They know my weaknesses!

We reach the Atbara, one of the Nile's greatest tributaries, but the old rail bridge, also the road bridge, is too narrow for *QE2*'s boat trailer. We are forced to wait and take the ferry that finally gets us across.

The hospitality of the Nubian people is overwhelming. Bribes are completely unheard-of. Offers to pay for hospitality are frowned on. At one village I make the mistake of admiring our host's Nubian costume. That is it – a tailor is called for, and three hours later I walk out decked in an *emma* and white flowing *galabiya*. I'm now a true Nubian, complete with beard.

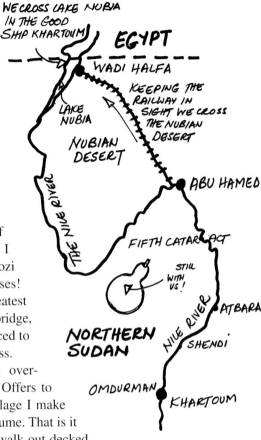

The locals tell Husham about one of the greatest desert guides in Nubia who might be able to help us. We find El Fakiya in his mud-brick house at the village of El Abediya some 40 kilometres north of Berber. Through Husham we do a deal and shake hands. He will guide us across the Nubian Desert to Wadi Halfa. El Fakiya is big and strong and sure of his knowledge of the desert. We travel at night on the full moon. Sand and rocks stretch forever, but our man never hesitates, moving forever onwards.

Sometimes we crawl through the sand at a snail's pace, our tyres deflated to minimum pressure, the vehicles growling in low gear. At other times we are able to cruise at 60 kilometres per hour or more on hard, pebbled sand. While our compass shows the right direction, only El Fakiya has any idea where we are. We're like ships in a sea of sand, the lead vehicle following El Fakiya's hand movements. If he gets lost we'll live for as long as it takes to finish our water supply. We are in the hands of El Fakiya and Allah!

It's about 2 am when El Fakiya motions us to stop by simply raising his hand. Without saying a word, he steps off the running board. He removes his sandals, puts them under his head as a pillow and, unwinding his huge *emma* from his head, he pulls it over himself and instantly falls asleep. A true man of the desert. Everyone follows suit, and within minutes we are all fast asleep.

Wednesday 1 December - 6 days to Cairo

With the Nile River a strip of green on our left, we roar into Abu Hamid. Once again the Sudanese hand of time intervenes, and we spend three hours having passports and papers checked. Fuel? No problem ... except that the diesel man has gone off with the key. While we wait, we eat delicious fatty mutton stew with our fingers and then throw our mattresses onto the mud-floored veranda of the local trading store. Abu Hamid marks the big bulge on the Nile where it swings away to the west before reaching Wadi Halfa. Our plan is to cross this harsh stretch of desert by following the old railway line that was built by General Kitchener in 1897 in his campaign to oust the Mahdi from Khartoum. This is the only route.

Soon the general populace turns out to view the travel-weary group having a siesta on the veranda. Everybody is polite and soft-spoken. Finally the diesel man arrives, walking slowly, keys dangling from his hand. *Salaam Alekum!* The fuel, he says sadly, is 'short'. Husham raises his eyebrows. El Fakiya returns to the mutton bowl.

We scrounge what fuel we can and head off into the desert, our wheels on either side of the railway track – a bad idea. The wheels scrub against the line at times and we bounce over the sand-covered sleepers. We'll rather drive through the desert, but keep the line in sight. It's 370 kilometres to Wadi Halfa – 370 kilometres of sand dunes and wide-open plains of nothing. The only people we see are the station crews, dark Nubians bound in white robes, who offer us water. Dirty fuel is a problem, and we run *Thirsty* at full revs in third gear 4x4, fully laden and pulling *QE2* across an intriguing landscape now lit by the full moon. We collapse in the desert at about 3 am, and are

Using Vulandlela's bonnet as a table, old Mohammed stamps us out of Sudan.

asleep within seconds of our heads hitting dusty pillows. We must get to Wadi Halfa early tomorrow or we will run into the day of prayer which starts at midday on Friday.

Thursday 2 December

We are up before sunrise and our crazy race continues. *Thirsty* ploughs through the dunes as we keep *Vulandlela* and the famous Naidi Khartoum (Kitchener's line) on our right. We stop to film *Vulandlela* and *Bathtub*, two small specks against a never-ending dunescape. In the distance I can see Wadi Halfa and I breathe a sigh of relief. We've completed the 1,500-kilometre journey from Khartoum. Now the challenge is to get the vehicles and trailers across Lake Nubia to Egypt. So we ride into Wadi Halfa in search of a solution. This time we go straight to the head of security. We've learnt that they are the masters. He's a pleasant man by the name of Ibrahim. Husham and I give him the full treatment – scroll of peace and goodwill, magazine articles on the Odyssey, the calabash. I think it is the introductory letter from the head of security in Shendi, however, that does it. Soon Ibrahim is all smiles. We must spend the night and tomorrow – *Insha Allah* – we can have the use of the government ship *Khartoum* to ferry the vehicles and trailers to the distant Egyptian shoreline of Lake Nubia. I just can't believe our luck. But first we must clear customs.

There's an old Bedford lorry leaving for Abu Hamed and the driver offers El Fakiya a ride. We shake hands. *Insha Allah*, we'll meet the great man of the desert again some time.

At 9 am we clear customs. The customs post is built of old railway sleepers – inside, Nubians in white robes run in every direction looking for stamps and a pen. The older Nubians talk with nostalgia about the old Wadi Halfa built by the British, which had decent roads and electricity way back in 1910, the good old days when Nile steamers plied between Aswan and Khartoum before the sell-out and the building of the high dam.

Immigration, in the form of a large white-robed gentleman named Mohammed, refuses to stamp us out of the Republic of Sudan until we are safely loaded aboard the good ship *Khartoum*. This means he will have to work on his day off. It worries us that he won't stamp us out immediately. Is this a reflection of the ship's reliability? Everybody, however, assures us that the boat will come, but this is the Sudanese way. Everything is always possible, you never says 'no' to your guests, but it will only happen *Insha Allah*. So, if it doesn't happen, don't be upset for such is the will of God. So here we are, with our Western ways, wanting things to happen immediately and needing to get to Cairo because we have been crazy enough to agree to a deadline.

Ross and I take Ibrahim and Husham out onto Lake Nubia in *Bathtub*. We cruise across the calm brown waters of the dammed-up Nile. Surrounded by the desert, the minarets, mud huts and palm trees of Wadi Halfa fade into the distance. It's dry and barren, lacking the beauty of lakes like Tanganyika, Victoria or George. Husham takes the controls. He has loved the adventure and I doubt we'd have made it without him. It's Husham the tuk-tuk man who is the hero of our journey.

The sun sets over Nubia. Back on the shoreline we all take the customary plunge. We camp in the desert between some rocky outcrops just outside Wadi Halfa. We discover that before coming into Sudan Mashozi hid some wine in the old tin grub box, having removed the original labels and called the bottles cooking vinegar. We celebrate our last night in the Nubian Desert.

Friday 3 December – 4 days to Cairo

Up at sunrise, we race off to Wadi. But there is no immigration – and no boat. Despondency sets in as we wait among the derelict fishing fleet. Ibrahim looks a bit crestfallen; he ordered the boat to come and pick us up. Ross, Ibrahim and I take off in *Bathtub*, and we find the ferry loading some farm machinery on the opposite bank. There is much shouting. Finally the ship *Khartoum* reaches Wadi to off-load the machinery. No cranes, just planks off the side of the boat and more shouting and screaming. Hilarious. They nearly drop the damn thing into the lake. Then it's our turn. We use our winches to pull the vehicles and trailers on deck and, with *QE2* and *Bathtub* being towed behind, we 'set sail' for Egypt. Mohammed only stamps our passports at the very last moment. From the deck we wave goodbye to Ibrahim, the head of security, and 'Tuk-tuk' Husham.

Egypt, land of the timeless river

The moment we thought would never come: emptying the Zulu calabash of Cape Point seawater into the Med!

On reaching Egypt we feel as if we have left Africa behind and are now part of an ancient world of pharaohs, pyramids, sphinxes and temples. It seems years ago that we honoured Nyaminyami, the great river spirit of the Zambezi. Now we'll need the blessing of Sobek, crocodile god of the legendary Nile.

Saturday 4 December - 3 days to reach Cairo

Our dock on the Egyptian side is a rocky bank in the middle of the desert. After much heaving, pushing and hopping about to avoid the countless scorpions, we have both vehicles and the trailers off the boat, and wave a cheery farewell to Captain Hussan Ibrahim and his merry crew. We have given them enough Sudanese pounds to buy themselves a sheep and have a meal on us.

The officer in charge of the border post is perplexed by our arrival. Obviously permission to cross this border into Egypt has never before been granted by the Egyptian Embassy in Nairobi. Who are we? Israelis come to blow up Lake Nassar perhaps (Lake Nubia is known as Lake Nassar in Egypt)? An Egyptian soldier in camouflage escorts us from the border (two army tents) to the military post just inside Egypt (a cluster of tents and army jeeps in the middle of nowhere).

We are offered *elba* – a hot drink that the head of the camp says will put lead in our pencils – while they radio through to Aswan to get us military clearance to cross this last remaining bit of the desert. This, after we have covered over a thousand kilometres of desert sand. We have a breakfast of carrot jam, flat bread and feta cheese, all army specialities, served with plenty of flies. But there is still no radio reply. And until it comes we cannot move. There is no mistaking the fact that we are now under arrest.

We wait in the desert. The officer in charge takes out a backgammon set. The heat and tension increase. Mashozi takes a bed and sleeps in the shade, a sensible thing to do. I write in the journal. We ask the radio operator how long they will keep us waiting. The reply comes in broken English: 'We like the visitors too much; maybe you stay one year! No, no, no, I mean one day.' Many a true word is spoken in jest.

Achmed, the cook, has been briefed to cook up a desert lunch, which consists of a huge Nile perch, prepared in a tasty tomato sauce and served with bowls of savoury rice. The plates of food are laid out and we all sit round, captives of army hospitality in a desert outpost on the Egyptian–Sudanese border. Only once we have eaten our fill are we finally allowed to drive down the strip of tar that leads to Abu Simbel.

But armed soldiers accompany us, riding with us in our vehicles. The armed sentries that we pass along the way have obviously been instructed to shoot on sight, and one eager conscript walks out onto the road, cocking his gun at the sight of our travelling circus. Fortunately, we have our own armed escorts, whether we like it or not. The elusive Cairo, will we ever get there? The obstacles seem stacked up against us.

We are escorted to the desert town of Abu Simbel, which is a pleasant surprise after the desert wastes of Sudan. There are smart hotels, pavement restaurants and Western music. We go through our normal *indaba* with security – what a cowboy show – with one of the officials so enraged at not being able to reach The Big Man on the phone that he pushes the instrument into the wastepaper basket. Nobody knows what to do with our merry band. There is a great deal of shouting and gesticulating. Everybody's friendly enough, but who is going to take responsibility for our being here? We get moved under escort to a military base in the middle of Aswan.

On our arrival at the base, the bald-headed 'Captain Apparition' comes out in his pyjamas to 'welcome' us. He's a truly horrible piece of work. We camp in the compound, and our every move is watched by armed men. Mashozi goes off to wee among the oil drums and I find 'Captain Apparition' sneaking a glimpse at her bare bottom. Mashozi is furious and tells him so. I start shouting at him. Ross wants to throw a punch and things get tense. Finally, reason prevails and we calm down – after all, they are the ones with the guns!

Sunday 5 December - 2 days to get to Cairo

I beg Aswan's head of security to contact the SA Trade Mission in Cairo, who, together with the media, is planning our arrival event for Tuesday evening. The Governor of Cairo will be accepting our peace and goodwill letter from Cape Town and all the major embassies will be present, as well as a South African delegation and many friends. We are less than 1,000 kilometres from our final destination!

'Oh no! It is not permitted to bring foreign-registered vehicles into the country, especially 4x4s and boats across the desert!' Before they will allow us to proceed we must register the vehicles in Egypt and have Egyptian number plates made. I'm about to blow, and my beard and moustache start to twitch ominously. After the race through Nubia I am on a short fuse. I hand over negotiations to Nkonkoni Rob and Ross. If they can find us a Land Cruiser half-shaft in the middle of Sudan, they can handle these assholes! I take off and go and sit down on the banks of the Nile to vent my feelings in the expedition journal.

After the peace and tranquillity of the desert wastes of Nubia, where everybody is quiet and polite, nothing can prepare you for Aswan. Here everybody wants to sell you something. 'Hey, Mr Moustache! Do you want to ride in horse carriage? Very cheap price! You special friend. Don't talk money now, talk later.' 'You good man – you want to buy papyrus? Genuine – not banana leaf. Look, see, feel! Very cheap, very good!' 'Welcome to Egypt – you special friend. Taxi, you want taxi? Make a very good price, very cheap!' 'You want to go in felucca? One hour for two Egyptian pounds – see Kitchener's Island and Botanical Gardens? No wait, you Mr Moustache, special friend. Make it 15 pounds. We go now!' 'You English? South African! Mr Mandela – good man. You want hotel boat to Luxor?' 'My friend, why not take a cheap taxi to Abu Simbel, beautiful ruins, very cheap?' 'You want hotel? Come with me, very good, very cheap, clean with bath!' 'You want camel ride? Donkey?' 'BUGGER OFF! LEAVE ME ALONE! We have got our own vehicles and our own boats.' 'Don't get angry, Mr Moustache, you best friend! Welcome to Egypt.'

Monday 6 December - 1 day to get there

Vehicle papers and numberplates will be ready by this afternoon. Meanwhile our vehicles and boats are impounded. Tomorrow is meant to be our big night in Cairo. I've phoned to say we're on our way. I gaze out over the Nile, without which there would be no ancient civilization here: the white sails of the feluccas moving slowly across the blue water, the green of the date palms, the yellow-brown sand dunes and the blue, blue sky. Despite our problems, there is only one Egypt and one Nile, and both are fascinating. I have three expressions for all our experiences here: *Insha Allah* – if God wills, *Malaysh* – never mind, and *burka* – tomorrow.

Finally we get the go-ahead. The Egyptian numberplates hang with wire from the front bumpers of our bravehearts *Thirsty* and *Vulandlela*. We're all quite gung-ho as we climb aboard. The narrow road to Cairo follows the Nile for most of the way, with all its livestock, old Peugeot taxis, lorries and pedestrians. The towns and villages buzz with activity. Fuel is cheap and plentiful, mouths fall open at the sight of our convoy and its wild-eyed occupants. We drink a few beers and smile and laugh at the police roadblocks that continue to hassle us all the way to Cairo. Around midnight we stop in a village where plump chickens are being roasted on the side of the road. We buy one each and tear them apart with our hands. The chicken fat runs through our fingers and down our cheeks. What a feast after our hard time in the Nubian Desert.

We continue to drive through the night, *Thirsty* and *Vulandlela* growling softly, happy at last to be out of the sand and on tarmac. Suspensions and wheel balance have really been knocked about and the brakes need to be pumped, but we're almost there. *Bathtub* and *QE2* bounce along faithfully on their buggered trailers, and to our right the moonshine glitters on the River Nile. For the exhausted Afrika Odyssey Expedition Team the end is almost in sight. Now we are running on sheer adrenaline.

Tuesday 7 December - Cairo

It's sunrise by the time we enter the hustle and bustle of the outskirts of Cairo. Ross navigates and I follow. Even at this early hour the choking traffic is crazy. We sit on our hooters, put on the flashers and 'put foot'. The taxis give way, pedestrians giving us curious glances. A couple of times we need to stop to ask for directions. After nearly a year in the African bush it's all a bit too much for us.

At 8.17 am on 7 December 1993, two South African vehicles and two red boats pull up outside the Nile Hilton in Cairo. Out leaps our motley crew, tired, but happy, pilgrims of adventure. There are tears in my eyes as friends rush out to greet us – the media team, Barry Leitch and Mike Boon, old friends from South Africa. Handshakes, bear hugs and kisses. We are all ecstatic. We've survived what at times seemed impossible, some 40,000 kilometres zigzagging across Africa, forever in search of new and exciting waterways. Our world-first has finally brought us to Cairo.

We sit down to a massive full English breakfast and hundreds of questions. Videos roll and cameras flash, but how can you in a couple of phrases explain what it was really like? The images, the simplistic joy of travelling in wild places, not knowing what to expect around the next corner, the beauty of Africa, the people, the pleasure and the pain, our family, Ross and Mashozi, the gallant pilgrims, we've finally made it to Cairo!

What a treat – real baths, showers and flush toilets, fluffy towels, air conditioning and room service ... luxury! And what an evening. We hand over the Cape Town letter of goodwill to the Governor of Cairo. Dignitaries in dresses and suits, imported South African wines and great sides of beef and lamb. Barry Leitch and Mike Boon perform a Zulu dance that makes the South African ex-pats homesick, and the Egyptians belly dance and play bagpipes. We join in and party well into the night. When I finally crawl into bed for the first time in two days, I find it too soft. Mashozi and I opt for the floor instead.

Saturday 11 December - Alexandria

The expedition is not yet over, and today we arrive in Alexandria. The city's governor is a delightful little fellow. We are received in his official chambers, he wearing suit and tie, we dressed in our rag-tag array of shorts and T-shirts, Ian wearing his old felt hat that looks as if it has been chewed by a dog. We produce the beaded calabash filled with

Grogan's journey down the Nile from Fahoda to Omdurman was more relaxing than our odyssey through Ethiopia. 'From Khartoum the Sudan railway soon carried us down to Wady Halfa, thence a steamer to Assuan (Aswan) and again the railway, and we once more stood in the roar of multitudes in the station at Cairo'. And now it is all over. A few dangers avoided, a few difficulties overcome, many disappointments, many discomforts, and those glorious days of my life are already dim ... my thoughts soar to the plaintive cry of the fish eagle, and my heart throbs in unison with the vast sob-sob of all created beasts, that mighty sound that is the very spirit of the veldt.'

Cape Point seawater and place it on a long shiny table, explaining that this afternoon we plan to launch both boats and empty it into the Mediterranean.

The governor insists on calling us 'Your Excellencies' which makes us feel good – almost like people who have crossed Africa. He explains that it has always been a dream of his to travel from Cape Town to Cairo, and that he is happy to see that our country is on the road to democracy. He ends warmly: 'Wercome to Egypt, Your Excerrencies. I not only rike you, but I ruv you!'

We presume he means 'love' and shake hands vigorously. He is a lovely man and presents us with a beautiful book on Alexandria. After a photo session we are ushered out to launch the boats. The ever-present security men follow us around as if we have come to blow up the palace. One of the heavyweights in a leather jacket who is armed with a big gun demands to know exactly where I am going. I explain patiently that prior to launching the boats I plan to go for a large hamburger and Coke, whereafter I will probably pass wind on the promenade. I ask if he has any trouble with flatulence, to which he replies: 'Welcome to Egypt.'

In the late afternoon, we launch both *Bathtub* and *QE2* into the Mediterranean from the Sea Scout jetty near the fishmarket. We are soon out of the harbour and into the deep blue. We cut the motors and without further ado we empty the calabash, which has travelled approximately 40,000 kilometres across Africa to the Mediterranean. The Cape Point seawater is dark brown and has become rather smelly after being inside the calabash for almost a year. It glugs slowly into the waters of the Med. We strip and leap overboard for the last time and in the true spirit of adventure, whooping with joy, ducking each other and shaking hands. Our Afrika Odyssey Expedition across the continent has come to an end. We have made it! *Siyabonga* Mama Afrika!

In the evening, seated on the balcony of a dingy hotel overlooking the ancient streets of Alexandria, I write my final notes in the sweat-stained expedition journal. Horse traps lit with old carriage lamps clip clop past. The muezzin's call to prayer floats on the Mediterranean night air. An old ceiling fan creaks and groans above me. The adrenaline drains from my body. The journey is over! I page to the front of the journal. Inside the cover an old friend scrawled this quotation from the famous Victorian explorer HM Stanley: 'For the traveller who is a true lover of wild life, where can she be found in such variety as in Africa, where is she so mysterious, fantastic and savage, where are her charms so strong ... her moods so strange ....' Like Stanley, my soul has been claimed by Africa.

The paths of the pilgrims

Kingsley and Mashozi: The Cape to Cairo Afrika Odyssey affected our lives and we've never settled down since. Countless other great adventures and expeditions have grown out of it, including an east to west crossing of Africa in the footsteps of Livingstone and Stanley; a circumnavigation of Lake Turkana and the Omo Delta; the Makgadikgadi by land yacht; tracking the Tugela River; and following in the path of Chuma and Susi, the two black heroes of African exploration, who carried Dr David Livingstone's salt-dried corpse all the way from Zambia's Bangweulu Swamps to Bagamoyo on the Tanzanian coast. Our latest expedition is a round-the-world Land Rover journey along the Tropic of Capricorn. Sometimes I think it's a tough life, but most of the time I think we're just bloody lucky, especially to have Ross as a travelling companion.

Ross and Nkonkoni Rob: Ross just couldn't get Africa out of his system. He and Nkonkoni Rob fixed up the vehicles in Cairo and, with a few adventurers to help pay for fuel and grub, went all the way back up the Nile, across Sudan and Eritrea, and finally down to Nairobi. For four years Ross and Rob ran a safari and expedition company specializing in the unusual; built a camp and cultural village with a Maasai community in the Maasai Mara; and generally added to their list of great African experiences and adventures. Ross continues to adventure, on his own and with his old man, but he no longer shows Africa to just a few clients in Land Rovers. The numbers have grown; with his camera skills, our adventures are now shown worldwide on the National Geographic channel. Nkonkoni Rob never went back to the UK; he now runs a successful bush school in Kenya. He's as wild as ever, and speaks fluent Swahili.

Jon: Like the rest of us, he is smitten by Africa. He left the family farm in Zululand and now owns and runs Nile River Explorers, a white water adventure company in Jinja, Uganda. The last we heard from him he was riding a motorbike from Kampala to attend a wedding in Zululand. By the time he reached Zululand via Kenya, Malawi and Mozambique, the wedding was off. So he turned around and went back to his beloved Nile, which he'd first discovered on our shared adventure.

Kiboko Caskie: After Cape to Cairo, farming in the KwaZulu-Natal Midlands seemed boring, so he took off with his camera and travelled the world in a series of great adventures. But Mama Afrika brought him home; if you travel to David Rattray's famous Fugitive's Drift, you'll find Rob Caskie as the colourful resident historian.

Ian: He went straight back to Zimbabwe and his beloved Zambezi. We've lost touch, but he was last heard of in a Harare pub, complaining about broken springs and half-shafts in Sudan. He was still wearing his old felt hat.

Nigel: Married with three children, Nigel now lives in Mozambique and speaks fluent Portuguese. Third-world Africa is his home and he has survived through thick and thin in his newly adopted country, where he still spends time exploring and enjoying this coastal paradise.

Warren: It didn't work out with the girl he rushed back from the Zambezi to be with, but he is now happily married with two children. He farms outside Eshowe, KwaZulu-Natal. He still spends every available moment in boats, fishing and diving the Zululand coast.

Understanding foreign tongues

Asanti sana – Thank you very much (Swahili)

askaris – armed guards or police officers (Swahili)

bamba – grab hold (Zulu)

baraza – veranda (Swahili)

boma – thatched shelter (SA English)

braai – barbecue (SA English from Afrikaans)

brak – water with lots of minerals (SA English)

buibui – long black veil worn by Muslim women (Swahili)

burka – tomorrow (Egyptian)

bwana – mister/sir (Swahili)

chai – a cup of tea or a bribe (Swahili)

chapati – a flour and water pancake (Hindi)

daaga – Tanganyika kapenta/sardine (Swahili)

dagga – marijuana (SA English from Afrikaans)

duka – a small shop (Swahili)

emma – a turban (Arabic)

faranji – foreigner (Amharic)

galabiya – white robes worn in Nubia (Amharic)

galawa – a large dugout with a single sail (Swahili)

goofed – high on marijuana (SA English)

Greens – the common name used for Carlsberg beers in Malawi

Habari? – How are you? (Swahili)

hakuna mutata – not a problem (Swahili)

indaba – discussions (Zulu)

induna – royal advisers (Zulu)

Insha Allah – If God wills (Arabic)

jahazi – a type of dhow (Swahili)

Jambo – Hello (Swahili)

jiko – small tin charcoal stoves (Swahili)

kanga/kanza – colourful cloth worn by women in East Africa (Swahili)

karibu – greeting

kocho – an Ethiopian dairy product mixed with oats (Amharic)

kraal – huts surrounded by a fence, or a pen used for animals (SA English from Afrikaans)

KwaHeri – Goodbye (Swahili)

laibon – a Maasai spiritual leader (Maa)

long drop – a toilet consisting of a deep hole dug in the ground (SA English)

Lala kahle – Sleep well (Zulu)

Lala salaam – Sleep well (Swahili)

litunga – the Lozi king (Silozi)

macho – good luck charm (Swahili)

madala – an old man (Zulu)

malaysh – never mind (Egpytian)

mamba – crocodile (Swahili)

mashua – a type of dhow (Swahili)

mbavu-za-mbwa – dog's stomach, the name for old Austin buses on Pemba (Swahili)

mealies – maize (SA English)

middelmannetjie – the ridge that runs between the two tyre tracks on an unpaved road, literally the middle man (Afrikaans)

miraa – leafy stems chewed for narcotic effect (Swahili)

(u)mlungu – a white person (*abelungu* – plural) (see also *wazungu*) (Zulu)

Mosi – popular brand of beer in Zambia

mtori – a type of dhow (Swahili)

mutato – East African minibus taxi (Swahili)

mzuri sana – very good (Swahili)

njire – a large flat round pancake made from tef; a staple food in much of Ethiopia (Amharic)

nkonkoni – wildebeest (Zulu)

nuka – to smell bad (Zulu)

nyama choma – roast meat (Swahili)

obrigado – thank you (Portuguese)

pesa – money (Swahili)

pombe – home-brewed sorghum beer (Swahili)

Renoster coffee – 'rhinoceros coffee'– strong coffee given the kick of a rhino with an added tot of Captain Morgan rum

rondavel – a small round building, usually with a thatched roof (SA English)

rubberduck – slang for an inflatable boat (SA English)

safari njema – a good journey (Swahili)

Salaam Alekum – Peace upon you (Arabic)

samoosa/samosa – deep-fried triangular pastry, usually with a spicy filling (Hindi)

sangara – Nile perch (Swahili)

sangoma – a diviner (Zulu/Xhosa)

Sawubona – I see you, traditional greeting (Zulu)

shamba – farm or fields (Swahili)

shukas – red or tartan cloth worn by Maasai (Swahili)

simba – lion (Swahili)

Siyabonga – We thank you (Zulu)

sukuma wiki – green leafy vegetables (Swahili)

tef – cereal grass grown in Ethiopia

telebiar – Arab dress

tembo – elephant (Swahili)

Tuskers – well-known beer brand in East Africa

ugali – a stiff porridge made from maize meal (Swahili)

velskoen – handcrafted leather shoes (Afrikaans)

vetkoek – deep-fried balls of dough (Afrikaans)

wat – spicy food or sauce served with *njire* (Amharic)

wazungu – white people (Swahili)

Index

Page references in *italics* indicate illustrations

Acknowledgements

To all the people who believed, shared and made possible this great adventure – *Siyabonga*! We thank you. Paul van der Westhuizen from Wilbur Ellis who sponsored the Mariner Outboards, and Graham Simmons and Carl de Villiers who provided the Gemini inflatables and Talon trailers – congratulations! Not only did *QE2* and *Bathtub* survive Cape to Cairo, but they went on to succeed in a number of other great adventures. Toyota's *Vulandlela* and *Thirsty* from Killarney Toyota are now veterans of African adventure. They continued to journey in East Africa, and to this day have survived thousands of kilometres of rough, tough adventuring. The superb Warn winches supplied by Mr Winch of Durban still operate – thanks! Protea Hotels, Sea King tents, Engen, Minus 40 camping fridges, Medical Rescue International and Continental Tyres, Castrol Oil and SAA – you are all part of the successful Cape to Cairo team. To Shirley Shearer, who headed up the media team and fell in love with Egypt, thank you. To *Getaway* and *Ski Boat* magazine, Leon Rautenbach and MNet, and the camera crew of Duncan McNeillie, Lourens van Rensburg and Tim Chevallier – Cape to Cairo was the beginning of many shared adventures. Patrick Wagner of *Getaway*, we're privileged to have had these shared adventures, and we miss you. To Jeremy Perks, Mike Boon, Barry Leitch and the Group Afrika team – thanks for all the friendship and logistical support, especially in Nairobi. *Asanti sana*. To François Meyer, Debbie Murray (for back-up support on the expedition), Lloyd and Hella Balcomb, Ann and Don Balmer, and to all the friends who shared in and supported this crazy adventure despite the hardships, wasn't it terrific? But most of all I thank Mama Afrika and the ordinary people along the way who extended a hand of help and friendship to our humble waterway odyssey across the continent. We could never have made it without you.

First published in 2002 by Struik Publishers
(a division of New Holland Publishing
(South Africa) (Pty) Ltd)

New Holland Publishing is a member of the
Johnnic Publishing Group

Garfield House
86–88 Edgware Road
W2 2EA London
United Kingdom
www.newhollandpublishers.com

Cornelis Struik House
80 McKenzie Street
Cape Town 8001
South Africa
www.struik.co.za

14 Aquatic Drive
Frenchs Forest
NSW 2086
Australia

218 Lake Road
Northcote,
Auckland
New Zealand

1 3 5 7 9 10 8 6 4 2

ISBN 1 86872 694 0

Publishing manager: Annlerie van Rooyen
Managing editor: Lesley Hay-Whitton
Design director: Janice Evans
Designer: Alison Day
Editor: Helen Keevy
Proofreader: Tessa Kennedy
Indexer: Sylvia Grobbelaar
Cartographer: Anthony Riley

Reproduction by Hirt & Carter Cape (Pty) Ltd
Printed by Tien Wah Press (Pte.) Ltd, Singapore

Log on to our photographic website
www.imagesofafrica.co.za for an African experience.